Our National Cathedrals: (the Richest Architectural Heritage Of The British Nation) ; Their History And Architecture From Their Foundation To Modern Times ; With Special Accounts Of Modern Restorations

Henry Winkles

Nabu Public Domain Reprints:

You are holding a reproduction of an original work published before 1923 that is in the public domain in the United States of America, and possibly other countries. You may freely copy and distribute this work as no entity (individual or corporate) has a copyright on the body of the work. This book may contain prior copyright references, and library stamps (as most of these works were scanned from library copies). These have been scanned and retained as part of the historical artifact.

This book may have occasional imperfections such as missing or blurred pages, poor pictures, errant marks, etc. that were either part of the original artifact, or were introduced by the scanning process. We believe this work is culturally important, and despite the imperfections, have elected to bring it back into print as part of our continuing commitment to the preservation of printed works worldwide. We appreciate your understanding of the imperfections in the preservation process, and hope you enjoy this valuable book.

OUR NATIONAL CATHEDRALS.

ST PAUL'S CATHEDRAL.

OUR
NATIONAL CATHEDRALS

(THE RICHEST ARCHITECTURAL HERITAGE OF THE
BRITISH NATION):

𝔗𝔥𝔢𝔦𝔯 𝔥𝔦𝔰𝔱𝔬𝔯𝔶 𝔞𝔫𝔡 𝔄𝔯𝔠𝔥𝔦𝔱𝔢𝔠𝔱𝔲𝔯𝔢 𝔣𝔯𝔬𝔪 𝔱𝔥𝔢𝔦𝔯 𝔉𝔬𝔲𝔫𝔡𝔞𝔱𝔦𝔬𝔫
𝔱𝔬 𝔐𝔬𝔡𝔢𝔯𝔫 𝔗𝔦𝔪𝔢𝔰,

WITH
SPECIAL ACCOUNTS OF MODERN RESTORATIONS.

ILLUSTRATED WITH FINE STEEL ENGRAVINGS BY WINKLES, AFTER ORIGINAL
DRAWINGS BY HABLOT K. BROWNE, R. GARLAND, AND OTHER ARTISTS,
AND MANY ORIGINAL WOOD ENGRAVINGS IN THE TEXT, THUS
FULLY ILLUSTRATING ALL THE CATHEDRALS FROM
MANY POINTS OF VIEW.

THE WHOLE CAREFULLY COMPILED AND REVISED WITH THE AID
OF DIGNITARIES OF THE ANGLICAN CHURCH.

"The native architecture of our own country, and that of our own forefathers."
"The more closely, constantly, and carefully we study its remains, the more entirely shall
we be convinced that our love and admiration cannot exceed what is due to its intrinsic
excellencies."—SIR GEORGE GILBERT SCOTT.

VOLUME III.

WARD, LOCK AND CO.,
LONDON: WARWICK HOUSE, SALISBURY SQUARE, E.C.
NEW YORK: BOND STREET.
1889.

ANDOVER-HARVARD
THEOLOGICAL LIBRARY
CAMBRIDGE, MASS.

H63.413

July 9, 1940

PREFACE.

In bringing to a conclusion this work on OUR NATIONAL CATHEDRALS, the Publishers take leave to point out that it contains over 150 illustrations in the text, in addition to the many separate steel plates originally engraved for Winkles' Cathedrals. This description of our Cathedrals is, therefore, quite unique in the number and variety of the representations of their various aspects during the present century. It is also the only work of the kind which includes, in addition to the new English Cathedrals, an account of the Scotch and Irish Cathedrals. The narratives of the modern transformations, improvements, or in some cases injuries which have taken place in the Cathedrals are also a very distinctive feature of the book, and as such give it a value which, the Publishers are glad to learn, has already been widely appreciated.

The Publishers have to thank, for kind aid in revision or in ascertaining the facts about the various Cathedrals described in this volume, in addition to the great majority of the Deans of the English Cathedrals, the Rev. A. T. Lloyd, Vicar and Canon of Newcastle Cathedral; the Rev. Canon Straton, of Wakefield Cathedral; the Rev. Canon Trebeck, of Southwell Cathedral; Mr. W. H. Purday (of Mr. Ewan Christian's), in relation to Southwell; Mr. W. Butterfield, to the Cathedral of the Isles and of St. Ninian's, Perth; the Rev. Dr. J. Cameron Lees, St. Giles', Edinburgh; the Rev. Dr. Burns, St. Mungo's, Glasgow; and Mr. John Honeyman, architect, of Glasgow.

During the progress of this work through the press, a new Cathedral, partially completed, has been opened at Truro, in the westernmost county of Cornwall, the result of the revived life of the Church in the West. This is the only really new Cathedral which the nineteenth century has produced in England. As yet the Liverpool Cathedral is but a project, but it is to be hoped that the nineteenth century may not be suffered to close before some further monument of architectural genius may be added to our National Cathedrals besides the Truro choir and the renewals or rebuildings which have at least preserved and strengthened some of the old work in which Englishmen justly take pride.

CONTENTS.

	PAGE
St. Paul's Cathedral	1
Modern History of St. Paul's Cathedral	21
Peterborough Cathedral	31
Modern History of Peterborough Cathedral	46
Chester Cathedral	51
Modern History of Chester Cathedral	64
Carlisle Cathedral	83
Modern History of Carlisle Cathedral	93
Ripon Cathedral	97
Modern History of Ripon Cathedral	111
Manchester Cathedral	117
Modern History of Manchester Cathedral	131
Southwell Cathedral	137
Newcastle Cathedral	157
Wakefield Cathedral	165
St. David's Cathedral	171
Modern History of St. David's Cathedral	179
Llandaff Cathedral	185
Bangor Cathedral	197
Modern History of Bangor Cathedral	205
St. Asaph Cathedral	211
Modern History of St. Asaph Cathedral	219
The Scotch Cathedrals	223
The Irish Cathedrals	265

LIST OF SEPARATE FULL-PAGE PLATES.

	PAGE
ST. PAUL'S CATHEDRAL—	
View from Southwark Bridge	*Frontispiece.*
West Front	*Facing* 1
North East View	8
The Crypt, with Nelson's Monument	9
Under the Dome (looking towards North Transept)	16
Nave and Choir	17
Ground Plan	20
PETERBOROUGH CATHEDRAL—	
West Front	31
North East View	33
West End	36
View across North Transept	40
The Nave	41
The Lady Chapel	44
Ground Plan	45
CHESTER CATHEDRAL—	
View from the Water Tower	51
South West View	53
South East View	56
The Lady Chapel	57
The Cloisters	60
Ground Plan	61
CARLISLE CATHEDRAL—	
North West View	83
South West View	84
South East View	85
Part of the Nave	88
The Choir	89
Ground Plan	92
RIPON CATHEDRAL—	
North West View	97
South West View	100

| | LIST OF SEPARATE FULL-PAGE PLATES. |

  South East View   104
  The Nave   105
  The Choir   108
  Ground Plan   109

MANCHESTER CATHEDRAL—
  South East View   117
  North East View   120
  South West View   121
  Interior, from West End   128
  View across Choir and Baptistery   129
  Ground Plan   130

ST. DAVID'S CATHEDRAL—
  South West View   171
  North West View   175
  View from the Ancient Bishop's Palace   176

LLANDAFF CATHEDRAL—
  West Front   185
  North East View   186
  Nave (looking West)   188

BANGOR CATHEDRAL—
  View (looking towards Beaumaris)   197
  South East View   200
  The Choir   201

ST. ASAPH CATHEDRAL—
  From the Bridge   211
  The West End   212
  The Choir   213

ST. GILES'S, EDINBURGH—
  Ground Plan   223

ILLUSTRATIONS IN THE TEXT

OLD ST. PAUL'S CATHEDRAL—
    Chapter-House and Cloisters
    Tomb of John of Gaunt
    North Aisle of Choir
    Tomb of John Beauchamp
    From the South East

ST. PAUL'S CATHEDRAL—
    The Gardens
    The Crypt
    The Choir, Reredos, etc.
    Tomb of Sir C. Wren
    The New Reredos

PETERBOROUGH CATHEDRAL—
    The East End
    View across South Transept
    From the South East

CHESTER CATHEDRAL—
    North Transept, Tower, and Chapter-House
    From the South East
    Choir Screen
    Pulpit
    Organ
    New Bishop's Throne
    Reredos
    Pulpit in Monks' Refectory

CARLISLE CATHEDRAL—
    From the South East
    The Great East Window

RIPON CATHEDRAL—
    From the South
    From the South West
    The Nave
    The Choir

MANCHESTER CATHEDRAL—
    The Choir
    From the South
    The Choir-Screen and Organ

SOUTHWELL CATHEDRAL—
    Before Restoration
    From the North West
    Central Tower and North Transept
    The Chapter-House
    The Nave
    The Choir, looking East

ILLUSTRATIONS IN THE TEXT.

NEWCASTLE CATHEDRAL—
    New Reredos 157
    " From the North West 161

WAKEFIELD CATHEDRAL—
    The Choir, looking East 165
    From the South East 167
    View across the Nave 169

ST. DAVID'S CATHEDRAL—
    North East View 179
    The Nave 181

LLANDAFF CATHEDRAL—
    From the South West 190
    The Choir 192

BANGOR CATHEDRAL—
    The Nave and Choir 205
    South View 208

ST. ASAPH CATHEDRAL—
    From the South West 220

THE SCOTCH CATHEDRALS—
    St. Giles' Tower and Steeple, Edinburgh 223
    " West End Restored 225
    " John Knox's Pulpit 228
    " The Choir 233
    St. Mary's Cathedral, Edinburgh, Exterior 237
    " " Interior 238
    St. Mungo's Cathedral, Glasgow, Exterior 240
    " " from the South 242
    " " The Choir 244
    " " The Lady Chapel 245
    " " The Crypt 246
    Cumbrae Cathedral: The Screen and Choir 248
    Inverness " from the North West 250
    Dunblane " The Nave 252
    Dunkeld " The Nave 253
    Brechin " West Front and Round Tower .. 255
    Aberdeen " from the South West 257
    Elgin " from the South West 259
    " East End 260
    Kirkwall " from the North 263
    Ruins of Iona 264

THE IRISH CATHEDRALS—
    St. Patrick's Cathedral, Dublin, Exterior 265
    " " Interior 267
    " " Nave and Choir 269
    Christ Church Cathedral, Dublin, from the South East .. 273
    " " Strongbow's Effigy .. 276
    " " The Crypt 277
    " " Norman Doorway .. 279
    " " The Apse and Eastern Chapel 281
    Cork Cathedral, Norman Doorway 284
    " Exterior 285
    Downpatrick Cathedral 286

ST PAUL'S CATHEDRAL,
THE WESTERN FRONT

OLD ST. PAUL'S: CHAPTER HOUSE AND CLOISTERS.

ST. PAUL'S CATHEDRAL.

THE see of London was established by Augustine of Canterbury, when the Anglo-Saxons first embraced Christianity, and a church was founded on the site of the present edifice by King Ethelbert, who dedicated it to St. Paul the Apostle: the structure was afterwards enlarged by St. Erkenwald, Bishop of London, but the Cathedral, together with great part of the city, was destroyed by an accidental fire in the year 1083.

Maurice, Bishop of London, in the year 1087, refounded the Cathedral, which he designed on a vast scale, but did not carry far towards completion. The building was carried on by his successor in the see, Bishop Richard de Belmeis, in 1108-1127, but was completed by Bishop Richard Fitz-Neal, about the year 1199. The choir was begun by Bishop Eustace de Fauconberg, (1221-1228), and completed by Bishop Roger Niger (1229-1241), together with the chapter-house. Bishop Henry Wengham originally erected the cloisters in the year 1260, on the northern side of the church; and the Lady chapel was chiefly built in the year 1310, during the prelacy of Bishop Ralph Baldock; near the high altar was a celebrated shrine of St. Erkenwald, the principal resort of the pious. The building was completed in 1315, while William Segrave was bishop.

The Cathedral was anciently encompassed by a wall which extended from the north-east corner of Ave Maria-lane eastward along Paternoster-row to the end of Old Change, in Cheapside, whence it ran southward to Carter-lane, and thence to Creed-lane, Ludgate-street, on the west. In the Cathedral wall were six gate-houses, the principal of which stood in Ludgate-street, near the end of Creed-lane, opening upon the western front of the Cathedral; the second was in Paternoster-row, at St. Paul's-alley; and the third at Canon-alley; the fourth, called the little gate, led from Watling-street into the Cathedral precinct; and the sixth gate-house fronted the southern porch of the church, near Paul's Chain.

In the middle of the churchyard, within the northern side of the close, stood a celebrated pulpit cross, at which sermons were preached weekly, and where the folkmote, or general convention of citizens, was formerly held. Paul's Cross was rebuilt by Bishop Kemp in 1449, but was destroyed, in accordance with the order of Parliament for the demolition of all crosses in the year 1643.

The ancient palace of the bishops of London stood at the north-western corner of the churchyard, and contiguous to it on the east was Pardon Church Haw, where Gilbert Becket founded a chapel in the reign of Stephen; this chapel was rebuilt in the time of King Henry V., by Thomas Moore, dean of St. Paul's, who also rebuilt the cloisters.

The cloisters of old St. Paul's environed what was usually called Pardon churchyard, and were only 91 feet square in extent. On the walls of this enclosure the Dance of Death was painted, accompanied by verses describing the several characters from the emperor to the beggar. The cloisters were two stories in height, a second range of open archways being placed over the lower, but were destroyed in the year 1549, at the very commencement of the Reformation, by the Protector, the Duke of Somerset, who used the materials in the erection of his house in the Strand.

On the eastern side of the churchyard was a campanile, or bell-tower, containing the Jesus bells, four great bells belonging to Jesus chapel in St. Faith's church.

The church of Saint Faith-the-Virgin was demolished about the year 1256, to enlarge the Cathedral, when a place of worship was granted to the parishioners in the eastern part of the crypt of

St. Paul's, under the choir, where divine service continued to be performed until the fire of London. The parish is now united to St. Austin's, in Watling-street, which is in the patronage of the dean and chapter. Part of the churchyard belonging to St. Faith's parish was taken to enlarge the street at the eastern end of the Cathedral, and the remainder, within the enclosure of St. Paul's churchyard, served as a burial place for the parishioners of St.

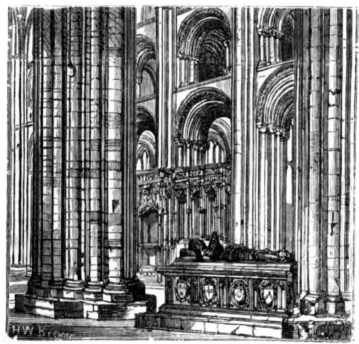

OLD ST PAUL'S: TOMB OF JOHN OF GAUNT.

Faith's. Fronting the eastern end of the Cathedral is St. Paul's School, founded in the year 1509, by Dr. John Colet, dean of St. Paul's, but rebuilt in 1670, and again in the year 1824.

Old St. Paul's represented a variety of styles from early Norman to Decorated. It consisted of a nave, choir, and transepts, each with two aisles. The nave, of twelve Norman bays with semicircular arches, had a triforium with similar arches, and a clerestory with Early English arches and windows. The nave was 290 feet long and 104 broad. The nave roof was vaulted in the thirteenth century. The transepts had five bays each, resembling the nave.[1]

The fine Early English central tower was remarkable for its lower range of long lancet windows and for its bold flying buttresses. The spire, of timber covered with lead, was greatly admired for its beauty. It was built about 1315, and was destroyed by lightning about 1561, and never rebuilt.

The entrance to the choir had a rich screen, and the choir extended beyond to twelve bays, all being of beautiful Decorated Gothic. The part behind the altar was the Lady Chapel. The east end had a large rose window of superb tracery over a seven-light window.

It is said by Stow that there were two western bell towers at the west corners, one of them being used for the Bishop's prison, but no other record or trace of them exists.

The dimensions of old St. Paul's have been carefully calculated by Mr. E. B. Ferrey from the plan given by Dugdale in his St. Paul's, and are given in Mr. W. Longman's excellent work.[2] The following are the chief of these: total length, 596 feet; breadth, 104 feet including aisle walls. Height of nave roof up to ridge of vaulting, 93 feet; of choir roof, 101 feet 6 inches; of Lady Chapel, 98 feet 6 inches; external height to ridge of choir roof, 142 feet; nave do., 130 feet; height of tower to base of spire, 285 feet; height of spire, 208 feet. The total area was 3 acres 3 roods 26 perches.

On the anniversary of the Conversion of St. Paul, held in the Cathedral, a fat buck was annually received with great formality at the entrance of the choir, by the canons in their sacerdotal vestments, and with chaplets of flowers on their heads. Camden, who was an eye-witness of this solemnity, says that the antlers of the buck were carried on a pike in procession round the church, with horns blowing, etc. On the buck being offered at the high altar, a shilling was paid by the dean and chapter as a fee to the keepers who brought it, which concluded the ceremony. This

---

1. The nave is termed Paul's Walk in many old plays, was much used as a fashionable lounge, and even as a business exchange in the latter part of the sixteenth and beginning of the seventeenth centuries.

2. "A History of the Three Cathedrals Dedicated to St. Paul in London," 1873.

OLD ST. PAUL'S : NORTH AISLE OF CHOIR: TOMBS OF THE EARLS OF PEMBROKE.

custom originated in the reign of Edward I., by grant from Sir William le Baud, in 1274.

King James I. appointed Sunday, 26th of March, 1620, to be present at divine service in the Cathedral: his majesty went on horseback, attended by the principal nobility and officers of the court. The king was met by the lord mayor, aldermen, and livery, in their formalities, at the western porch, and upon entering the church the king knelt near the brazen pillar and prayed: then his majesty was received under a canopy supported by the dean and residentiaries, the prebendaries and dignitaries, with the whole company of singing men advancing before him to the choir, which on this occasion was hung with rich tapestry. Here the king heard an anthem, and then proceeded to Paul's Cross, where the Bishop of London preached a sermon from this text given him by his majesty, the 13th and 14th verses of the 102nd Psalm; the sermon was afterwards circulated with considerable effect in the promotion of public zeal through the whole kingdom. After divine service was ended, the king and the whole court were entertained at the bishop's palace. At the same time it was agreed to issue a commission under the great seal to raise money for carrying the repairs of the church into execution. Inigo Jones was employed afterwards to erect a portico, of the Corinthian order, at the western end of the Cathedral.

The monuments of the following bishops of London remained in the church when Dugdale wrote his History of St. Paul's. St. Erkenwald, ob. 695; his shrine was restored with great splendour in 1339. William the Norman, bishop of London, ob. 1070. Bishop Roger Niger, ob. 1241. Bishop Richard Newport, ob. 1318. Bishop John Chishull, ob. 1279. Bishop John Elmar, ob. 1594. Bishop Richard Fletcher, ob. 1596. Bishop Eustace de Fauconberg, ob. 1228. Bishop Henry Wengham, ob. 1261. Bishop Ralph Baldock, ob. 1313. Bishop Hobert Braybrooke, ob. 1404. Bishop John Stokesly, ob. 1539. Bishop John King, ob. 1621. Bishop Thomas Kemp, ob. 1489. Bishop Richard Vaughan, ob. 1607. Bishop Richard Fitz-James, ob. 1521. Bishop Thomas Ravis, ob. 1609. Most of the Anglo-Saxon bishops of London, besides those already mentioned, were also interred in this church.

The other remarkable monuments in the old church, which were destroyed by the fire, were those of Henry Lacy, Earl of Lincoln, who died in 1312. Sir John Beauchamp, one of the founders of the Order of the Garter, who died in 1360. Sir Simon Burley, K.G., ob. 1388. John of Gaunt, Duke of Lancaster, who died in 1399. Dean Colet, ob. 1519. William, Earl of Pembroke, ob. 1551. Sir Nicholas Bacon, ob. 1579. Sir Philip Sidney, ob. 1596. Sir Christopher Hatton, K.G., ob. 1591. Sir Francis Walsingham, ob. 1590; and that of Dr. Donne, ob. 1631.

OLD ST. PAUL'S NAVE: TOMB OF JOHN BEAUCHAMP ON THE RIGHT.

Sir Anthony Vandyck, the painter, who died in 1641, was also buried in old St. Paul's.

The great fire of London in the year 1666 destroyed the chief part of the building, and irreparably damaged the remainder. The vast magnitude of the work, and the contemplation of the great expense requisite for building a new Cathedral, occasioned a lapse of some years, as well as a loss of considerable labour and materials, before it was finally determined that all attempts at reparation were hopeless. A commission was appointed in November, 1673, consisting of several peers, spiritual and temporal, together with other persons of rank, having authority to superintend the plans for

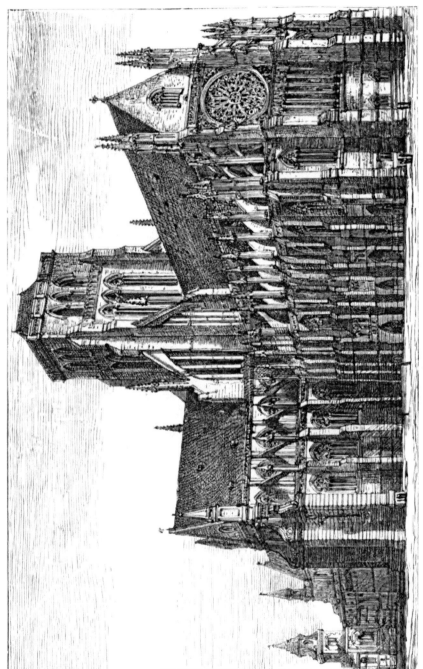

OLD ST. PAUL'S: FROM THE SOUTH-EAST.

OLD ST. PAUL'S FROM THE SOUTH-EAST.

rebuilding the Cathedral; and a design having been approved by the king, his majesty issued a warrant on the 1st of May, 1675, for the commencement of the works. The removal of the ruins of the old Cathedral was not accomplished without difficulty, and repeated efforts were found necessary to level the walls of the venerable edifice. The foundation commenced at the western end, was carried on eastward, and the first stone was laid by Sir Christopher Wren on the 21st of June, 1675. In ten years the walls of the choir and aisles were finished, together with the northern and southern porticoes, and the great piers of the dome were brought to the same height.[a]

The choir of the church was first opened for divine service on occasion of the Thanksgiving for the Peace of Ryswick, 2nd December, 1697, concluded in that year between the allied powers and France; service was first performed in the morning prayer chapel, on the southern side of the church, on the 1st February, 1699; and in 1710 the highest and last stone, on the top of the lantern, was laid by Christopher Wren, son of the architect, in the presence of Mr. Strong, principal mason, and others who had been employed in the execution of the work. Thus the Cathedral Church was completed in the period of five and thirty years, under the superintendence of one architect, under the direction of one principal mason, and during the occupation of the see of London by one bishop: it may also be mentioned that it remains without alteration or addition since its original erection.

Dr. Henry Compton, son of the second Earl of Northampton of that name, was appointed Bishop of London by King Charles II. in 1675.[b] After King James ascended the throne, he was, however,

---

[a] From an account of St. Paul's Church printed in the year 1685, by John Tillison, clerk of the works, it appears that the general depth of the foundation below the surface of the ground is 22 feet, and in many places 35 feet; that the large vaults below the church are 18 feet 6 inches from the ground to the crown of the arch, and that each of the great piers sustaining the dome stands upon 1360 feet of ground superficial measure, and each lesser one upon 380 feet. The whole space occupied by the piers and covered by the dome contains half an acre, half a quarter of an acre, and almost four perches.

[b] In the same year this bishop was made dean of the Chapel Royal, and the king committed to his care the education of his two nieces, the princesses Mary and Anne; they were both confirmed by him in 1676, and both likewise married by him, Mary to William, Prince of Orange, in 1677, and Anne to George, Prince of Denmark, in 1683.

suspended from the execution of his episcopal office, during his majesty's pleasure, when the bishops of Durham, Peterborough, and Rochester, were appointed commissioners to exercise ecclesiastical jurisdiction within the diocese of London. Bishop Compton was restored in 1688, and was chosen by King William to perform the ceremony of his and Queen Mary's coronation in 1689. He died at Fulham in 1713, at the age of eighty-one, and was buried in the churchyard there.

St. Paul's Cathedral, one of the most conspicuous objects of the British capital, stands in the very centre and most elevated part of the city of London, having Ludgate Hill on the west, Cheapside on the east, and St. Martin's-le-Grand on the north. The edifice is entirely built of fine Portland stone,* and on the plan of the Latin Cross, a form which approaches to perfection, expands easily to the eye of the spectator, and exhibits its beautiful combination at one view. The whole length of the church with its portico is 500 feet, the width of the western front with the towers is 180 feet, and the length of the transept within the doors of the porticoes is 250 feet; the circumference of the building being 2292 feet. At the intersection of the nave and transept rises a magnificent dome, 145 feet in diameter, from the top of which springs a lantern enriched with columns, and surmounted by a gilded ball and cross, the *croix aveline*. At the western end of the church are projections northward and southward, answering the purposes of a morning chapel and consistory court, an expedient for giving more importance to the western front. There are also, at the internal angles of the cross, on the plan, small square bastion-like adjuncts, the real use of which is to strengthen the piers of the dome, but which are made serviceable, internally, as vestries and a staircase. The nave and choir are separated by the area over which the cupola rises; from this area a transept diverges to the north and south, extending each way one severy, or arch, in length. The choir is terminated eastward on

---

* The Portland stone which has been used in many of the magnificent buildings of the kingdom, was first brought into repute in the reign of James I., and was employed in the construction of the Banquetting House, part of an intended new palace at Whitehall. After the fire of London this stone was used by Sir Christopher Wren in rebuilding almost every edifice of magnitude in the metropolis.

the plan by a semicircular apsis or tribune, which is equal in diameter to the width of the choir.

The architectural elevation of this grand edifice consists throughout of two orders; the lower one Corinthian, the upper Composite. In both stories, excepting at the northern and southern entrances, which are enriched with semicircular porticoes, and on the western front, the whole of the entablatures rest on coupled pilasters; between these, in the lower order, a range of semicircular headed windows is introduced, and in the order above, the corresponding spaces are occupied by dressed niches, on pedestals pierced with openings, which give light to passages over the aisles. The upper order of architecture is merely a screen to hide buttresses which are carried across from the outer walls to resist the thrust of the great vaulting.

One of the principal objections made by architectural critics is, that the body of the church is divided into two equal orders, instead of an attic only being added, as in the instance of the church of St. Peter's at Rome, also, that the surface of the building is crowded with festoons, and broken into minute rustic to the very summit. It is known that the original design which Sir Christopher Wren gave for the Cathedral of St. Paul, was more approved by himself than that adopted in the present building, and it had apparently some points of superiority; the whole fabric in the first design consisted of one order only, instead of an equal division into two, and the grand portico projected with a space and elevation not unequal to that of the Pantheon at Rome.* An architect of eminence, after a comparison of St. Paul's with the churches of St. Peter, St. Mary, at Florence, and that of St. Geneviève, or the Pantheon, at Paris, three of the largest modern churches of Europe, admits that St. Paul's ranks high in point of constructive merit; but it appears there is least waste of interior effect in St. Mary's, at Florence, and that St. Paul's and the church of St. Geneviève, are very far from being economical in this view of their merits.† The

---

* The dome of the intended church did not rise from a peristyle as at present, but was supported by buttresses. The plan and elevation have been published, and the model is exhibited in the Cathedral.

† Account of St. Paul's Cathedral, by Joseph Gwilt, architect, who is the author, also, of "A Comparative View of the Magnitude of the Four principal Modern Churches in Europe;" and besides extensive information on architecture, possessed a highly cultivated taste.

greatest defect in the architecture of St. Paul's Cathedral, says the same intelligent critic, arises from the multiplicity of breaks and incongruous forms in every part; hence a want of breadth and repose throughout, the cupola and its peristyle only excepted, in which a very opposite practice has produced the most delightful result. Another defect is the almost universal absence of even the semblance of tie and connexion which the want of continuous lines of entablature produces; pediments with the horizontal corona omitted, besides many minor abuses, such as deficiency of architraves, fritter in the ornament, etc. In short, all the details appear to have been copied from the worst examples of the worst Italian and French masters.

With respect to the general division of the body of the building into two orders of architecture, it is stated in the Parentalia, that Sir Christopher Wren was obliged to yield to circumstances, as the Portland quaries would not afford stones of the required dimensions;[8] but Mr. Gwilt says these excuses are unsatisfactory, it would have been far better to have had the columns in many pieces, and even with vertical joints, than to have placed one portico over another on the western front.

The lower division of the western portico is composed of twelve coupled columns of the Corinthian order, on a basement formed by a double flight of steps of black marble, and the upper of only eight columns supporting an entablature and pediment, the tympan of which is a bas-relief, representing the Conversion of St. Paul, the patron Saint of the church,[9] sculptured by Francis Bird.[10] On the apex of the pediment is a colossal statute of St. Paul, and at the extremities are figures of St. Peter and St. James. On the sides of the portico are towers, each of which is surmounted

[8] Parentalia, or Memoirs of the Family of the Wrens, but chiefly of Sir Christopher Wren. London, 1750.

[9] The Conversion forms the subject of one of the oldest pictures in the National Gallery, a production of the Ferrarese school, obtained from the Aldobrandini collection.

[10] This artist was employed by Sir Christopher Wren in the sculptural enrichment of the Cathedral; for the pediment, 64 feet by 17, and consisting of eight figures, of which six are equestrian, he received £650, for the reliefs under the western portico, the acts of St. Paul, he received £300, and £75 each for the panels. Lord Orford says, that "the many public works by his hand are not good testimonies in his favour;" but it must be admitted that he succeeded well in monumental figures; that of Dr. Busby, in Westminster Abbey, by the same master, is sufficient to prove his ability.

ST. PAUL'S CATHEDRAL.

by an enriched steeple of two orders, in light pierced work, covered with a dome formed by curves of contrary flexure, and terminated by a majestic pine-cone 222 feet from the ground. At the angles of these towers, on the western front, are colossal statues of the Evangelists with their attributes. In the south-western tower is the clock, and the great bell on which it strikes.[11] The diameter of this bell is about 10 feet:[12] on it are the words, "Richard Phelps made me, 1716."

In the centre of the area before the western front of the Cathedral is a statue of Queen Anne, sculptured by Belt, in 1886; it stands on a circular pedestal, having four pilasters at equal distances, supported by trusses, on which are seated four allegorical female figures, representing England, France, Ireland, and America. It is a replica of Bird's statue (1712).

The fronts of the northern and southern transepts are terminated upwards by pediments, over coupled pilasters at the quoins, and two single pilasters in the intermediate space: each front is surmounted by five colossal statues of apostles. On the front of each transept is also a grand semicircular Corinthian portico, the southern raised on a semicircular terrace, having, on each side, piers of entrance surmounted by rich vases, ornamented with arabesque work, which are placed on elegant circular pedestals, enriched with cherubim heads, and festoons of fruit and flowers. It has been justly observed of these porticoes, that they are not inferior in beauty to the dome itself; they are objects equally admirable whether considered separately or in connexion with the building which they adorn, and diversify by affording a contrast of curved with the straight lines of the architecture, and of insulated columns with engaged pilasters.

---

[11] The clock is of great magnitude, and is wound up daily; the outward dial, 18 feet 10 inches in diameter, is regulated by a smaller one withinside. The length of the minute hand is 8 feet, and its weight 75lbs.; the length of the hour hand is 5 feet 5 inches, and its weight 44lbs.; the length of the hour figures is 2 feet 2¼ inches. It appears that the art of making large clocks is every day retrograding, and exhibits a singular instance of a branch of mechanical science, and one of very great importance, in which we are infinitely surpassed by the French, amongst whom the art of turret clock making, as an object worthy of public attention, is carried to an unrivalled degree of perfection.—*Vulliamy's Considerations on the Subject of Public Clocks.* 4to, 1828.

[12] Its weight, which is not to be compared with the great bells of Oxford or Exeter, is generally stated at 4¼ tons, but is also said to be only 3 tons 15 cwt., or 8400lbs.

The walls of the nave and choir are decorated with two stories, of coupled pilasters, arranged at regular distances, the lower range being of the Corinthian, and the upper of the composite order; the intervals between the Corinthian pilasters are occupied by large windows, and those between the composite pilasters, by niches; the entire summit of the side walls is crowned by a regular balustrade. The projecting semicircle, which terminates the eastern end, is more highly enriched, and appears to have been completed in the reign of William III., as the royal initials are sculptured beneath the eastern window. Over the choir at the extreme eastern end is an ornamented attic, which breaks the line of balustrade.

The dome, the most remarkable and magnificent feature in the building, is generally spoken of in terms of unqualified admiration; objections, it is true, have been raised to the columns of the peristyle, for their excess in height, over that of either of the orders below, and the objections are not groundless; but none, says Mr. Gwilt, can lament this violation of rigid propriety. The same gentleman affirms, that for dignity and elegance no church in Europe affords an example worthy of comparison with the cupola of Paul's. The peristyle stands on an immense circular basement, rising about twenty feet above the roof of the church, and supported on the piers and great arches of the central area: the columns, thirty-two in number, are of a composite order, every fourth intercolumniation being filled with masonry, but so disposed as to include an ornamental niche; by which arrangement the buttresses of the cupola are judiciously concealed, and converted into a decoration of a beautiful character. The colonnade is crowned with a complete entablature and balustrade, which forms an entire circle, connecting all the parts in one grand and harmonious whole. Above the colonnade, but not resting upon it, rises an attic, the detail of which is simple and appropriate, and whence springs the exterior dome of a very bold and graceful contour; it is covered with lead and ribbed at regular intervals. At its summit is another gallery of gilded iron work, from the centre of which rises a stone lantern enriched with columns and crowned by a ball and cross.[12] The view of the city

---

[12] In 1826 a new ball and cross were placed on the lantern in lieu of the originals, which had become so decayed as to render this measure necessary.

of London from the stone gallery, round the dome, over the colonnade, is very fine, but by no means equals the extensive prospect obtained at the superior elevation of the golden gallery at the apex of the dome round the lantern. The outward diameter of the dome is 145 feet, the inward diameter of the same is 108 feet.[14] The entire height from the ground to the top of the cross is 365 feet.

The principal entrance to the crypt is by a flight of steps in the south-eastern angle of the great transept: in this, the basement story, vast piers and arches sustain the superstructure, the space being formed into three avenues corresponding with those of the nave, transept, and choir above. In the very centre of the crypt repose the remains of Admiral Lord Nelson, who fell at the battle of Trafalgar in the year 1805. The colours of his own ship, the Victory, were deposited in the same grave, which is covered with an altar tomb of granite, supporting a large square sarcophagus of black and dark coloured marbles. In the crypt is also the grave of the architect, situated under the southern aisle of the choir.

The nave and choir of the Cathedral are each flanked by three arches springing from piers, which are strengthened as well as decorated on their inner faces by pilasters of the Corinthian order, crowned by an entablature. Over this order of architecture rises a tall attic, the pilasters of which form abutment piers for the springing of the semicircular arches of the vaulting. The vaulting of this part of the church is light, elegant, and very judiciously constructed; each division forms a low dome, supported by four spandrils, the face of each sphere being encircled by an enriched course of foliage. In the upright plane space on the walls a clerestory is introduced over the attic; the aisles, which are low in comparison with the nave, are vaulted from the small pilasters, and terminated in a manner similar to that of the vaulting of the nave and choir. At the western termination of the nave is a small transept, which on the south is occupied as a morning prayer chapel, and on the north was used as the court of the chancellor of the diocese; these are divided from the aisles by screens of ornamental

[14] The diameter of the inside of the Pantheon at Rome is about 149 feet English measure, exclusive of the walls, which are about 18 feet thick, so that the diameter of the whole circle is about 185 feet; the roof of this ancient temple, now covered with lead, was formerly covered with plates of gilded brass.

carved work. In the story above the consistory court is the Cathedral library: over the chimney-piece is a portrait of Dr. Henry Compton, Bishop of London, painted by Sir James Thornhill; he is represented with a plan of the Cathedral in his hand; this prelate presented the whole of his books to the library. At the opposite extremity of the transept, and exactly corresponding in situation and dimension with the library, is another apartment, in which is preserved the model which was made under the direction of Sir Christopher Wren, and valued by him as the most perfect of all the designs he made for the Cathedral. The central area under the cupola is circumscribed by eight large piers, equal in size, but not equi-distant. The four larger openings occur in the spaces where the nave, choir, and transept diverge from the great circle, the lesser ones between them. These latter are surmounted by arches which spring from the architrave of the main order, but by extending the springing points, above, in the attic so as to break over the re-entering angular pilaster below, such an increase of opening is acquired in the attic, that the eight arches which receive the cantilever cornice of the whispering gallery are all equal."[18] Above the cornice a tall pedestal, or dado, receives the order immediately under the dome; its periphery is divided into eight portions, of three intercolumniations each, pierced for windows; each of these divisions being separated from that adjoining it by a solid pier, one intercolumniation wide, decorated with a niche. The piers so formed connect the wall of the inner order with the external peristyle, and thus serve as counterforts to resist the thrust of the inner brick cupola, as well as that of the conical wall which carries the lantern.

The ascent to the whispering gallery, as it is universally called is by a circular staircase, constructed within the north-western projection of the great transept. This gallery, composed of richly-ornamented iron-work, encircles the drum of the dome, and extends to the extreme edge of the cornice. The staircase contracts on approaching the gallery to afford room for various passages, through the apertures of which the immense buttresses of the dome may be seen.

[18] The mitering of the archivolts over the eight great arches of the cupola is a sad abuse, it makes the lofty works which rise above them seem to stand on points.—*Gwilt.*

ST PAUL'S CATHEDRAL.

Mr. Gwilt, an architect who has written an account of St. Paul's Cathedral, seems to have exercised the strictest impartiality in the observations he has made relating to this great work; he admits that Wren was a consummate mechanician, but as an architect he considers him by no means so distinguished. It is obvious to every one who has given the matter due consideration, that in estimating the merits of a building and the constructive skill of its architect, that is superior in which the greatest effects are produced by the use of the slenderest materials. Amongst the most elegant applications of science ever introduced into a building is the conical wall, between the inner and outer domes, upon which the stone lantern of enormous weight is supported. This was truly the thought of a master, but however admirable the science which directed the use of the expedient, it has induced two defects which are scarcely pardonable. The first of these is, that the exterior dome is constructed of timber, which however well attended to, must necessarily decay within a comparatively short period, should even the carelessness of plumbers spare it. The other defect is, the immense waste of section which it has caused, and the consequent loss of interior effect sustained.

In the height of this cone are three tiers of circular perforations, not alone contrived to admit the necessary currents of air in order to keep the walls dry, but to light, and render visible, the framing of the timbers bearing the external dome, and also to keep them free from moisture. The framing of these timbers is most scientific; each of the thirty-two frames stands on a stone abutment, with a circular perforation conjoined, with the three cones, at the springing lines. The whole frame is in three stages, three principal upright timbers rise through the said stages, with occasional struts and braces; having from frame to frame successive tiers of horizontal timbers, running with the curvature of the dome, whereon the external covering of lead is laid. Although the appearance of the several frames from their seemingly complex admixture, in the circuitous line round the cone, may, at first view, confound and astonish the beholder, yet, upon examination, the nature of the carpentry becomes familiar to the eye, and from its simplicity, and true geometrical principle, satisfies the mind in the great security afforded to the whole by these auxiliaries of the dome.[16]

The interior of the cupola is painted in two colours, relieved with gilding, by Sir James Thornhill; it is in eight grand compartments, representing the principal events in the life of St. Paul.

The dome is pierced with an eye in its vertex, and through it a vista is carried up to the small dome in which the great cone terminates. When the whole height is seen through the opening from below, the gaze becomes truly fascinating; this view is very justly considered the prime scenic feature of the whole building. The architectural embellishments of the more lofty parts of the structure are all painted and gilded.

The western end of the choir commences at the piers supporting the cupola, which are wider than the other piers, and are flanked by Corinthian pilasters at the angles, having a square recess in the intercolumniation; uniform with these, there are, at its eastern end, piers of the same dimensions, excepting that they are pierced for a communication with the aisles. In other respects the leading architectural features of the choir resemble those of the nave with the addition of the tribune, wherein the altar stands which is domed over from top of the attic.

The choir screen was a Corinthian colonnade, supporting a gallery for the organ, and bore the following tribute to the memory of the architect, now removed to the inner face of the north entrance:—

SVBTVS . CONDITVR . HVJVS . ECCLESIÆ . ET . VRBIS . CONDITOR . CHRISTOPHORVS . WREN . QVI . VIXIT . ANNOS . VLTRA . NONAGINTA . NON . SIBI . SED . BONO . PVBLICO . LECTOR . SI . MONVMENTVM . REQVIRIS . CIRCVMSPICE.

The organ was constructed in 1694 by Bernard Smydt, a German; but was entirely taken to pieces and repaired in 1802.

On each side of the choir is a range of fifteen stalls, exclusive of the bishop's throne, on the southern side, and a stall for the lord mayor on the northern; these are beautifully enriched with carving by Grinling Gibbons.[17] The pulpit was designed by Robert

---

[16] Survey of the Cathedral Church of St. Paul, by John Carter, F.S.A., an architect whose descriptive remarks are highly interesting.

[17] This artist, celebrated for his excellent carving, was introduced by Evelyn to Sir Christopher Wren and to King Charles II.; the king gave him an appointment to the

Mylne, clerk of the works, and carved by Edward Wyatt; it was erected about the year 1802. The reader's desk, representing an eagle with expanded wings, supported by a pillar and enclosed within a railing, is a fine example of the kind, entirely brass, richly gilt. The apsis, or tribune, at the eastern end of the choir, is enriched with pilasters painted in imitation of lapis lazuli, with capitals, and ornaments of the entablature, richly gilded. The intercolumniation is panelled with marble.

In the year 1773 a design was formed for decorating the Cathedral with the works of our most eminent painters and sculptors, when the presidents and members of the Royal Academy offered to fill some of the compartments with pictures without charge; but the scheme. although approved of by his majesty, was discouraged by the Archbishop of Canterbury and the Bishop of London as savouring of "Popery." About the year 1793 another suggestion to break the monotonous uniformity of the architecture in the interior of the Cathedral, was the admission of national monuments raised in commemoration of eminent characters. The two first monuments erected in this building were those of John Howard, the philanthropist, who died at Cherson, in Russian Tartary, in 1790, and Dr. Samuel Johnson, the famous author of the "Dictionary of the English Language," who died in 1784; both statues were the work of John Bacon, R.A.,[18] and occupy corresponding situations in the angles in the front of the smaller piers of the dome. In another angle is a third statue by the same sculptor, erected to the memory of Sir William Jones, an accomplished scholar, who died at Bengal, in 1794. The fourth statue in a corresponding angle of the dome is that of Sir Joshua Reynolds, who died in 1792.[19]

All the monuments in the church are of white marble, with the exception of the plinths of those which stand upon the pavement.

---

board of works, and employed him in the ornaments of most of his palaces, particularly at Windsor; but his principal performance is at Petworth. Gibbons died in 1721.

[18] This eminent sculptor died in 1799; there are few of our Cathedrals without some specimen of his skill, but one of his grandest efforts is the monument of Lord Chatham, in Westminster Abbey, completed in 1783.

[19] In the vaults of the Cathedral were also buried the following members of the Royal Academy: James Barry, R.A., who died in 1806. John Opie, R.A., who died in 1807. Benjamin West, President of the Royal Academy, who died in 1820; and Sir Thomas Lawrence, President of the Royal Academy, who died in 1830.

The expenses attending the erection of the Cathedral were defrayed by an imposition on sea coal imported into London, the annual proceeds of which were sometimes less than the yearly charges for materials and labour, the deficiency was supplied by the contributions of the king, the nobility, the clergy and gentry, and by the sale of some of the old materials. The whole expense of erecting the edifice, deducting the money expended in attempts to repair the old Cathedral, was £736,752 2s. 3d., in addition to which the stone and iron inclosure which surrounded it cost £11,202 0s. 6d.; total, £747,954 2s. 9d.

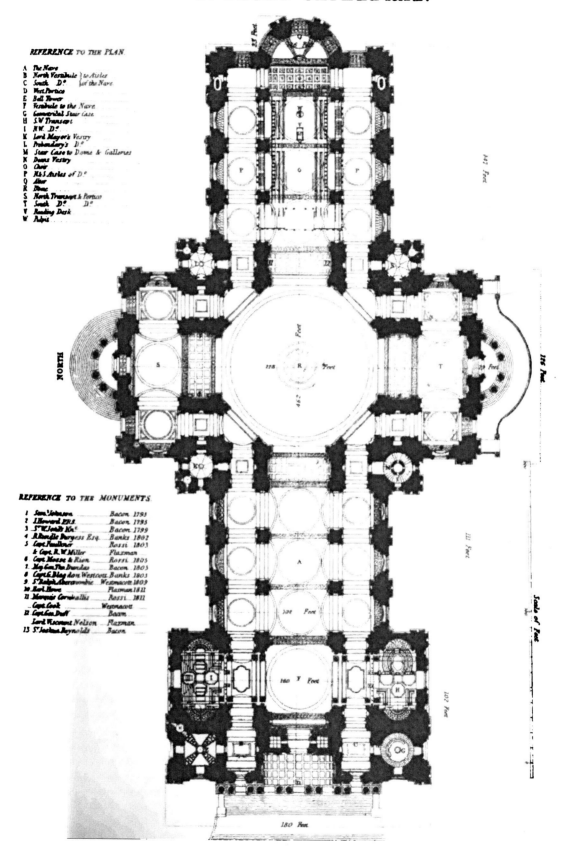

ST. PAUL'S CATHEDRAL: THE GARDENS.

MODERN HISTORY OF ST. PAUL'S CATHEDRAL.

THE era of restoration and improvement at St. Paul's began in 1858, with a suggestion from the Bishop of London (afterwards Archbishop Tait) that special Sunday evening services should be held in the Cathedral. Dean Milman, in reply to this, brought forward his ardent desire that something adequate should be done to relieve the "cold, dull, unedifying, unseemly appearance of the interior," and make it worthy of its exterior grandeur and beauty. "I should wish to see," he wrote, "such decorations introduced into St. Paul's as may give some splendour, while they would not disturb the solemnity or the exquisitely harmonious simplicity of the edifice; some colour to enliven and gladden the eye, from foreign or native marbles, the most permanent and safe modes of embellishing a building exposed to the atmosphere of London. I would see the dome, instead of brooding like a dead weight over the area below, expanding and elevating the soul towards heaven. I would see the sullen white of the roof, the arches, the cornices, the capitals, and the walls broken and relieved by gilding, as we find it by experience the most lasting, as well as the most appropriate decoration. I would see the adornment carried out in a rich but harmonious (and as far as possible from gaudy) style, in unison with our simpler form of worship."

A committee was soon formed, and subscriptions were collected, amounting to many thousands of pounds. In order to make the building more available for worship, arrangements were successfully made for warming it, and the organ-screen was removed, the organ being placed under one of the arches of the choir, and greatly improved and extended in compass. It has since been divided, and placed half on either side of the choir. The entire space under the dome, together with parts of the nave and transepts, was adapted for public worship, and has since been usually filled by vast crowds on Sundays.

The work of decoration has been but partially completed, largely owing to divergence of opinion as to what should be done.

Two fine mosaics have been placed on spandrels of the dome; they represent Isaiah and St. Matthew, and are the work of Signor Salviati, from designs by Mr. G. F. Watts, R.A. Painted windows have also been placed in the apse.

During investigations made in 1878, Mr. Penrose found a portion of the foundations of the old Paul's Cross (demolished in 1642), on the north-east side, showing that the platform on which it stood was octagonal, about 37 to 40 feet from angle to angle. An ornamental enclosure has been made to indicate the site. This was done in connection with a scheme for lowering the remaining iron railings round the Cathedral and laying out the churchyard as a garden, at the expense of the Corporation of the City of London. The railings before the west front had previously been removed, and the space thrown open, much to the improvement of the western view. A stained-glass window inserted in 1879 in the north-western chapel, in memory of Dean

Mansel, representing the incredulity of St. Thomas, has had a very good effect in giving a warm tone to the interior. Two fine

ST. PAUL'S CATHEDRAL: THE CRYPT.

adjacent lights, representing St. Peter and St. Paul, have an excellent effect.

The north-west tower, which had been specially designed to receive bells, remained with only one bell till 1878, when a fine peal of twelve bells, presented by the Corporation of London, some city companies, and Lady Burdett-Coutts, was placed in the tower. The tower bell weighs three tons two hundredweight; its note is B flat. In 1881 a much larger bell was cast at Loughborough, and in 1882 was placed in the same tower. "Big Ben" sinks into comparative insignificance by the side of "Great Paul," which is among the six or eight heaviest bells in Europe. Its diameter is 9 feet $6\frac{3}{4}$ inches from lip to lip; its perpendicular height is 8 feet 10 inches. Its weight is more than $17\frac{1}{2}$ tons, and its principal note is E flat; but for various reasons it has not proved entirely satisfactory.

The principal monuments in the Cathedral, in addition to those mentioned on p. 19, are the following, with the names of the sculptors:—North transept—Generals Gore and Skerrett (Chantrey), killed at Bergen op Zoom, 1814; Sir C. Napier (Adams), died 1853; Admiral Lord Duncan, the victor of Camperdown (Westmacott); Sir W. Ponsonby, killed at Waterloo; Henry Hallam, the historian (Theed), died 1859.

South aisle of choir—Bishop Heber (Chantrey), died 1826; C. J. Blomfield, Bishop of London (Richmond), died 1857; J. Donne, Dean of St. Paul's; Dean Milman (Williamson), died 1868.

South transept—Sir Henry Lawrence, who died in the Indian Mutiny; Admiral Earl Howe, victor in the battle of Ushant, 1794 (Westmacott); Admiral Lord Collingwood, Nelson's comrade (Westmacott); J. M. W. Turner, R.A. (Macdowell), died 1851; General Lord Heathfield, defender of Gibraltar (Rossi), 1790. At the angle of the south transept, against the east face of the great pier, is Nelson's monument. Opposite to this is Lord Cornwallis's monument; Sir Astley Cooper, the celebrated surgeon (died 1842); General Sir John Moore, of Corunna; General Sir Ralph Abercromby, died 1801.

South aisle of nave—In the recess formerly used as the Consistory Court of the diocese is the magnificent monument of the great Duke of Wellington, by Alfred Stevens, only completed after twenty-five years' labour and after Stevens' death. Stevens designed it for a position between two arches of the nave, where it could have been much better seen. It is no less than thirty-six feet high, but was intended to have been surmounted by an equestrian statue. The Duke's large effigy in bronze lies on a sarcophagus of white marble, decked with rich military trophies

ST. PAUL'S CATHEDRAL: THE CHOIR, REREDOS, ETC., FROM THE CENTRE, UNDER THE DOME.

and wreaths in bronze. Over the effigy is a massive broad arch or canopy supported on either side by four white marble Corinthian columns, the shafts being carved in foliated diaper. At either end on the cornice is a group of sculptured bronze, the one a seated female figure plucking out the tongue of Falsehood; in the other,

Valour thrusting down Cowardice at her feet. There are many other details which are best examined on the spot. The east and west walls of the chapel are decorated with relief in white marble. The central eastern one by Mr. Calder Marshall was suggested by these passages: "Righteousness and peace have kissed each other," and, "Young men and maidens, old men and children, praise the name of the Lord." The central western one, by Mr. Woodington, represents Melchisedek blessing Abraham.

North aisle of nave—Lord Melbourne (Marochetti), a gloomy mass of black marble; Mountstuart Elphinstone, Governor of Bombay (Noble), died 1859; Admiral Lord Rodney (Rossi); General Sir T. Picton, who fell at Waterloo; Admiral Lord St.

CRYPT OF ST. PAUL'S: TOMB OF SIR CHRISTOPHER WREN.

Vincent (Bailey); General Sir W. Napier, historian of the Peninsular War.

Much has been done in recent years to improve and bring out the beauties of the crypt, the windows having been glazed, and stained glass representing the entombment of the Saviour having been inserted in the eastern one. The central space beneath the choir and dome has received a tessellated pavement; an altar has been placed at the east end, rendering it available for daily services. The part representing the old church of St. Faith is marked by two mosaic inscriptions on the pavement. Fragments of tombs which escaped destruction at the Great Fire are placed west of the altar.

The crypt contains the remains of most of those whose monuments appear in the Cathedral. Nelson is laid in the centre under the dome. His black marble sarcophagus was designed originally for Cardinal Wolsey, and not having been used, was removed from Windsor to receive Nelson's remains. In a space between two large supports of the dome is the Duke of Wellington's sarcophagus, on a massive granite base. The sarcophagus is cut out of a great block of a rare Cornish stone named luxulyanite, a kind of porphyry with large crystals of red felspar in a mass of quartz and black tourmaline. The funeral car in which the Duke's coffin was conveyed to the Cathedral is at the extreme west end. The remains of Sir Christopher Wren are at the east end of the crypt, in the south aisle; a black marble slab has these words: "Here lieth Sir Christopher Wren; the Builder of this Cathedral Church of St. Paul, etc., who dyed in the year of our Lord mdccxxiii, and of his age xci."

Not far from Wren's feet are many noted artists: Sir Joshua Reynolds, Benjamin West, Sir Thomas Lawrence, Barry, Opie, Fuseli, Turner; Robert Mylne, and C. R. Cockerell, architects; and near them Dean Milman. A monument to Sir Bartle Frere is the latest addition.

The library, the large room over the Wellington Chapel, has many Biblical treasures, Fathers, and works on the Councils of the Church. It is rich in books and pamphlets on the history of the Cathedral. It has in recent years received the large collections of pamphlets formed by Bishop Sumner of Winchester, and Archdeacon Hale.

The most important structure added to St. Paul's in recent times has been the new reredos, dedicated on January 26, 1888. The central portion is suggested by Wren's original design; but in the opinion of many this idea has been greatly improved upon and developed, so that the first impression is that the reredos was originally designed for the Cathedral, and belongs naturally to it. It is certainly the finest as well as the largest piece of modern classical sculpture in England. The design is the work of Messrs. Bodley and Garner, but especially of Mr. Garner. The work has been executed by Mr. Brindley, of the firm of Farmer and Brindley, the whole of the models for the sculpture having been the work of M. Guillemin.

ST. PAUL'S CATHEDRAL: THE NEW REREDOS.

The reredos is connected with the side arches of the easternmost bay of the choir by a semicircular marble colonnade, ranging in height with the architectural lines of the building.

The design consists of a basement, against which the altar stands, with a small doorway on each side to give access to the apse behind. Over these doors, which are of pierced brass, are angels supporting shields of the crossed swords and keys, the arms of the diocese and St. Paul and St. Peter, and they are flanked by sculptured festoons of fruit and flowers separated by marble panels. Above this is a range of sculptured panels with coloured marble backgrounds, supporting an open colonnade of semicircular plan. A large group of sculpture, in bold relief, occupies the centre, flanked on each side by twisted columns of rich Brescia marble (both being monoliths) wreathed with foliage in golden bronze. These support an entablature and rich pediment. The frieze is of Rosso Antico, bearing the inscription, "Sic Deus dilexit mundum," in gilt bronze letters. The whole is crowned by a central niche and surrounding statues at a height of between 60 and 70 feet from the ground.

The general idea of the sculptured subjects is to express the incarnation and life of our Lord, beginning with the two figures at the extremities of the colonnade, which are those of the angel Gabriel and St. Mary, and represent the Annunciation. The panel on the north side is the Nativity, the large subject in the centre the Crucifixion with the entombment underneath it, and the group on the south side the Resurrection. The panels of the pedestals are filled with angels bearing instruments of the "Passion." The niche above the pediment is occupied by a figure of the Virgin Mary with the Divine Child in her arms, with the statues of St. Paul and St. Peter on either hand. The figure on the summit of the niche is an ideal one of the risen Saviour.

The entire reredos is executed in white Parian marble with bands and panels of Rosso Antico, Verde di Prato, and Brescia marble. The enrichments are generally gilt. The steps in front of the altar are of white marble, and the pavement of Rosso Antico, Brescia, and Verde di Prato, like the reredos.

It is intended to place wrought-iron screens at the sides of the sanctuary, using some very fine iron gates of Sir Christopher

Wren's design now in the crypt, which were removed from the choir at the time of the alterations.

There can be no doubt in most minds as to the gain to the Cathedral by this magnificent work. No other style could be appropriately introduced in such a church, and it is fortunate in every way that it has been added at the present period in art, when the true spirit of all forms of architecture is better understood and reproduced than at any former time. The cost has been about £37,000, largely defrayed from the Cathedral funds, but supplemented by about £14,000 mainly from the accumulated interest on the funds subscribed for the decoration of the Cathedral.

PETERBOROUGH CATHEDRAL.

The see of Peterborough is comparatively of modern date. It is one of those erected by Henry VIII. soon after the dissolution of the abbey. The charter by which it was erected into a bishopric bears date September 4, 1541, and before the end of the same year John Chambers, the last abbot, was chosen first bishop, and the abbey church became from that time the Cathedral.

No part, however, of the present fabric has been built since it became a Cathedral, and therefore in giving its history, we must necessarily begin with the history of the famous monastery to which it once belonged.

The name of the place was originally Medeshamsted, from a pit in the river Nen called Medeswell, which tradition says was a little below the present bridge. But this well, together with another called St. Lawrence's, of great celebrity in former days for its miraculous properties, is now entirely lost. The locality of the latter indeed is only guessed at by Gunton in his valuable history of this once abbey and now Cathedral Church. His conjecture is a very reasonable one; there was a chapel dedicated to St. Lawrence, the chancel of which is yet standing, and forms the hall of one of the prebendal houses: near the chapel must have been the well of St. Lawrence, if the chapel itself was not built over it, as was often the case with wells supposed to be possessed of supernatural virtues.

Medeshamsted being a part of the county of Northampton was of course within the kingdom of Mercia. Penda is reckoned by most antiquaries to have been the first king of the Mercians. He had five children, three sons, Peada, Wulfere, and Etheldred, and two daughters, Kyneburga and Kyneswitha. Penda being dead, was succeeded by his eldest son Peada, who in the year 656, or as some say 655, founded the monastery of Medeshamsted; the stone of which it was built was certainly brought from Barnack, near Burleigh, in the same county, and those laid in the foundation, are said to have been of so large a size, that eight yoke of oxen could with difficulty draw one of them. But Peada did not live to finish his work, for his wife Alfleda (unmindful of the pious memory of her grandfather Oswald, the martyred king of Northumberland, king Oswine her father, and king Alfred her brother), betrayed him to death at the feast of Easter, after he had reigned only four years; when his crown and kingdom descended to Wulfere his next brother.

Wulfere was converted and baptized by Finanus, a Scotch bishop, and upon his coming to the throne vowed to purge his kingdom from idolatry, and to the utmost of his power promote the Christian religion. He married Ermenilda, daughter of Egbert, king of Kent, a very virtuous and pious princess, who was afterwards canonized; on this occasion he solemnly repeated his vow, which however not long afterwards he entirely neglected to fulfil, through the persuasion of his steward Werbode, so that the Christian religion rapidly declined, and heathenism again prevailed. By his wife he had two sons, Wulfade and Rufine, who were both converted to the Christian faith by St. Chad. Their conversion was concealed from their father for some time, but they were betrayed at last by the same Werbode, who so inflamed the king against his sons, that having watched them both into an oratory, slew them with his own hands, whilst they were praying before the altar. Werbode and the king then demolished the place, and left the bodies of the murdered princes buried in the rubbish. Soon after this Werbode is said to have hanged himself, and king Wulfere being deeply wounded in conscience, consulted his queen Ermenilda, who advised him to go to St. Chad, to which he consented; and having made a full confession of his heavy crimes, and manifested his repentance, he was readmitted into the bosom of the church, and upon his promising to perform any penance St. Chad should think fit to impose upon him, he was only desired by that good man to be ever mindful of his former vows in future, and so to restore the Christian religion in his kingdom, to repair its ruined temples, and to build new ones.

The monastery of Medeshamsted, begun by his brother, became, as we may well suppose, the object from henceforth of Wulfere's peculiar care and favour. In his zealous endeavours to complete it, he was assisted by his brother Etheldred, and his sisters Kyneburga and Kyneswitha. When finished, he dedicated it to St. Peter, and on this account in after times the place obtained the name of Peterborough, and lost its original appellation of Medeshamsted. At the

same time King Wulfere bestowed upon this abbey many great and valuable privileges and immunities, and very large possessions. The bounds of its jurisdiction established by him were from Croyland on the east, to Walmesford, or Wansford Bridge on the west, and so northward to Easton and Stamford, and all along by the river Welland to Croyland again; as it may be seen in the charter which he sealed and confirmed in the presence of kings, nobles, and bishops, in the year 604, and the seventh of his reign.

King Wulfere died without issue, in what year is not exactly known; but his brother Ethelred succeeded him both in his throne and in his good affection for the monastery of Medeshamsted. Ethelred reigned thirty years, and then laid down his crown and sceptre, and became first a monk, and afterwards abbot of Bardney, according to William of Malmsbury, about the year 704. But (observes Gunton), speaking of the completion of the monastery of Medeshamsted, the nest being thus fitted and prepared, care was taken to furnish it with birds: and first with an abbot, who should become a sort of call bird to others, till the nest was full.

The first abbot was Saxulfus, an earl, who thought it no degradation to be the head of the religious establishment in this place. His reputation for piety was very great, so that he soon gathered a convent of monks, who flocked to him from all parts. He presided over this monastery with great fidelity and zeal for thirteen years and was then elected bishop of Durham, and was succeeded by Cuthbaldus, one of the monks, who from his extraordinary sanctity, was thought the fittest person to fill the place and dignity thus vacated.

The monastery continued in a flourishing condition till the year 870, when the Danes, having burnt down Croyland Abbey, and put to death the monks there, proceeded to Medeshamsted, slew both the abbot and the monks, eighty-four in number, set fire to the convent, and utterly destroyed the church, the altars, monuments, and library, with all the adjacent buildings. At this time Hedda was abbot: the fire continued burning for fifteen days together; the sight was terrible, and the desolation complete. In this ruinous condition the monastery remained for a whole century, till the year 970, when King Edgar rebuilt it, and called together the princes, nobles, bishops, and abbots of his kingdom to be present with him at its consecration. It was dedicated to St. Peter, and on this occasion, and for this reason, the name of the place was changed from Medeshamsted to Peterborough. Edgar procured Adulphus his chancellor to be elected abbot of the re-edified monastery, who after having enjoyed this dignity for twenty years, was advanced to higher places, being first promoted to the see of Worcester, and afterwards translated to the archiepiscopal see of York. Kenulphus, a learned, eloquent and pious man, succeeded him, who inclosed the monastery with a wall, and was afterwards elected Bishop of Winchester.

Leofric, a person of the blood royal, and in great favour with the king, became abbot a little before the Norman conquest, and was a great benefactor to the abbey. His means must have been ample enough, for he held at the same time with this of Peterborough four other abbeys, viz. Burton, Coventry, Croyland, and Thorney. He was however more fitted to be a soldier than a churchman, as he put himself at the head of the English army to oppose William the Conqueror, but sickness obliged him soon after to return to the monastery, where he died on the first of November, in the year 1066.

Thorold was elected abbot in 1069, and has made his name infamous as a waster of the abbey goods; when he entered upon his office they were valued at £1500, and when he died they were reduced in value to £500. Soon after he was elected he became weary of his situation, and contrived to obtain the bishopric of Beauvais, in France, and carried off with him many things which belonged to the abbey of Peterborough. He was, however, so unwelcome to the church of Beauvais, that he was expelled thence in four days after his arrival. He then desired nothing so much as to return to his former situation, and by large presents to the king he was reinstated in the abbacy of Peterborough.

In the year 1116 a great fire happened, which was all but as destructive as that which was lighted by the Danes; how it originated historians have not informed us, but they tell us gravely that it was a judgment upon the abbot, who was an impetuous man, and had been cursing and blaspheming all the day because a fire in his lodgings would not burn; at length he concluded his malediction upon it with these words, "*The Devil kindle thee!*" upon which the whole monastery was in a blaze, and the church rebuilt by King Edgar destroyed by the conflagration.

In the month of March 1117, John de Sais, at that time abbot, laid the foundation of a new church, but did not live to finish it. The work was interrupted at his death, which happened in the year 1125, and for the three years after that event, during which time the place of abbot was vacant; neither did the work go on under the next abbot, Henry de Angeli, who held the place for five years. But in the year 1133, Martin de Vecti was elected abbot, who proceeded with the work of re-edification with the greatest assiduity, and had the satisfaction of seeing it completed. It was re-dedicated to St. Peter in the year 1140 according to some, or in 1143 according to others. This ceremony was performed with the greatest pomp in the presence of the Bishop of Lincoln, the abbots of Croyland, Thorney, and Ramsay, many barons and knights, and a vast number of inferior ecclesiastics.

This, which may be called the third abbey church, is in great measure still remaining, and forms the present Cathedral.

Martin de Vecti's church, however, has undergone several important alterations, and received some considerable additions. We find that abbot William de Waterville, who was deposed in 1175, after governing the establishment for twenty years, almost rebuilt the transept and great central tower, added the cloisters, and founded a chapel, which he dedicated to St. Thomas-à-Becket. His successor, Benedict, prior of Canterbury, who was elected in 1177, finished these works, and built the nave of the church after a better manner than before, from the central tower to the porch. But as the church is said to have been entirely finished and dedicated in the year 1143, and nothing disastrous is recorded to have happened to the building after that period, we cannot suppose that the works of abbots William and Benedict amounted to a total re-edification of the nave and transept, which had only been finished between thirty and forty years by Martin de Vecti. Possibly therefore they made considerable alterations in these portions of the church, according to the taste of the times; perhaps raised the clerestory, or at least enlarged the windows, and gave a different form to them. Perhaps Benedict also gave a new roof to the nave; the one which still exists is certainly as old as his time.

Abbot Robert de Lyndsey after this gave glass to about thirty of the windows in the church, which having been left unfinished by his predecessor had till now been stuffed with straw.

Of the west front no date has been assigned, and no name mentioned of the benefactor or architect. In the absence of all documentary evidence, Mr. Britton assigns this most magnificent part of the present Cathedral to abbots Acharias and Robert de Lyndsey, whose united government of the abbey comprised a period of twenty-two years, viz. from the year 1200 to the year 1222.

Richard de London elected abbot in 1273, erected the great bell steeple before that date while prior. The Lady Chapel, which was destroyed in Cromwell's time, was built by abbot William Parys.

Robert Kirton, elected abbot in the year 1496, finished the building at the east end of the church, which was in Gunton's time known principally by the name of the new building. Abbot Robert died in the year 1528, and was succeeded by John Chambers, the last abbot, who in the year 1539 surrendered the abbey to king Henry VIII., and had a pension assigned him of £266 13s. 4d. per annum, which he afterwards resigned upon being appointed the first bishop of Peterborough, which happened only two years after the suppression of the abbey.

It is said that Henry VIII. spared this abbey church, and made it a Cathedral, an account of the remains of his first queen, Catherine, which still repose within its walls. Those of Mary queen of Scots, which were also first interred here, were afterwards removed by her son James I. and again interred at Westminster, where a magnificent monument is erected to her memory. Pity it is, says Brown Willis, that Henry VIII. did not likewise spare another magnificent abbey, that of St. Edmund's Bury, in Suffolk, for the sake of another queen buried there, in his lifetime, viz., his own sister Mary, the French queen.

Great and extraordinary were the privileges which this monastery enjoyed from the earliest times, through the favour of kings, popes, princes, and nobles. It is said that the documents confirming these privileges were preserved during the Danish invasion by the pious care of some of the monks, and were discovered and exhibited to King Edgar at the dedication of the new church, who wept for joy that he had a second Rome in his own kingdom; for one of the privileges was, that if any desired to visit Rome, and could not, by reason of the great distance or any other impediment, it should suffice to visit this abbey; here they may pay their vows, obtain abso-

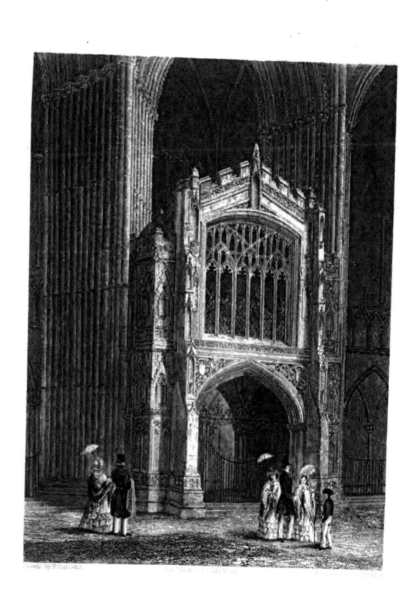

lution, and receive the apostolical blessing. So great, indeed, was the esteem in which this abbey was held, that whoever came, whether king, bishop, baron, abbot, or knight, they took off their shoes at the gate of the monastery, and entered its sacred precincts barefoot, and when any of the monks were seen in the neighbouring villages, they were treated with the profoundest reverence.

The abbots were called to parliament in the reign of Henry III., but had not the honour of wearing the mitre till the year 1400. It was a benedictine abbey, in which at the time of the dissolution there were forty monks. It was a very wealthy establishment, though there were others in the kingdom still more so. Its possessions were valued at £1721 14s. per annum, according to Dugdale, and £1972 7s. according to Speed.

When Henry VIII. converted the abbey into a Cathedral, he placed therein a bishop, a dean, six prebendaries, a divinity reader, eight minor canons, the same number of lay-clerks or singing-men, the like number of choristers, and a master over them: two other school masters, twenty scholars, six alms men, and some inferior officers.

In the king's books the bishopric is charged at £4141 7s. 8d. per annum, and the gross annual value of the same is now fixed at £4,500.

Since it became a Cathedral this church has suffered much and gained little till recent years, when Dr. Monk, who was afterwards made Bishop of Gloucester and Bristol, proposed and liberally supported a subscription for the refitting of the choir, but of this we shall take occasion to speak in its proper place. We repeat that this Cathedral suffered most lamentably in Cromwell's time, the cloisters being then destroyed, together with many of the adjacent buildings; and no doubt the whole of this magnificent fabric would have soon perished, had not the church been re-established, with the restoration of the king to the throne of this kingdom. For by an act passed August 19th, 1651, the minster (as it was then called) was granted to the inhabitants of Peterborough both for a place of worship and for a workhouse, at the same time, to employ the poorer sort in manufactures—the inhabitants, at their own costs and charges, repairing and maintaining the same.

Such, then, is the history of the abbey, and origin of the see of

Peterborough. We come now to speak more particularly of the Cathedral itself, of the several portions of which we have given the dates, as far as they can be ascertained either by documentary or architectural evidence. The situation of the Cathedral is something like that of Ely, placed on gently rising ground, and surrounded by a vast extent of level country, which is oftentimes inundated. Its appearance at a distance is not very prepossessing. Having no tower or spire, or any important feature which rises much above the roof ridge, it looks a huge heavy lump of building when it first breaks upon the view, and of no describable form or shape. On a nearer approach, however, the mass appears broken by bold projections. The transept and low central tower, with its angular turrets, are plainly discernible, and, within a mile, the magnificent western façade, with its tower, turrets, pinnacles, and gables, is seen rising majestically far above the chimneys of the highest houses of the city.

EXTERIOR.

The Cathedral of Peterborough is far less encumbered by adjacent buildings than most others. The precincts are entered from the town under a gothic gateway, when the visitor has the most superb and imposing portion of the fabric immediately before him, viz., the west front, to which there is nothing superior in gothic architecture, if there be anything equal. If there be anything in England that can be brought into competitition with it, it is the west front of Wells Cathedral—if anything in France, it is the west front of Rheims. In respect to extent they may vie with Peterborough, in respect to the quantity of decoration they may, and Rheims certainly does exceed it, but in respect to form, proportion, and general effect, the west front of Peterborough is far superior to them both, and perhaps is unrivalled in the world. The west fronts of Rheims and Peterborough have been thought to resemble each other by some, but it would puzzle a good gothic architect to discover the resemblance. Rheims has, indeed, three deep-pointed portals side by side, the middle one being higher and wider than the other two, and Peterborough has three lofty arches side by side, of equal height, and supported on clustered columns; so that unless a colonnade can be said to be like a door (for it is not pretended that there exists any other point of resemblance), these two west fronts cannot be said to be in the least degree alike.

But what a grand conception is here! The front of the cathedral is adorned with a gigantic and finely-proportioned portico, flanked with towers adorned with lofty pinnacles; such is the design. The ornamental detail is both well selected and judiciously applied, and of the effect of the whole, it is not too much to say, that it is not in the power of the pencil or the pen to do it justice; it must be seen to be duly appreciated. Strictly speaking, the west front is perfectly finished and perfectly uniform; but behind it are two towers, one of which is finished, while the other wants the upper story. The finished one appears over the gable towards the north, and being seen in connection with the west front, seems to form a part of it; but the other to the south not being seen above the corresponding gable gives from some points of view an unfinished and irregular appearance to the whole, and injures the effect. Nevertheless it must be confessed that the first view of this façade is striking and imposing in an unusual degree. There is a solemnity in the effect which it produces such as is observable in no other Cathedral, and which is not unmixed with awe. The architects of the thirteenth century certainly understood better what a temple for the Deity ought to be, than any that have appeared before or since from the first establishment of Christianity to the present times.

It is with reluctance we quit this most attractive portion of Peterborough Cathedral, to describe the rest of its exterior; which, however, is not wanting in any part of it in respect of dignity and importance. Let us then turn round the corner of the north-west tower, and the whole length of the nave with the side aisle, north wing of the transept and central tower, burst upon the view; all in the same style originally, and all altered as to the lower windows in the same taste at a subsequent period. Some of these windows had been stopped up with plaster, but the late dean, Dr. Monk, had them re-opened with the best effect both externally and internally; the dean also ornamented the ground on this side of the Cathedral, and all round the east end, by tastefully laying it out in flower beds and walks, and planting trees and shrubs: it had before the character of a common churchyard, and was not kept in the very best order.

The north front of the transept has three rows of windows, one above another, and three in each row, and one single window above all in the gable; it is also adorned with two rows of arcades, one above the second tier of windows and one above the third, running under the base of the gable. This front is also flanked by turrets, which are square, as high as the upper row of windows, and octagonal in their upper portions, which rise to the height of the gable point, and are finished with battlements.

Before we pass this front, it will be well to look back towards the west end of the nave, and call the reader's attention to the tower (before mentioned as appearing above the portico of the west façade), and to the adjacent portions of the fabric. It will be here perceived how much wider the façade is, not only than the nave, but also than even the building which forms at that point a sort of second transept. The tower flanks the nave to the north, and beyond the tower is a short transept, whose north front is adorned with a large and beautiful pointed window of decorated Gothic, and flanked with towers similar to those of the north front of the greater transept.

Passing now the north wing of the transept, we have the choir and building to the east of it in view; to the east side of the transept, both north and south wing of it, is attached an aisle. The choir with its aisle is nearly of the same age and style of architecture with the nave and transept, and similar alterations have been made in the windows. The choir ends circularly, plainly indicating its Norman origin, but at the points where the circular wall begins on each side are built square buttresses engaged in the walls, which at the point where they rise above the parapet become octangular, and are terminated by plain spires.

The beautiful building which surrounds the circular termination of the choir is of an oblong form, having four pointed windows of four lights each, with perpendicular tracery in the sides of it to the north and south, and five of such windows in the length towards the east; between the windows are buttresses with statues in the place of pinnacles; and an elegantly pierced and embattled parapet, very similar to that of King's College Chapel, in Cambridge, runs all round the building.

The south side of the choir is too similar to the north to need any particular description of it; the south wing of the transept is enclosed

PETERBOROUGH CATHEDRAL.
VIEW ACROSS THE NORTH TRANSEPT

PETERBOROUGH CATHEDRAL.

within a garden of a private house; this is the only point of the whole exterior of the fabric which is not open. This front of this transept is also so like the other that nothing more need be said upon the subject. The same is true with regard to the south side of the nave, and the south wing of the less or western transept differs from the north only in not having its tower completed; the upper story is wanting — whether it was ever built does not seem certain—and is now nearly the only thing wanting to make Peterborough Cathedral both perfect and uniform in every respect.

The central tower, or lantern, as it is called, alone remains to be noticed. The best view of it is obtained from a spot a few paces from the building to the north-east, and is given in one of the accompanying plates. It had been greatly metamorphosed since it was erected, and received additions within the present century, which greatly disfigured it; we allude to the octagonal turrets at the four corners, which Dean Kipling carried up to a most disproportionate height above the embattled parapet of the tower. The tower itself was originally much richer and more lofty; when it was altered is not precisely known, but by the windows and panelling, and other detail upon its surface, we may conclude that it was of about the same date with the porch at the west end. The rebuilding of this tower is described in the modern chapter.

We will now conduct the reader back to the matchless west front, and through the porch, inserted between the clustered columns which support the centre arch of this sublime arcade, introduce him at once into the

INTERIOR.

On entering the Cathedral, to the right and left is the west transept, of the same age and style of architecture with the west front, which forms as it were a screen before it. As far as the internal view is concerned, the towers of this transept are finished, and are exactly alike; lofty, well-proportioned, pointed arches open into the nave on the one hand, and into the short wings of the transept on the other, so as to give an uninterrupted view of the whole of this west transept on first entering the Cathedral, as well as of the nave and choir. This general view of the interior is very grand and imposing. The dimensions, simplicity, and symmetry of the nave are most remarkable. Here we find vastness, solidity, and massiveness combined with a degree of lightness of effect which is unusual in buildings of this age, and of which we should hardly have supposed the Norman style of architecture capable. This is mainly to be attributed to the more than ordinary span of the arches both of the lower arcade and of the open triforium immediately over it. The arch mouldings of the lower arcade are bold and simple, but more in number than is usual, and the columns are broken into more than the usual number of members, though their bases and capitals are exceedingly plain. The arches of the triforium are of equal span with those below, and are adorned with the zigzag moulding; within the larger are two smaller arches, semicircular also, resting on a short cylindrical column with plain capital. The upper triforium, or clerestory, is composed of a succession of semicircular arches, three together in each compartment, the middle one rising higher than those on each side, and resting on two short cylindrical columns, with simple capitals; the three arches are comprised within the same space as each single arch of the lower triforium and nave. Behind the middle arch of the three is a round-headed window, which has been filled with mullions and tracery of a later date. A plain cylindrical shaft, a quarter of which is engaged in the walls, runs up between each arch of the nave from the pavement to the ceiling dividing the whole length of the nave into compartments, and two horizontal bands of simple mouldings divide it again into three stories; the band is also repeated by way of finish above the arches of the clerestory. These bands are continued round the shafts before mentioned, and appear as fillets to them.

The ceiling of the nave is of wood, and Mr. Blore, who, several years ago, examined it minutely, in order to its being repaired, pronounced it to be coeval with the walls on which it rests, and it is a very curious and rare specimen of the ceilings which were in use before stone vaulting was introduced. The central and by far the greater part of this ceiling is flat, and being higher than the walls of the nave, the side portions are consequently placed in a sloping direction to meet them. It is painted in panels of a lozenge form, in various colours and patterns, the panels themselves being also adorned with figures, probably of saints and angels, abbots, kings, and princes, and other benefactors of the abbey. The aisles of the nave are vaulted with stone, and the windows which light them are the insertions of a subsequent age, divided by mullions into several lights, with good simple tracery in the heads of them.

We come now to the transept and central tower. Both wings of the transept have an aisle to the east; no longer open, indeed, but divided into rooms now used as vestries. The south wing has an aisle also to the west, which is closed up and forms a room, which now serves for a practising room. Of the columns of the transept, some are cylindrical and some octagonal, of vast diameter, and the lower arches have an ornamented moulding, which is wanting in those of the nave. The roof of the transept is of wood, and flat throughout; it is elegantly painted in a pattern composed of octagons recurring, and filled up with subdivisions, while the intervening squares are ornamented with flowers and other devices.

The central tower was built upon four clustered columns and the same number of arches, of which those which open into the transept are semicircular and original, and the others, opening into the nave and choir, are pointed. This change was made in the 14th century, and in the rebuilding of the tower it has been exactly reproduced. Over the semicircular arches which remain, the form of a pointed one is traced upon the wall by a single moulding, which seems to indicate what was wished and intended, but was never effected. The mouldings of the pointed arches are many but plain; those of the semicircular are equally numerous, and the outer ones adorned with the zigzag. Above the arches of the tower are the windows which light it, two in each of the four faces of three lights each, with decorated tracery in their heads, which are pointed, and having between them and in the angles of the tower clustered shafts, from which spring the ribs of the wooden vaulting.

We come now to the choir and its aisles, a work of the same age and style with the nave and transept; it has (as all Norman churches had) a semicircular termination, and the windows in the apse, although they retain their original form, have been since filled with tracery which belongs to the second period of the pointed style. The ceiling of the apse is perfectly flat and of wood, and painted in a pattern of circles and lozenges. The lower arches of the apse are covered with a rich facing of Decorated feathered detail, and the inter-columniations, as high as the stall work, have been filled up with a screen of stone in imitation of Decorated Gothic, by Mr. Blore. The state of the choir previously was mean and incongruous to the last degree. Dean Monk proposed a restoration, which was liberally supported by subscriptions. The means being thus raised, Mr. Blore was selected as architect. The stalls, throne, pulpit, seats, and organ-case are all of oak, carved from Mr. Blore's designs in the style of Decorated Gothic.

The organ screen, which is of stone, has been removed, and will not be replaced in its old position. The design is exceedingly beautiful; in the centre is the arch of entrance, of most graceful proportions, deeply feathered and adorned with a straight canopy richly crocketted, and surmounted by a finial of the most elegant description. This entrance arch is flanked by octangular buttresses, decreasing gradually towards the top, and terminated by crocketted pinnacles with finials. On each side of the entrance are four deep and long niches, with projecting canopies in the best taste, with buttresses and pinnacles between each; the whole front of the screen is flanked at each end with buttresses and pinnacles exactly similar to those which flank the entrance, and the parapet is straight at the top, and adorned with open trefoils. The old choir extended nearly as far as the first columns of the nave, but when it was newly fitted up it was confined to its natural and architectural position, leaving the transept open and the new screen placed under the eastern arch of the central tower. The roof of the choir from that arch to the apse (the roof of which has been already described) is of wood, and partly vaulted and partly flat: the ribs of the vaulting being continued over the flat part in squares, which are each of them twice crossed diagonally, and with the same description of mouldings.

The interior of the building which surrounds the apse is as to its

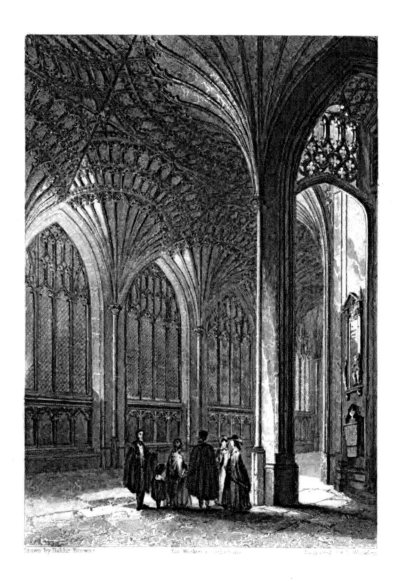

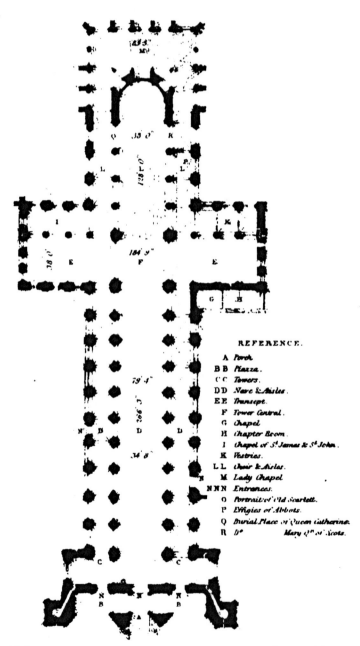

groined roof and its windows so very like the interior of the chapel of King's College, in Cambridge, and so nearly of the same date, that it is probable the same architect was employed about both. The only defect in this addition to Peterborough Cathedral is a want of due elevation.

Of the cloisters very little now remains; they were on the south side of the nave, and judging from what is still to be seen, they must have been of considerable extent and beauty. Under the north-east and north-west angles were entrances into the abbey church, which still remain, though seldom used.

Peterborough Cathedral, as will be evident to the reader from the plates and from the description, is certainly one of the first class as regards size, magnificence, and architectural importance.

Its dimensions are as follow:—Breadth of western facade, 156 feet; length of nave from the western wall to the choir entrance, 266 feet 3 inches; breadth of do., 35 feet 5 inches; total breadth in the clear of outside walls, 79 feet 4 inches; length of transept, 184 feet 9 inches; length of choir from the entrance to the eastern extremity of the apse, 128 feet; thence to the east wall, 35 feet; breadth of Lady Chapel, 83 feet 5 inches. Total external length of the Cathedral, 479 feet; general height from the pavement to the ceiling, 81 feet; height of lantern, 135 feet.

In former years few of the bishops of Peterborough were men of great distinction. In the present century Bishops Herbert Marsh (1819-1839), translator of Michaelis' "Introduction to the New Testament;" George Davys, tutor of Queen Victoria (1839-64); and Francis Jeune (1864-68), have been succeeded by Bishop Magee, one of the most eloquent and outspoken prelates that have ever adorned the English Church.

PETERBOROUGH CATHEDRAL: THE EAST END (BEFORE THE RE-BUILDING OF THE TOWER).

MODERN HISTORY OF PETERBOROUGH CATHEDRAL.

The roof of the apse, which is flat, and also the eastern screen, have been decorated after the designs of Sir G. G. Scott. In the centre of the roof is Christ in majesty, surrounded by half figures of the apostles among vine branches. The whole is bordered by the inscription: "I am the Vine," etc. This is believed substantially to reproduce the original decoration, destroyed by Cromwell's soldiers in 1643. The north and south windows of the transepts have been filled with stained-glass by Messrs. Heaton and Butler, and Gibbs. Among several other modern windows may be mentioned the east window, to the memory of Bishop Davys.

A pulpit was erected against the north-east pier of the central tower, in memory of Dr. James (died 1878), but was removed when the central tower was taken down, and will be placed further westward in the nave. It is of red Mansfield stone, resting on polished-marble columns.

The central tower, or lantern, was discovered to be in a dangerous state in 1882, and in 1883 a contract was entered into for its reconstruction. As the work of removal was proceeded with, it was found that the state of the structure was such that it could not possibly be preserved, and must be rebuilt entirely. During this removal several Norman fragments and portions of the Norman arcading were found. In consequence Mr. J. L. Pearson, R.A., the chapter architect, submitted designs for a reconstruction of the original Norman arches. But his

PETERBOROUGH CATHEDRAL: VIEW ACROSS SOUTH TRANSEPT.

proposals were overruled, and the arches, as they had last stood, were rebuilt, the old stones being replaced as far as possible. The tower is now completed as far as funds would allow. The decoration of the repaired and replaced ceiling of the lantern has been completed at the cost of Mr. H. P. Gates, Mayor of Peterborough. The south transept roof has also been rebuilt, and the north transept roof repaired. Much remains to be done, notably the underpinning of the transept gables and portions of the eastern chapel or "new building," and the refitting of the choir.

About £24,000 has already been expended on the Cathedral, but at least £20,000 is required for necessary works, independently of the choir and of possible expenditure on the west front, which is known to be in a doubtful state.

PETERBOROUGH CATHEDRAL FROM THE SOUTH-EAST: SHOWING THE CENTRAL TOWER AS REBUILT.

Canon Argles has offered the cost of a new bishop's throne and new pulpit, when the plans for the fittings of the choir have been agreed upon. Lady Elizabeth Villiers has undertaken to erect a new screen between the choir and the nave.

The monuments at Peterborough are very few, nearly all

having been destroyed or defaced by the Puritans. At the west end of the south choir aisle is the effigy probably of Abbot Andrew (1193-1200), treading on a dragon, whose mouth his staff pierces. There are three other effigies of early abbots by the south wall of this aisle, each holding a book.

A plain slab of stone outside the north door of the choir marks the resting-place of Queen Katherine of Aragon, and a corresponding one on the south that of Mary Queen of Scots' remains from 1587 to 1612, when they were removed to Westminster Abbey. These slabs, however, do not cover the vaults, which are within the choir.

Entering the "new building" from the south aisle in the wall, on the left hand is seen the Jacobean monument of Sir Humphrey Orme, almost destroyed by Cromwell's troops. At the back of the apse is a small monument of Barnack stone, dating from the early part of the twelfth century, containing on each of its sides six figures, probably of Christ and the apostles. This was long assigned to the Abbot Hedda and his monks, slaughtered by the Danes in 870, but is probably a part of the shrine of St. Kyneburga, which was brought from Castor. Other monuments in this neighbourhood are those of Thomas Deacon (died 1721), a benefactor to Peterborough, and an Early-English effigy of an abbot, and monumental slabs of various bishops. Under the north window of the apse is a monument formed of portions of previous ones, the Perpendicular portion supposed to belong to the shrine of St. Ebba.

In 1839 the Archdeaconry of Leicester was added to this Diocese, being taken from Lincoln. In 1875 a new archdeaconry of Oakham was formed out of the archdeaconry of Northampton.

CHESTER CATHEDRAL.

OF all the Roman stations in Britain, Chester seems to have been the most important. It was called Chester *par excellence*, all other stations or chesters had some addition to distinguish them from one another and from this, which was *the* chester, *the* camp, *the* station of stations. What it might have been before the Roman invasion, may be left to the inquiry of those who delight to roam at large in the wide and pleasant regions of conjecture. To those who would rather tread the paths of certainty, it will be sufficient to trace the history of this city no higher than the settlement of the Romans on this spot, of which there can be no doubt. Proofs of this fact are numerous enough in and near the city of Chester, such as pavements, brickwork, vessels, and coins of Roman workmanship.

It is more, however, in accordance with the object of this work to make inquiry concerning the first introduction of the Christian faith, and first foundation of a religious establishment in this famous city. It is more than probable that the Gospel was known here during the greater part of the time that the Romans occupied it, but on their quitting it, and soon after the Saxon invasion, some Christians fled into Wales, and others, it may be feared, adopted the idolatry of their heathen and savage conquerors, and allowed their children to be nurtured to it. Thus all traces of Christianity were lost until the conversion of the Saxons themselves. In Ormerod's "History of Chessire," there is a discourse concerning the foundation and endowment of the Abbey of St. Werburgh, in Chester, written by N. N. That author says, "Touching the original foundation of a monastery in this place, there is not anything that I have seen from our historians, or records, which may make a perfect discovery thereof; but by circumstance I do conclude that Wulpherus, king of the Mercians, who flourished about the year of Christ 660, perceiving his daughter Werburgh much disposed to a religious life, caused her to be veiled, and first built it for her, and such other pious ladies who resolved to dedicate their lives to the service of God therein; for, William of Malmsbury, an ancient author and of great credit, speaking of this devout virgin, saith, that she was buried at Chester, in the monastery there, afterwards re-edified by Earl Hugh. Neither doth the charter of King Edgar import less than that the abbey here was of great antiquity. How long it continued a monastery of nuns (for such they were at first), I cannot take upon me to say, having no certain information thereof from any good authority, but do conclude it was so till towards the Norman conquest, and then it seems that canons secular were placed in their stead, which remained therein till Hugh, earl of Chester, in the sixth year of William Rufus, began the foundation of a new monastery for monks of St. Benedict's order in this place, having procured Anselm, abbot of Bec, to come over into this realm, chiefly for the ordering of that great work, which being accordingly performed, one Richard, a monk of Bec, and chaplain to the said Anselm, was by him first instituted abbot here. Hugh, the pious founder of this great monastery, had such an affection thereto, and so great devotion towards his latter end, that three days before his death he caused himself to be shorn a monk therein, and so departing the world the 6th Cal. of August, 1101, left issue, Richard, who succeeded him in the earldom of Chester, and not only confirmed all his father's grants to this abbey, but added many more himself, as also did many of his successors in the earldom; and thus in great glory, as the greatest ornament of the city and the parts thereabouts, stood this opulent monastery till the 30th of King Henry VIII. his reign, that all the great houses went to wreck, and that by a public instrument the then abbot and his convent surrendered it to the king, who thereupon of the six new bishopricks then made constituted one in this place, designing the buildings of the abbey for the bishop's palace, and the conventual church for his Cathedral, wherein were instituted a dean and secular canons; by which means the ancient title that the bishops of Lichfield and

CHESTER CATHEDRAL.
S.W. VIEW.

Coventry, while they resided here (this being within the diocese), had used, became again to be revived."

To this account should be added that which is given by the learned and judicious ecclesiastical antiquary, Bishop Tanner, who says, "Though this city is deservedly famous on account of its antiquity, being unquestionably a colony of the Romans, and the station of one of their legions, yet the building of a Cathedral Church here to the honour of St. Peter and St. Paul, in the time of King Lucius, must be looked upon as a fiction of later writers. Of not much better authority is the tradition concerning Wulphere (who was the first Christian king of Mercia), his founding here, about the year 670, a nunnery for his daughter Werburgh, and other virgins disposed to lead monastic lives. It is more certain that, before the end of the seventh century, an episcopal see for part of the Mercian dominions was placed in this city. This was some time under different, but for the most part under the same bishops with Lichfield, and to that at length was united; but, after the conquest, Bishop Peter and his successor Robert de Limesay, removing wholly from Lichfield, fixed their residence almost thirty years here at Chester in St. John's Church, where Bishop Peter was buried, till A.D. 1102, when Bishop Robert, taking greater liking to the rich monastery of Coventry, made that one of his Cathedrals and left Chester." With regard to the Benedictine Abbey, Tanner adds, "In this city there was, pretty early in the Saxon times, a religious house, probably a nunnery, and dedicated to St. Peter and St. Paul, whither, as to a place of safety, the remains of St. Werburgh were brought from Heanburgh, A.D. 875. But this monastery was ruined by the wars or injury of time, and in the reign of King Ethelstan re-edified for secular canons by the noble Elfleda, countess of Mercia; and afterwards it was more amply endowed by the munificence of King Edmund, King Edgar, Earl Leofric, and other benefactors, in honour of the above mentioned royal holy virgin St. Werburgh. In the year 1093, at the instigation of the famous Anselm, afterwards archbishop of Canterbury, Hugh Lupus, earl of Chester, expelled from hence the seculars, and settled here an abbot and convent of Benedictine monks from Bec in Normandy, in whose possession St. Werburgh's church continued till the general dissolution of monasteries in England by King Henry VIII., who, anno regni 33, restored the same to a dean and prebendaries, and made this city once more the seat of a bishop, independent of any other see, with a diocese of its own."

As a distinct bishop's see, therefore, Chester can go no higher than the time of Henry VIII., and owes its origin to that monarch.

The abbey, now the Cathedral Church, though of no great magnificence, is an interesting edifice. It is in the form of a cross, but very irregularly so, the south wing of the transept not agreeing at all with the north; the whole fabric is wanting in elevation and dignity, and will bear no comparison with the other Cathedrals of England except those of Rochester, Bristol, and Oxford, to each one of which it is certainly in all respects superior. Its situation is not favourable to its external appearance, being low and crowded by other buildings; nor does the red and crumbling sandstone of which it is built aid the effect of it.

There is nothing about the present Cathedral of Chester to indicate a date anterior to the time of Hugh Lupus; the church which Leofric, earl of Mercia, is recorded to have repaired in the time of Edward the Confessor, has entirely disappeared; but, says Dean Howson, in his "Handbook to Chester Cathedral," "the remains of Norman architecture, which are found in the present church, have a special interest; and, though not conspicuous on the outside, they are not inconsiderable; and recent research enables us, by their help, to ascertain with approximate correctness the size and form of the church of the time of Henry I. The character and dimensions of the north transept can be seen at a glance, and those of the south transept can consequently be inferred. We also know that the length of the nave must have been the same that it is at present; for the whole of the wall of its north aisle is Norman. This may be seen, not only by the easternmost door which enters from the cloisters, and by the round arches conspicuous on the exterior in the south cloister, but by an examination of the masonry throughout, and especially by the really fine Norman architecture which we find at the north-west angle of the church, where it is hoped that a baptistery will soon be formed, so as to bring these long concealed features well to view. Beyond this point, to the west, is the lower stage of a Norman tower, with a passage, also Norman, leading from the west front of the cathedral to the cloisters; and to this must be added the Norman crypt, running the whole length of the west cloister, and forming the lower part of which was once the abbot's house, which always was in absolute contact with the church in this place.

"Turning now to the choir, we have in curious fragments, gradually discovered evidence sufficient to enable the imagination to reproduce the appearance of the old Norman church, with tolerable accuracy. During the restoration of the choir, in 1846, Mr. Hussey discovered under the pavement the 'foundations of the Norman pillars which carried the arches between the choir and the aisles of the central apse'; and this discovery was published in the fifth volume of the 'Journal of the Archæological Institute.' During the recent restoration (1868—1876) the actual curves of the two subordinate apses have been discovered, as well as the curve of the apse which terminated the north transept aisle on the east, and which shows how the south transept aisle was terminated eastward. It has also been ascertained that the piers of the choir were, in their simple rotundity and immense size, similar to those of St. John's Church in this city. In external appearance the east end of the church must have resembled that of some of the Romanesque churches of the Rhine, though, of course, with less of lightness and elevation."

The present cathedral is chiefly of Decorated and Perpendicular work. To the Early English period, however, about the middle of the thirteenth century, belong the Lady chapel, the chapter-house and its vestibule. The Early Decorated work, superintended by Abbot Simon of Whitchurch, includes parts of the choir and its aisles, with geometrical tracery. The later Decorated style appears in the south nave aisle, the eastern aisle of the south transept, and at the south end of both its aisles. In the Perpendicular period, under the superintendence of Abbot Simon Ripley, were

[1] For full and exact details of the Norman architecture in Chester Cathedral reference may be made to Mr. Ayrton's paper in the first volume of the "Transactions of the Chester Archæological Society," and to Sir Gilbert Scott's lecture (printed in the second volume of these transactions) which was delivered in 1870, on "The Architectural History of Chester Cathedral, as developed during the present work of Restoration."

added the main features of the upper part of the nave and south transept.

EXTERIOR.

The west front of this cathedral is by no means the best portion of its exterior; it is now in an incomplete state, but had the original design been executed, it would not have been very imposing. It is now partly concealed by a portion of the King's School, which has been built on the site of the old bishop's palace. The original intention seems to have been the usual one, viz., a square tower on each side of the west end of the nave. The foundations of that on the north side existed till lately. The site of that on the south is now occupied by a building called the consistory court, once perhaps a chapel, in the west wall of which is a window of four lights, with Perpendicular tracery, and flowing crocketed canopy with rich finial; above the window is a belt of panelled tracery, and on each side of it is a niche with overhanging canopies, adorned with pendants and pinnacles, and resting on good brackets. The statues are gone. The parapet of this building is quite plain. The west entrance is a singular and beautiful composition. The doorway itself is modern Perpendicular, inclosed within a square head, the spandrils are filled with rich and elegant foliations, the hollow moulding along the top is deep and broad, and filled with a row of angels half-length; all this is deeply recessed with another Tudor arch, under another square head, with plain spandrils of ordinary panelling. On each side of the door are four niches, with their usual accompaniments of crocketed canopies, pinnacles, and pendants, and instead of brackets, the statues stood on pedestals with good bases and capitals. Above this entrance is the great west window of the nave, deeply and richly recessed; it is of eight lights, with elaborate tracery, of some breadth just below the spring of the arch, and above this some simple Perpendicular tracery. The arch of the window is much depressed, and has above it a flowing crocketed canopy; the gable has no parapet, but is finished off with a simple coping. The flanking turrets before mentioned are octagonal, and have belts of panelled tracery and embattled parapets.

Leaving the west front, and turning to the south, a rich and

deep porch presents itself behind the consistory court. The south face of that court is very similar, in all respects, to the west, already described. The porch is flanked by buttresses which once had pinnacles. The entrance is under a Tudor arch, within a square head, the spandrils richly pannelled; over the square head is a broad belt of quatrefoil panelling, above that a hollow moulding adorned with the Tudor flower. Above this are two flat-headed windows, of two lights each, with a deep niche between them, resting on a projecting bracket. The statue is of course gone, but the projecting and richly decorated canopy remains, on both sides of which the wall above is adorned with two rows of panelling. The open embattled parapet which once crowned the whole has disappeared. The south side of the nave and its aisle is plain, but not without dignity; the windows are all pointed and of Perpendicular character; those of the aisle have straight canopies, with projecting buttresses between, which still have niches, and once had both pinnacles and statues. The aisle has no parapet. The windows of the clerestory are unusually large and lofty, and their canopies are flowing in form, but perfectly plain, and without finials; they have no buttresses between them, and the parapet is very shallow and quite plain.

The next feature of this cathedral, which is now to be described in due order, is a very singular one, and indeed unique, viz., the south wing of the transept. It is no uncommon case to find the two portions of the transept unlike each other in some respects; but in no other instance are they so perfectly disimilar as at Chester. Here the south wing is nearly as long as the nave, and of equal length with the choir, and considerably broader than either, having, like them, aisles on both sides; while the north, which probably stands upon the original foundations, has no aisles, is very short, and only just the breadth of one side of the central tower. The east and west faces of this south portion of the transept are nearly similar. The aisles have no parapet; the windows are pointed, of four lights each, with Late Decorated tracery and small intervening buttresses. The clerestory has a parapet similar to that of the nave; the windows are pointed, large, and lofty, with Perpendicular tracery, and two transoms. The south front of this transept, flat at top, is flanked with square embattled turrets and buttresses, and has a large Perpendicular window filling up nearly all the space between them, the debased tracery of which was inserted early in the present century, but was removed in 1837 by Lord Egerton. The south face of the aisles on each side have pointed windows, similar to those already described, and sloping tops without parapet, but flanked by double buttresses at the external angles, without pinnacles.

The south face of the choir, with its aisle, is in nearly all respects similar to the south portion of the transept; but the aisle was lengthened out beyond the choir, and became the south aisle of the Lady chapel. It had an octangular turret near the east end, with embattled parapet, and beyond it a plain heavy clumsy buttress: the sloping parapet of the east face of this aisle met at the top the flat plain parapet of the most eastern compartment of the Lady chapel which projected beyond the aisle, to that extent. The windows of the Lady chapel are now all of good Early English character; the projecting portion has double buttresses at the external angles, and the eastern face had a low gable point. This chapel was very little higher than the aisles of the choir, the east face of which is seen over it, with a large lofty pointed window, with Perpendicular tracery and several transoms, flanked with octagonal turrets, engaged, and terminated with something like domes of Elizabethan architecture. The parapet of this east face of the choir was flat. The north side of the Lady Chapel was similar to the south; the choir and its aisles exhibit features of Early English character on this side, but the chapter-room conceals a considerable portion of it, which is a small building of an oblong form, and also of early English architecture. Over its vestibule and the arched passage leading into the east walk of the cloister, is seen the large window in the north front of the transept; the arch is much depressed, the old tracery was very plain, and it has two transoms; the walls of this wing of the transept are very plain, flat at top, with no parapet. The whole north side of the nave can be seen only from the cloister-yard. The south walk of the cloister was gone, and in the wall of the aisle, below the windows, are still seen several enriched semi-circular arches resting on short cylindrical columns evidently belonging to the original church of Hugh Lupus. The windows of the aisle are Perpendicular, with the ordinary tracery of this period; but, owing to the cloister once existing beneath, are necessarily curtailed of half their due length: there is a thin flat buttress between each; the aisle has no parapet. The clerestory is lofty, and the windows pointed, and not so much depressed as those in the aisle beneath: they are not so lofty as those in the south side, nor have they any canopies. There is a thin buttress between each, without pinnacles, and the parapet is quite plain, but not so shallow as that on the south side.

The central tower is perhaps the best external feature of this cathedral; it is indeed only of one story above the roof ridge, but it is loftier than such towers usually are; in each face of it are two pointed windows, divided down the middle with a single mullion, with a quatrefoil at the top, and all of them have flowing crocketed canopies with finials. At each of the four angles of the tower is an octagonal turret engaged, all of which, like the tower itself, are terminated with an embattled parapet. From what has been already said of this cathedral, it is plain that it was not all the work of one age, nor of one architect; although some traces of the Norman work are still visible, and much more of the early English, yet by far the greater part must have been erected in the fifteenth and altered in the sixteenth century. The refectory, now a school-room, is built at the back of the north walk of the cloister. The east window of this room consists of several lancet-shaped lights side by side, and the whole building is evidently of Early English date.

INTERIOR.

Entering through the west door-way by a descent of several steps into the nave, we see a view full of dignity. Both the breadth and height of the nave are good, and the fine view of the east end is very satisfying. The new fan vaulting, though in wood, is far superior to the old flat roof. The nave is of six bays, differing north and south. Those of the south side are Decorated; those of the north, whether originally contemporary or not, were afterwards altered, apparently by Simon Ripley, whose initials are on the foliage of the capital of the first pillar from the west end. There is no triforium gallery, simply a considerable space of plain wall between two plain string courses. Though the clerestory windows are large, their tracery (like the springers) has no cusps. The clerestory is unusually lofty, which in some measure makes up for the absence of the triforium; the windows are deeply recessed, and galleries are constructed through the intervening piers. The pillars of the nave are clustered, and have rich bases and foliated capitals; the arches are pointed, formed from two centres, of good span and proportion. The eastern bay of the nave differs from the others, and is of earlier date; both the windows and the springers are cusped, and there is additional ornamentation at the base of the triforium. Formerly the choir was made to extend across into the first bay of the nave. It now ends at its natural termination under the eastern arch of the tower.

The transept, though in one straight line from north to south, yet the two portions of it beyond the central tower on either side, are, as was observed in the description of the exterior, perfectly disimilar. In its plan and architectural detail it very much resembles the nave, having four columns and arches on each side, a triforium gallery and lofty clerestory. The central tower stands on four massy piers; and they were designed, according to some accounts, to support a lofty spire upon the tower. The flat wooden ceiling above the arches has a bad effect in itself, and conceals some good stone work. The north portion of the transept was formerly open, and has a flat ceiling, no aisles, and windows of Late Perpendicular character. The lower portion of the walls is probably the original Norman work. The organ and screen were formerly set between the two eastern piers of the tower; it was heavy, as was also the organ case, which did not accord with anything that is seen in connection with it. The choir was entered by an archway in the middle of the screen, which is of stone, and had a projecting porch in the form of a half hexagon, standing on clustered pillars, supporting three pointed but depressed arches with flowing canopies.

The choir is separated from the aisles by five pointed arches on each side; above them is an arcade of pointed arches, resting on slender shafts; and above it are the clerestory windows. The pavement of the choir is of black and white marble. At the west

GROUND PLAN OF CHESTER CATHEDRAL

A West Entrance
B Nave
C Choir
D South Transept now the Parish Church
E North Transept
F Lady Chapel
G Cloisters
H Chapter Room
I Vestibule to D°
J School
K Vestry
L South Porch
M Consistory Court

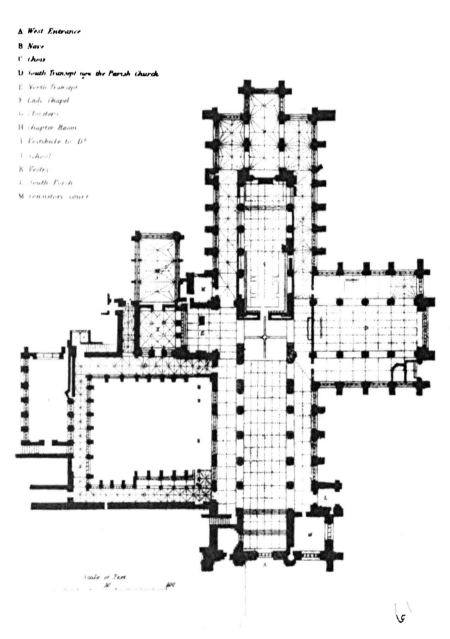

Drawn by Benj.ⁿ Baud   Engraved by B Winkles

end of it are four stalls on each side of the entrance, and there are twenty others on each side of the choir; over these are rich canopies, with pinnacles and pendants in great profusion. Above the stalls, on the right hand opposite the pulpit, was the stone base of the shrine of St. Werburgh, then adapted as the bishop's throne. Under the east window is an arch opening to the Lady chapel, the stone vaulting of which is adorned with richly carved keystones.

There is no crypt under this cathedral. The cloisters are on the north side of the church, and form a quadrangle of about 110 feet square; originally there were four walks, but the south walk was destroyed till lately. The general style of the cloisters is that of the fifteenth century, with carved keystones at the intersection of the vaulting, the arches of the windows are depressed; a lavatory, similar to that at Gloucester, projects from the west walk of the cloister, and did extend along the south walk; over the east walk was a dormitory, which was destroyed many years ago, and which is greatly to be regretted.

In the east walk of the cloister is the entrance into the chapterhouse, or rather its singular vestibule, 30 feet 4 inches long, and 27 feet 4 inches wide. The vaulted roof of this apartment is supported by four columns without capitals, surrounded by eight slender shafts. The chapter-room itself is an Early English building 35 feet high, 50 feet long, and 26 broad. The stone vaulting rests on clusters of slender shafts with foliated capitals. All the windows are in the lancet style; those at the east and west ends consist of five lights each. A gallery goes round three sides of the room, and where it passes the windows is carried between the mullions and a corresponding series of light shafts connected with them, which have elegantly sculptured capitals, and support the mouldings of the lancet arches above; notwithstanding the soft nature of the stone, the carving is all in the most perfect state of preservation.

The north walk of the cloister contained the chief entrance into the refectory of the convent, which still remains, a magnificent apartment, now divided by a modern passage, the eastern and greater portion being used as a school-room. It was 98 feet long, and 34 high, with a roof of oak resting on brackets, which was removed more than half a century ago. Six pointed windows, with intervening buttresses, light the north side, and four the south; at the east end were three lancet-shaped windows, with slender detached shafts, all included within one greater arch. In the south-east angle of this once noble room is a flight of steps within the wall, with a projection at the upper end like a stone pulpit; these steps led to the ancient dormitory, and open into the refectory by an elegant range of pointed arches, trefoiled within, whose spandrils are pierced with a series of quatrefoils.

The dimensions of this cathedral are as follows: Length from east to west, externally 372 feet, internally 350 feet; nave, 175; choir, 110; Lady chapel, 65; transept from north to south, 200; breadth of nave, choir, and aisles, 74½ feet; south wing of transept, 80 feet square; height of nave and choir, 78; tower, 127; Lady chapel, 33; north wing of transept, 39 feet broad.

Upon erecting the see, Henry VIII. caused the church to be dedicated to Christ and the Blessed Virgin Mary, and refounded it for a dean, six prebendaries, six minor canons, or priest's vicars, a deacon, six singing men, six choristers, two masters of the grammar-school, twenty-four scholars, six almsmen, a verger, two sextons, two porters, of which one to be a barber also, one cook, one under-cook, in all seventy-eight by the charter, which bears date August 4, 1541.

There are now attached to this cathedral a dean and four canons.

The old diocese of Chester contained the entire counties of Chester and Lancaster, parts of Westmorland, Cumberland, and Yorkshire: the chapelries of Holt and Iscoed, county of Denbigh: the churches of Hawarden, Hanmer, Bangor, Worthenbury; and chapelry of Orton Madock, county of Flint. By subsequent changes, the last of which took effect in 1880, the diocese has been restricted to the county of Cheshire.

There were two archdeaconries belonging to this diocese, viz., those of Chester and Richmond, but the latter is now replaced by an archdeaconry of Macclesfield. The bishopric of Chester was valued, temp. Henry VIII., at £420 1s. 8d. per annum; but its present annual value is £4,200.

Of the abbots of St. Werburgh nothing remarkable is recorded, except that some of them were great benefactors to their own abbey, both in respect of its revenues and its buildings. All the bishops have been of the reformed church; among them was John Pearson, D.D., the famous author of an Exposition on the Creed, a work of great learning and usefulness, who was consecrated bishop, February 9, 1673, and died July 16, 1686. He was master of two colleges in Cambridge, first of Jesus and then of Trinity College. He was buried within the altar rails of his cathedral without any memorial. Other notable bishops have been William Markham (1771-1776), afterwards Archbishop of York; and Beilby Porteous (1776), afterwards Bishop of London. The present bishop, Dr. Stubbs, is famous for his writings on the constitutional history of England.

CHESTER CATHEDRAL: THE NORTH TRANSEPT, TOWER, AND CHAPTER HOUSE.

MODERN HISTORY OF CHESTER CATHEDRAL.

IN consequence of the perishable nature of the stone of which it was built, this cathedral has undergone much restoration. In 1818-19, under Dean Hodgson, repairs were carried out, Mr. Harrison being the architect, at a time when knowledge and judgment on such questions were still rudimentary. The exterior of the transepts was most affected, and, as Dean Howson says, the new work, though strong and solid, deviated disastrously from the true style and character of the cathedral. The south transept still remains outwardly much in the same state in which this restoration left it.

Dean Copleston (afterwards Bishop of Llandaff), in 1828, carried out at his sole expense the objectionable walling off of the south transept from the rest of the cathedral, now again thrown open.

In 1844 Dean Anson began a transformation of the choir, Mr. R. C. Hussey being the architect. New seats were substituted for the old pews lined with faded baize. The pavement was relaid. The stalls were repaired and removed to a position under the tower. A new organ by Gray and Davison was placed on the choir screen, having a large case with Gothic pinnacles. The former organ is now in St. Paul's Cathedral, La Valetta, Malta. A new pulpit was erected, given by Sir Edward Walker; and the Bishop's throne, on the base of St. Werburgh's shrine, was reconstructed by Canon Slade, in the Decorated style, as a memorial of Bishop Law. At this period also stained windows were inserted in the choir aisles; a screen was erected between the choir and Lady Chapel, and the vaulting was plastered!

In 1855 was carried out the restoration of the interior of the Lady chapel, under the auspices of Dean Anson. The roof and walls were ornamented and coloured by Mr. Octavius Hudson, at the cost of Mrs. Hamilton, of Hoole House, reproducing, he believed, much of the ancient design. The glass mosaics at the east end, forming a low reredos, were designed by Mr. A. Blomfield. They represent scenes connected with the nativity of Christ. A pavement of encaustic tiles and marble was also introduced.

The woodwork at the west end is an adaptation of Bishop Bridgeman's fine pulpit, formerly in the choir.

Various improvements in and near the chapterhouse were made at the time.

The great cathedral bell, which for long rang the curfew at a quarter to nine, was broken by an accident on Nov. 9th, 1866. A public subscription was made, and a new curfew bell was cast. At the same time three new bells were added, the Dean and Chapter contributing £500; thus the peal was raised to eight. The oldest bell bears date 1604, and is inscribed

"I, sweetly tolling, men do call
To taste the meat that feeds the soul."

Before the death of Dean Anson, Mr. Ewan Christian had made a careful examination of the cathedral, and estimates of the cost of needful restorations. A grant of £10,000 was made by the

Ecclesiastical Commissioners in aid of the proposed works. An appeal was issued in 1868, in response to which large subscriptions were received. Sir Gilbert Scott was chosen as architect, and the work was in progress many years under the unremitting supervision of Dean Howson.

As regards the exterior, a beginning has been made of a green Cathedral close by the demolition in 1878 and 1881 of some old houses on the north-east side of the building. It is much to be desired that this process may be still further carried out. The exterior of the chapterhouse has been repaired, but the high roor which it naturally requires has not been added, because it would interfere with the view of the north transept.

The north end of the north transept has been restored in a very befitting style to a correct perpendicular architecture, the tracery of the great window being most carefully designed by Sir Gilbert Scott.

The clerestory windows of the choir had, all but two, gone to utter decay before 1870; from these two all the rest were restored both north and south. In the north wall the greater part of the old stone is untouched, the decay having been much less serious than on the south side.

The walk along the city walls at the east of the cathedral has been widened, and the churchyard made much more neat and seemly.

The central tower in 1868 was in a very bad condition, and in no little danger of falling, owing to the extreme shallowness of its foundations. After the underpinning was successfully accomplished, the whole tower was carefully repaired, following precisely the best ancient evidences, not modern accretions. A new set of four large turrets was added, each with a pair of crocketed pinnacles nestling under it; a pinnacle also rises in the middle of the new battlement of each face of the tower. Respecting these new erections there is much difference of opinion. There is a different impression according to the point of view. From some points the corners of the tower appear to curve outwards in ascending.

The peculiar slope of the rock accounts for the fact that at the west end the cathedral is entered by a double flight of descending steps, being here based directly upon the rock, while at the east end the rock is many feet below. The old builders, however, did not dig down to the rock, and their work was consequently very

CHESTER CATHEDRAL FROM THE SOUTH-EAST.

insecure. During the recent restoration, the whole of the foundations, where necessary, were underpinned, and strong foundations built from the rock upwards. This especially applied to the choir and Lady chapel, at the east end; thirteen feet, in depth, of massive foundations underground had to be built, a work of great expense and considerable danger.

The interior view of the cathedral from the west end is now unquestionably an attractive one. Previous to 1869 it was most unattractive. Its masonry was injured, and disfigured by whitewash. Springers showed that interior vaulting had been intended but never erected. The main roof was in a dangerous condition in consequence of the decay of the great beams. The nave aisles were separated by wooden partitions from the choir aisles, and there were merely doors for passage; while the heavy organ screen, surmounted by the large organ, effectually hid the choir.

Under Sir G. G. Scott, the whitewash was removed and the masonry renewed where necessary. The greatest improvement, however, was the construction of a fine oak vaulted roof, it being judged unsafe to vault in stone. In the centre are the Prince of Wales's arms, and in bosses to the east and west, those of the Duke of Westminster, the Earls of Derby and Sefton, and Lord Egerton of Tatton. The pulpit given by Sir E. Walker was removed to the nave from the choir. The south porch also received a new fan-vaulting, designed by Mr. Gilbert Scott, jun. The nave aisles were vaulted in stone, that of the north aisle being the gift of Mr. R. Platt.

The completion of the nave restoration was marked by a formal opening, in 1872, and all services were thenceforth held in it during the restoration of the choir.

The large Norman arch on the east side of the north transept, which formerly gave entrance to an eastern chapel, now the canons' vestry, is still walled up, as it was found that its opening might be prejudicial to the safety of the tower. The small row of triforium arches above still shows the old Roman rudeness and massiveness, and on the west side three round-headed Norman windows, now closed, may be traced. The arms of Cardinal Wolsey may be noticed, carved on one of the cross-beams of the flat roof.

In 1844 the coffin of Bishop Pearson was found during the restoration of the east end of the choir. It was ultimately removed to the north transept, where a handsome monument,

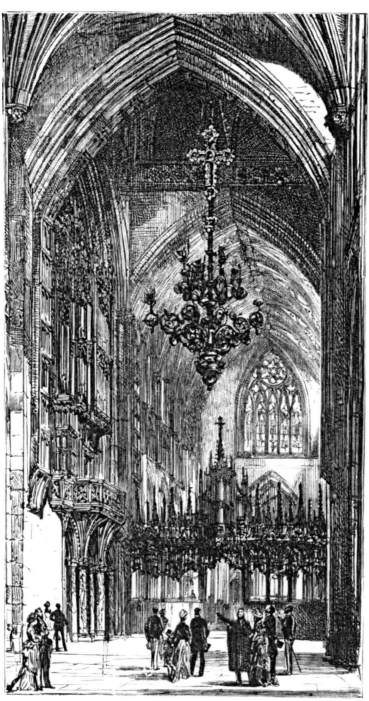

CHOIR SCREEN, CHESTER CATHEDRAL.

designed by Mr. A. W. Blomfield, has now been erected to his memory, partly by subscriptions from the United States. The monument, raised on steps, is surrounded by heads of the twelve apostles, with sentences from the Creed. Above is a recumbent effigy of the bishop, surmounted by a fine canopy of metal work, by Skidmore, of Coventry, richly inlaid with coloured marbles and precious stones.

It is designed to fill the north window with stained glass, illustrating the Seven Churches of Asia on the lower lights, with figures of the Seven Deacons on the upper.

The new organ, and especially its new position, have been subjects of considerable discussion. It was completed in 1876, and is one of the largest cathedral organs in the kingdom, the best parts of the former organ having been incorporated by the builders, Messrs. Whiteley, of Chester. It has four manuals, and may be said to form seven complete organs—the choir, the small organ on the choir screen, the great, the swell, the echo, the solo and the pedals—with seventy-two stops, sixty-three of which are sounding stops. It is blown by steam power, the engine-room being constructed underground in the north side of the chapter-house, the bellows being 100 feet from the organ, in a chamber above the canons' vestry. The large thirty-two feet pipes of the organ are placed under the large window of the north transept; but the main portion of the organ occupies the north arch of the tower, concealing to a large extent the north transept. Though this is better than the first intended position in the south aisle, it cannot be said to be made quite acceptable by the consideration that the north transept is so inferior in size to the southern.

The organ is raised on an open and strongly-built arcade, supported on sixteen columns of rich Italian marble, presented by the Duke of Westminster, who also gave the capitals and arches above the columns, which have been richly carved by Messrs. Farmer and Brindley. Thus a free communication and considerable view between the transept and main body of the building are afforded. The organ case is of beautiful design (by Sir G. G. Scott), and forms a conspicuous feature in the Cathedral.

The south transept, which enveloped, absorbed, and finally obliterated the old parish church of St. Oswald, in the latter part of the fifteenth century, was given up to the parishioners for their services, and the great wall of partition erected by Dean Copleston was only in recent times removed. In 1880 grants were made by the Ecclesiastical Commissioners which aided largely in the building of a new church (St. Thomas') for the parish of St. Oswald, and the transept is now fully restored to the Cathedral. Some repairs have been done to the interior, and the flying buttresses originally intended have been added, but the general aspect of the south front remains, as Sir Gilbert Scott expressed it, " as mean a work as the present century has produced." The inner masonry is still disfigured with whitewash, and there is no vaulting, but only springers on which the vaultings hould be based. There was, however, one bay of vaulting remaining, at the south end of the east aisle, which has served as a guide to the completion of the whole vaulting of the east aisle.

The choir has been greatly improved by the removal of the heavy stone screen and the large organ case. The new screen preserves the Decorated woodwork, and is constructed to suit its style: the small portion of the organ still remaining on this screen is enclosed in a handsome case designed by Sir G. Scott, and the view is now practically open throughout from nave to choir, instead of quite closed.

The stall work and misereres have been renovated, the restoration of each stall being the subject of special gift. Mr. Bridgeman, Mr. Armitage, and Mr. Thompson have executed the restoration, and such new work as was necessary. It may be said that no series of stall-work surpassing this can be found in England. The list of subjects of the work on the misereres is most interesting, but it is too long to be given here.

The new pulpit was given by the Freemasons of Cheshire, and represents the building of Solomon's Temple, the preaching of John the Baptist, and the showing of the new Jerusalem to St. John. The new bishop's throne opposite includes stalls for two chaplains. It is a lofty structure of woodwork, according in character with that of the stalls. Both pulpit and throne were executed by Messrs. Farmer and Brindley.

The plaster vaulting has been replaced by oaken vaulting, given by Mr. R. Platt. It has been decorated by Messrs. Clayton and

Bell. In the eastern bays are represented the sixteen prophets, each with a scroll, bearing a sentence in Latin from his own prophecies. In the western bays, on the seats of the choristers, are

PULPIT, CHESTER CATHEDRAL.

angels with musical instruments. The bay between has various orders of angelic beings.

The new pavement represents in incised marble, at the east of the stalls, the heads of the apostles in a circle, and at the corners the heads of four doctors of the church—St. Ambrose, St. Augustine, St. Athanasius, and St. Chrysostom. The raised steps approaching the communion table contain representations of the Passover in incised marble, and the border round these consists of fragments of tesselated pavement brought from the Temple area at Jerusalem.

The altar table is constructed of olive, cedar, and oak wood

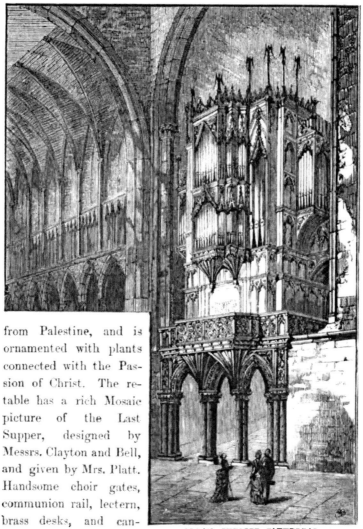

ORGAN, CHESTER CATHEDRAL.

from Palestine, and is ornamented with plants connected with the Passion of Christ. The retable has a rich Mosaic picture of the Last Supper, designed by Messrs. Clayton and Bell, and given by Mrs. Platt. Handsome choir gates, communion rail, lectern, brass desks, and candelabra are among the important additions in metal work which the choir has received.

The great eastern arch opening into the Lady chapel has been made firm and symmetrical, but only after considerable difficulty.

In the north choir aisle traces of the Norman period can now be distinctly seen. "On the right," says Dean Howson, "at the entrance of this aisle, we see the base of one of the old Norman piers, which was brought to view in the process of re-laying the floor during the recent restoration: and we perceive at once that the piers of the choir, in the earliest period of the church, were of immense size and of perfect simplicity, like those of Durham Cathedral or of St. John's Church in this city. Close to this base we have the proof that an inverted capital of one of these old massive piers has been used for the support of a pier of later date. Between these two remains of Norman times are the fragments of some old tiles of various patterns. Further to the east a curved line of dark marble in the floor shows where the Norman apse ended. One of the stones used in the construction of this apse still remains. But the most perfect memorial of the Early Plantagenet times in this part of the cathedral is in what is termed the Canons' Vestry. This is an ancient chapel which formerly opened out of the north transept, on its east side. Two dates of architecture can easily be distinguished in the chapel. The arch and the supporting columns in the east wall of the transept are of early Norman; and a fragment of masonry at the edge of the floor, by the door which enters from the aisle, shows the curve in which the apse originally terminated. Afterwards the chapel was rebuilt and terminated in a square form, with vaulting of the Transitional period. About twelve years ago it was in urgent need of restoration; and the work was done at the cost of Robert Platt, Esq., whose arms are in the window. This chapel ought not to be left behind without observation of the very beautiful ironwork, and of a curious lock of early date, in a cupboard in the west wall.

"The second, or Early English period, of the history of this aisle can likewise be very easily traced by looking upwards at the vaulting. It will be perceived at a glance that this vaulting suddenly changes its character at a point some little distance beyond the above-mentioned curve in the aisle-floor. Here also a piscina, of very beautiful form, on the right, shows that there was formerly an altar at this point. The slit too in the masonry which once held the glass of one of the windows, can be clearly seen on the right. In the Early English period the aisle terminated here in a semi-hexagonal form: and the place of its termination can be very well marked on the outside by a heavy mass of masonry on the roof. At this point a round-headed Early English window on the left leads to a staircase, and ultimately to the triforium of the choir; and this fact again is indicated on the exterior of the cathedral by a plain projecting masonry, which was very insecure a few years ago, but which has now been made safe and strong by the footing of the base of the wall outwards. Here too must be named the re-appearance of a doorway which partially invades one of the windows. This fact, though utterly lost to view, was only so lost during recent years; for it appears in one of the engravings of Lysons' 'Britannia.'"

The alterations effected at the east-end of the north aisle, in the Late Perpendicular period, by which an outer aisle or projection of the choir aisle encased the Lady chapel, were not seriously interfered with, since the only entrance to the Lady Chapel is here; but the old buttresses have been restored.

In the south aisle the form of the Norman apsidal end is also shown by a curved line on the floor; but the termination of the apse has been restored to the form it had in Edward I.'s time, so that the whole south wall of the Lady chapel is now once more external. The eastern or apsidal part of the aisle has been restored as a memorial of Mr. Thomas Brassey, the eminent railway contractor, by his sons. On the north wall is a memorial bust of Mr. Brassey. Mosaics on the wall are commemorative of Mrs. Brassey. They were executed at Venice by Salviati, after designs by Clayton and Bell, and represent the Widow of Sarepta and Elijah, Phœbe receiving the Epistle to the Romans from St. Paul, and Priscilla with Aquila instructing Apollos. The windows are described later. The tiles on the floor, reproduced from ancient fragments found here, depict the twelve months. The choir aisles are closed by beautiful iron gates of Spanish work given by the Duke of Westminster.

The old bishop's throne has been placed near the western extremity of the south choir aisle. The fragments of St. Werburgh's shrine, or rather of its base and canopy, which it contains are genuine Early Decorated work; and other fragments were found during the late restoration, inserted in a wall which blocked up the west end of the north nave aisle. When Canon

NEW BISHOP'S THRONE, CHESTER CATHEDRAL.

Slade restored the throne he greatly modernised it. It is chiefly the lower part, and the small gilt figures, supposed to represent the kings and queens of Mercia, that are old.

In 1868 the Lady chapel presented externally an utterly flat and mean appearance, the original lofty roof having been long removed. At the south-east corner of the choir was a turret, much lower than the choir, added apparently about 1820; and a horribly ugly and disproportionate buttress bolstered up the south-east corner of the prolonged choir aisle. The junction of the choir and Lady chapel was extremely unpleasing. These features are depicted in our coloured plate (south-east view).

The underpinning we have already described was a most serious piece of work, as regards the Lady chapel. Its roof was raised to a dignified loftiness, and by finishing it westward in an apsidal shape, the blocking up of the east window of the choir was avoided. A good gable was added at the east end of the Lady chapel, including a triplet lancet window designed after an example at Wells. Handsome turrets, flanked by improved buttresses, complete this extreme east end. The removal of the old south prolongation of the choir aisle and the substitution of the Brassey Chapel, have been already recorded.

This Lady chapel is now used for early morning prayer and other services. Visitors should note a sculptured boss in the vaulted ceiling, probably of the 13th century, which contains a group of figures representing the murder of St. Thomas à Becket, which appears to correspond very closely with the early traditional description.

The windows had been filled with bad Perpendicular tracery, which has been removed. Its general Early English aspect, the original style, has been revived. The east window was reconstructed, according to Sir G. G. Scott's design, of five lancets, symmetrically rising to the centre. The two central bays were once more closed half way up, and an Early English window (not opening to the exterior) of three unglazed lights has been inserted, looking on to the eastern prolongations of the choir aisles.

The theory formerly held that the piers of the tower are Norman in their core has been upset by discoveries in the course of restoration. It was found that the north-eastern pier was actually supported " upon several floriated tombstones of the 13th century, placed cross-wise upon one another. One of these stones has been removed, and carefully kept, in testimony of this unexpected fact; and the rest have been covered up under the pier."

Sixty years ago Chester Cathedral had no stained glass windows; but many have been inserted since, by no means always of good design or colour. We cannot give the subjects or dates of all these. The great west window is the largest, and is a memorial by Mrs. Hamilton, to her husband, Rev. E. P. Hamilton (died 1858). The glass is by O'Connor, and represents Resurrection scenes, and Christ seated in judgment. In the south transept two windows, the northern and southern in the east aisle, are military in character, in memory of General Harding and Colonel Twemlow respectively. The tracery of the great south window has been given by Lord Egerton of Tatton, and filled with very beautiful stained glass, as a memorial of his father. The tracery was designed by Mr. A. W. Blomfield, and the glass was wrought by Heaton, Butler, and Bayne. Several windows in the south choir aisle are given by Dean Anson or are memorials of his family. The Brassey apsidal chapel has windows by Clayton and Bell, representing scenes illustrative of Faith, Hope, Charity, etc. The glass which had been inserted in the three Perpendicular windows of the part now removed has been adapted and placed in the eastern windows of the choir clerestory on the south side. That which had been in the eastern windows of the Lady chapel when they were Perpendicular in character, has been placed in the clerestory windows of the east side of the north transept. The best window at Chester is the west window of the chapter-house, by Heaton and Butler. It is in memory of Dean Anson, and depicts very successfully the legend of St. Werburgh, the Saxon and Norman Earls of Chester, and various scenes of the history of the cathedral.

The monuments in Chester Cathedral are comparatively unimportant. Besides Bishop Pearson's, already referred to, there are on the right of the western entrance, monuments to Bishop George Hall (died 1668), son of Bishop Joseph Hall; and Bishop Stratford (died 1707). The inscription which Bishop George Hall wrote for his tomb says that he is a hearty though useless servant of the Church, worthy of notice only as the son or rather the shadow of his father, and that he is glad to be burnt out, if only meanwhile he may give light in the House of God (alluding to the representation of a lighted candle at the base of the monument). The recumbent effigy of Bishop Graham (died 1865) is behind the north wall of the Lady chapel in the north prolonged aisle. Deans Arderne (died 1682), Fogg (died 1692), and Smith (died 1758) are the only deans of Chester who have monuments there; but several Archdeacons of Chester are thus commemorated, including Archdeacons Travis (died 1797) and Wrangham (died 1843). On one of the piers under the tower is an inscription in memory of a New York citizen, representing forcibly the feelings with which he found himself separated from the mother country. On the north wall of the north nave aisle is a monument to one of the Napiers who died during the Sikh war.

A brass in memory of Dean Howson (died 1885) has been fixed to the wall of the north choir aisle; it is contained in a sunken panel of Runcorn stone with carved Early English border.

In the south wall of the south choir aisle are two sepulchral recesses, with a stone coffin in each. One of them is probably an abbot's, dating from the twelfth century. At the further end of the aisle is a coffin-shaped altar-tomb, bearing quatrefoiled panels, and between them small painted figures of kings and bishops. There is a tradition that this tomb, probably dating from the fifteenth century, is that of Henry IV. of Germany, who died and was buried in his own country. It is probably the tomb of an abbot.

A new door on the north side of the vestibule of the chapter-house was made by Sir G. G. Scott to communicate with rooms to the north. The wooden ribs inserted in the vaulting of the chapter-house from a mistaken idea are now removed. The east side of the exterior has been fully restored, the north side partially. The library, though it contains no great treasures, is in a much better state than formerly.

One side of the cloister (the southern) has been restored, beginning at the Norman doorway into the church. Other Norman arches are seen in the exterior of the wall of the north nave aisle. A Norman passage, formerly blocked up, leads round to the west front of the Cathedral. Remains of monumental stones of several abbots of Chester were discovered in the eastern part of the cloister, and may now be seen where found.

It is singular that this restoration was due to Mr. Platt's offer to vault the north nave aisle itself. It was found that this could not be done without adding the external support which had been lost; for the whole south side of the cloister had disappeared, except three bases of the vaulting shafts, and the east and west ends. Its form is interesting, as it consists of a double arcade, the inner

REREDOS, CHESTER CATHEDRAL.

recesses being used for the monks to write in. The double arcade extends for some distance along the west cloister also, but the three unrestored sides remain in a state of considerable decay.

Several portions of the old monkish buildings still remain in connection with the cloisters, and have been restored in modern times, including a fine vaulted chamber on the east, probably the fratry of the monks. The western part of the (Early English) refectory has been cleared of rubbish, and many of its interesting features can be made out. It was originally about 90 feet long by 34 wide. The beautiful stone pulpit and staircase in the

PULPIT IN MONKS' REFECTORY, CHESTER.

south-eastern corner are unique in England. This room was long used as the King's School. It is now the practising room of the Cathedral choir.

In 1886 was completed an extensive series of marble mosaics, executed by Burke, etc., from designs by Clayton and Bell, for the decoration of the north wall of the nave, at the cost of Mrs. Platt. The work is composed of a very large number of small tesseræ, like those in old Roman pavements. The grouping of coloured marbles in these panels is excellent for softness of tone. In each bay is represented a conspicuous figure in Old Testament history (Abraham, Moses, David, and Elijah), and on either side are panel spaces filled with grouped compositions illustrating scenes in the life of the character in the centre. Above are canopied niche-like panels with other Old Testament characters.

CARLISLE CATHEDRAL.

CARLISLE CATHEDRAL.

THE city of Carlisle is not indebted for its origin, as many others are, to the Cathedral or any other religious establishment. Some authors attribute it to Luel, a British prince, before the Roman invasion; but this opinion is discarded by others as resting on no certain foundation, who say, with much more reason, that it was a Roman station, built by Severus, about the same time with his famous wall. "That it was a place of consequence in the time of the Romans," says Camden, "appears plainly from the various evidences of antiquity occasionally dug up, and from the frequent mention of it in the writers of those days, and even after the ravages of the Picts and Scots, it retained something of its ancient splendour, and was accounted a city." In the Itinerary of Antoninus it is called Lugo-vallum, and this name Dr. Burn imagines to have been formed from the British Llu gyda gwal, signifying the army by the wall. This appellation was, by the Saxons, contracted into Luell and Luall, to which the British Caer, a city, being afterwards prefixed, it became Caer-luell, which by an easy transition has, in more modern times, been changed into Carlisle.

The priory of Carlisle was founded in 1101, and was finished and endowed by Henry I. The see of Carlisle, taken out of Durham, was founded in 1133. The early records of the Cathedral are very scanty; the styles of the different parts are given on page 96. The transept and nave are coeval with the priory; a large part of the nave was destroyed during the Commonwealth. The choir was rebuilt after an accidental fire in 1292, after which indulgences were issued, an effectual means of raising money in those days: they were of forty days' duration for all such who should, by money, materials, or labour, contribute to this pious work: and the bishop's register abounds with letters patent, and orders for the purpose. Camden says the belfry (meaning probably the central tower) was raised, and the bells placed in it, at the charge of William de Strickland, bishop, in the year 1401. Hutchinson says, that several portions of this sacred edifice were enlarged or improved by Prior Gondibour in 1484, and judges so from the initial letters of his name appearing in those portions. Prior Senhouse, he says, repaired the square tower about 1507; judging again from sentences inscribed on the beams in the middle room of it, containing a moral maxim often used by him, " Lothe to offend." The door on the south side of the choir, with its ornaments, the same author says, was the work of Prior Haythwaite, about the year 1480, his name having been seen on the back of it; and the opposite door, with its ornaments, is supposed to have been erected by Prior Senhouse, about the year 1500, from the sentence inscribed thereon, *Vulnera quinque Dei, sint medicina mei*, which was that prior's common adage. The tabernacle work of the choir, he adds, was done at the expense of Bishop Strickland before mentioned. The chapter-house and cloisters stood on the south side of the Cathedral, but were destroyed during the civil wars. Traces of the dormitory yet remain. The refectory is now used as the chapter-house. It is not known when, or by whom, these buildings were erected. Though this church has been despoiled of its fair proportions by the misapplied zeal of the puritans, it is still an imposing and interesting object on every approach to Carlisle, especially from the north-east, where it is seen crowning the whole city, rising far above the highest buildings which surround it, backed by a graceful line of hilly country; while the foreground of the picture consists of rich meadow and river scenery, rendered still more picturesque by a handsome stone bridge of many arches.

EXTERIOR.

Beginning as usual with the west front, the visitor of Carlisle Cathedral looks for it in vain; it is gone, and with it 92 feet

CARLISLE CATHEDRAL.

of the nave, the remaining portion being only 43 feet in length; the opening made by the destruction of so much of the nave and its aisles was afterwards closed up with a plain wall, supported by very ugly sloping buttresses. What remains of the nave, aisles, and clerestory is very plain, and of the original work; the windows are of one light, and roundheaded. The north wing of the transept has a small round-headed door in the west wall of it, which is plain solid masonry, and has a large inserted window of three lights, and of Late Decorated character. The north face of the transept has a much larger window, inserted to the memory of five children of Dean (afterwards Archbishop) Tait; it occupies the whole space, which is flanked by double buttresses at the angles, above which to the west rises an octagonal turret; the wall is a straight line at top, and without a parapet. The east wall of this wing of the transept is quite plain, except that there are three parallel string courses upon it about midway, horizontally disposed, a few feet from each other.

The north side of the choir, with its aisle and clerestory, next presents itself to view; the parapet of both is perfectly plain; the windows of the aisle are of various forms, some narrow and highly pointed, of one light, and three together; others wide, of many lights, and much good tracery within the arch; the buttresses between the windows are perfectly plain, do not project far, and their pointed heads only rise above the parapet. The clerestory has no buttresses; the windows are in clusters of three together; the centre one, of three lights, rises higher than those on each side of it, which are of one light only; the middle ones also contain some elegant tracery. The east end of the choir, with its aisles, is rich and magnificent, though by no means uniform; the east face of the north aisle is straight at top, and has an enriched parapet, it is flanked with a double buttress at the angle, and an octagonal turret engaged rising above, the window is large and contains good decorated tracery; the east face of the south aisle has a plain sloping top, with a window similar to that just described, and is flanked by a double buttress at the angle, surmounted by lofty crocketed pinnacles. The east face of the choir itself is lofty and well proportioned, and contains a window perhaps the most superb in England—it has nine lights, and is filled at top with tracery of the most rich and elegant design; above this is another, in the form of a triangle, whose sides are curved, which is also filled with tracery of the like description; above this is the gable point, surmounted with a cross. There is no parapet, but an enriched cornice instead, upon which there are a series of crosses which form a sort of open parapet. The whole is flanked on each side by gigantic buttresses, enriched with crocketed canopies, niches, and statues, and terminated by lofty crocketed pinnacles, almost deserving the name of spires. On the south side of the choir the clerestory is, in all respects, the same as on the north side, already described. In the aisle a little difference is observable: the windows are all original, except those in the first and third compartment from the east end, which are of later date. That in the third compartment, which Prior Gondibour had altered to Perpendicular, has now been restored to an Early English triplet form like the rest. From the fifth compartment from the east end formerly projected a small chapel, now removed. To the east wall of the south wing of the transept is appended another chapel, dedicated to St. Catharine; to the east it has a triplet window like some of those in the aisles of the choir, but all enclosed within one arch formed by a pointed dripstone; the parapet is plain, and the whole has the appearance of an aisle to the transept. The clerestory of this wing of the transept is like that of the nave, and its round-headed windows are two in number. The south face of the transept was very plain. But during the restoration, in 1856, a handsome doorway was inserted here which is now the main entrance to the building; there is also an octagonal turret rising out of the buttress at the angle of St. Catharine's Chapel, which forms part of the south front of the transept.

The tower is perhaps the worst feature of this Cathedral; it rises only one story above the ridge of the choir roof, but two above those of the transept and nave. In the lower story are two windows of two lights each, and plain tracery; the upper has only one in each face of the tower, of three lights, and plain tracery; the whole surmounted with an embattled parapet very plain; and at the north-east angle is placed a turret which rises a little above the battlements.

INTERIOR.

The small part of the nave which now remains was used for many years as the parish church of St. Mary's. The old pews shown in our plate are now removed. The arches are semicircular, with a few simple mouldings of Early English character. The columns which support them, four in number, two on each side, are extremely massive, the height of them being only fourteen feet two inches, while their circumference is seventeen feet and a half. The arches nearest the tower are crushed out of place, and the aisle wall is much out of the vertical. This nave formerly had eight bays.

The choir is entered by a low doorway in the woodwork of the stalls at the north-west. The organ screen is inserted between the two eastern piers which support the tower. The aisles of the choir are entered by arches in the transept wall. The first view of the choir itself gives the beholder quite another idea of this cathedral. From the remains of the nave he passes into a transept unusually narrow, and is next ushered into one of the very finest choirs in England—spacious, lofty, well proportioned, and in all its detail rich and elegant. The columns are clustered, and have beautiful sculptured capitals of leaves and flowers. The arches are highly pointed, and adorned with a great variety of elegant mouldings, among others, that graceful one so common to this age of the pointed style, which resembles a flower of four petals turned back towards its stem. The triforium is low, composed of three pointed arches of equal height side by side in each compartment, with a good string course above and below. The clerestory is lofty, having also three pointed arches side by side corresponding with the windows, which are seen through them, and have been already described. Beneath the windows is a gallery pierced with quatrefoils. The original ceiling was of wood; this from time and neglect became very ruinous, and on examination it was found to be too far gone to be repaired. In the year 1764 it was agreed to take it down and put up a plaster vaulting in its place. During the restoration of 1856 a facsimile of the original wooden wagon roof was put up. The stalls for the dean and chapter, and other members of the cathedral establishment, are elaborate Perpendicular structures. A multitude of foliated canopies and sculptured pendants, together with a grove of crocketed pinnacles rising above all, create a striking effect. But the chief glory of this choir is the great east window, which nearly occupies the whole east end. Upon the whole, this window is deemed by many to be the very finest in England. It is beautifully proportioned, divided by upright mullions into nine lights, and the upper part filled with tracery of the very best design and execution. Too much cannot be said in commendation of this magnificent window. The admirer of this period, of the pointed style in particular, will dwell upon it with delight, and quit it with regret.

The chapel of St. Catherine on the east side of the south transept, opens by a massive Norman arch, of two orders. The lower part is closed by a beautiful late decorated screen. The chapel, now used as a choristers' vestry, is of Early English architecture. Above it is a room in which are some Roman tiles, and various fragments of sculpture found during the restoration. In the wall between the choir aisle and the chapel is a pointed doorway formerly leading to a well, from which water was formerly raised by a windlass. It was closed during the restoration. A similar well, long closed, exists in the north transept.

The chapter-house and cloisters stood on the south side of the cathedral, but were taken down for their materials during the civil wars. They were probably erected when the choir was rebuilt, and if so, their destruction cannot be too much regretted. The refectory, now used as a chapter-house, is a building of good proportions, and, from the style of its architecture, seems to have been erected about the time of Richard II.

Many of the bishops of Carlisle have been interred in the cathedral, but it is uncertain to which of them the few ancient monuments remaining were erected. In the middle of the choir on the pavement is a very fine brass monument to the memory of Bishop Bell. Under a triple canopy, adorned with crockets, pinnacles, and pendants, is the figure of the bishop in his pontificals, with a crosier in one hand, and an open book in the other, and over his head a motto in a brass fillet, and an inscription on a brass margin, within which the whole is enclosed. Bishop Henry

Robinson was also buried in this cathedral, and there is this remarkable entry in the parish register of Dalston, that he died at Rose Castle (which is the episcopal palace) on the 19th day of June, 1616, about three o'clock in the afternoon, and was buried in this cathedral the same evening about eleven o'clock, from which it is concluded that he died of the plague. In taking down the old hangings and ornaments of the high altar, says Hutchinson, to make the late repairs, at the north corner was discovered a brass plate finely engraven, which had been put up to his memory. The bishop is there represented in his pontificals, kneeling, with one hand supporting a crosier, while in the other is a lighted candle and a cord, to which three dogs are attached, who appear guarding an equal number of sheepfolds from the attack of wolves. Below the candle is a group of figures, bearing implements of agriculture and peaceful industry; near their feet is a wolf playing with a lamb, and various warlike instruments scattered and broken. Each part is accompanied with appropriate sentences in the learned languages, chiefly taken from Scripture. Behind the bishop is a quadrangular building inclosing an open court, and doubtless intended to represent Queen's College, Oxford, which he had so much benefited. On it are the words, *Invenit destructum, reliquit extructum et instructum.* Above this building is the delineation of a cathedral, over the entrance is inscribed, *Intravit per ostium;* on a label across the entrance is, *Permansit fidelis;* and below on the steps, under a group of figures, one of whom is kneeling and receiving a benediction, are the words *Recessit beatus.* Near the top of the plate is the angel of the Lord, bearing a label, inscribed, Του Επισκοπου. Above are the words, *Erunt pastores in eadem regione excubantes et agentes vigilias noctis super gregem suam.* At the bottom is a Latin inscription, stating that he was a most careful provost of Queen's College, and afterwards a most watchful bishop of this diocese for thirteen years; that on the thirteenth of the calends of July, in the year from the delivery of the Virgin 1616, and of his age sixty-four, he devoutly resigned his spirit to the Lord; and that Bernard Robinson, his brother and heir, set up this memorial as a testimony of his love. Beneath are the following lines:

Non sibi, sed patriæ, præluxit Lampadis instar,
    Deperdens oleum, non operam Ille suam:
In minimis fide servo, majoribus apto,
    Maxima nunc Domini gaudia adire datur.

There are other more modern monuments, but chiefly mural tablets. This cathedral has no crypt; its dimensions are as follows—length of the choir 137 feet; of the transept 124; breadth of the choir and its aisles 71 feet, of the transept 28. Height of the choir from the pavement to the centre of the vaulting 75 feet; of the tower to the top of the parapet 127 feet.

It was dedicated to the Virgin Mary, but Henry VIII., after dissolving the priory and erecting a new foundation, called it the church of the Holy and Undivided Trinity, and placed therein a dean, four canons or prebendaries, eight minor canons, a sub-deacon, four lay clerks or singing-men, a master of grammar, six choristers, a master of the choristers, six alms-men, one verger, and two sextons; and granted them the site of the priory, and the greater part of the revenues of it.

The only way in which the Act of Parliament interfered with this establishment was that the eight minor canons were done away with; the sub-deacon's place had not been filled for many years.

The old diocese of Carlisle consisted of the better half of Cumberland and Westmorland, under the government of one archdeacon, viz., of Carlisle; the new arrangement was that the sees of Carlisle and Sodor and Man should be united, and the Isle of Man added to the diocese, but after a strong remonstrance and petition on the part of the Manx clergy, the commissioners gave up the plan. The new diocese now consists of all the old, together with those parts of Cumberland and Westmorland which were in the diocese of Chester, of the deanery of Furness and Cartmel in the county of Lancaster, and of the parish of Ulverston in the diocese of Durham. Two new archdeaconries have also been created, viz., those of Westmorland and Furness.

The revenues of the bishopric were valued 26 Henry VIII. at £577 in the whole, and £531 4s. 11d. clear per annum; its present value is £4,500.

The most worthy of all the bishops that ever yet filled the see of Carlisle, deserves special mention—James Usher, " a man," says Nicholson, " of deep erudition, and a zealous Protestant, without bigotry and fanaticism, with which the age was too much tinctured. He was born in Dublin, January 4, 1580, and had his education in the college of that university. In 1620 he was promoted to the bishopric of Meath, and upon Dr. Hampton's death, in 1624, was advanced to the archbishopric of Armagh, but suffered such great losses in the troubles of Ireland that he was obliged to quit that country, and came to England in the year 1641, when Charles I. granted him the bishopric of Carlisle in commendam, upon the revenues of which, diminished as they were by the quarterings of the English and Scotch armies, he contrived to support himself till Parliament seized on all the episcopal revenues, and then, in consideration of his great merits, a pension was granted him of £400 per annum; which, however, he never received above once or twice at most. He died March 21, 1655, at the house of the Countess of Peterborough, at Reigate, in Surrey, aged seventy-five years. Cromwell ordered him a magnificent public funeral in Westminster Abbey, and signed a warrant to the Lords of the Treasury, to pay to Dr. Bernard £200 to defray the expense of it."

On the restoration of the church and kingdom, Richard Stern was elected bishop of this see; he was educated at Cambridge, and took the degree of doctor in divinity, and became master of Jesus College in that university. He was also domestic chaplain to Archbishop Laud, and attended that ill-fated prelate on the scaffold at his execution. He was a prisoner in the Tower with several other persons, upon a complaint made by Cromwell, who was then one of the burgesses of Cambridge, that they had conveyed the college plate for the king's relief to York; from this cause he was dispossessed of his several appointments, and lived in obscurity till the Restoration. In the year 1664 he was translated to York, and died there in 1683. Two almost opposite characters are given of this prelate, perhaps the truth may be between the two. Burnet calls him " a sour ill-tempered man, chiefly studious of measures to enrich his family;" and says, "that he was particularly attached to the court, and servile in adopting the measures then moved in; that he was zealous in the affairs of the Duke of York (afterwards James II.) and strongly suspected of Popery." Another account states that he was greatly respected and generally lamented, that "all his clergy commemorate his sweet condescensions, his free communications, faithful counsels, exemplary temperance, cheerful hospitality, and bountiful charity." These two opposite opinions of the same person, prove perhaps how high party spirit ran in those times.

Edmund Law, appointed bishop in 1768, was father of two bishops (of Bath and Wells, and Elphin), and of the first Lord Ellenborough. The most notable bishop of recent times is Bishop Harvey Goodwin, appointed in 1869.

GROUND PLAN OF CARLISLE CATHEDRAL.

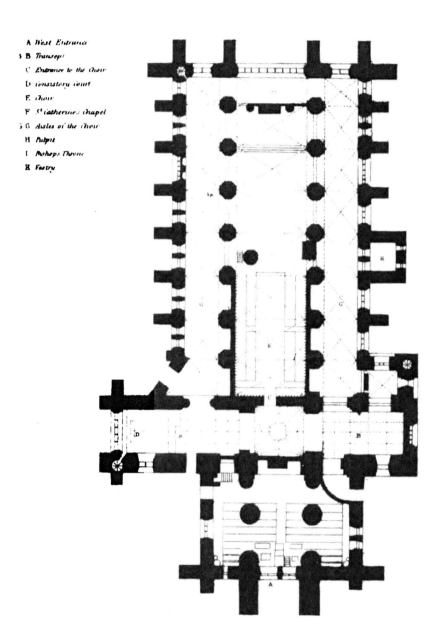

A West Entrance
B Transept
C Entrance to the Choir
D Consistory Court
E Choir
F St Catherine's Chapel
G Aisles of the Choir
H Pulpit
I Bishops Throne
K Vestry

MODERN HISTORY OF CARLISLE CATHEDRAL.

THIS cathedral, much as it needed it, did not come under restoration till 1853-7, when Mr. Ewan Christian designed and superintended extensive repairs, at a cost of £15,000.

A new doorway, richly sculptured, was inserted in the south front of the transept. The window above it is also new work; in fact, all except the masonry of the wall is modern. The north transept is also mostly modern Decorated. The north end has been rebuilt. The large window, of geometrical Decorated character, is filled with stained glass in memory of five children of Dean (afterwards Archbishop) Tait who died of scarlet fever between March 6 and April 9, 1858. The Early English window in the west wall is filled with stained glass in memory of Chancellor Fletcher (died 1846). In the west wall, protected under glass, is a Norse Runic stone found in this position during the restoration. The inscription signifies, "Tolfihn wrote these runes on this stone."

During the restoration the original form of the wooden roof was restored. It is semi-circular in section, and divided into square panels by moulded ribs at the intersections. From the feet of three of the main ribs project hammer-beams, perhaps originally intended to have lamps suspended from them. They are terminated by large angels, and connected with the vaulting shafts by wall-pieces and curved ribs. The roof has been somewhat too showily painted under the direction of Mr. Owen Jones, but is said to follow the original colouring.

The east window has had its tracery renewed in stone, reproducing most carefully the original design. The stained glass in the tracery is, however, quite old and good, dating from Richard II.'s time. It illustrates the Resurrection, the Last Judgment, and the New Jerusalem. The stained glass in the series of lights below is modern, and contains much blue which does not quite accord with the colouring in the tracery. It forms a memorial to Bishop Percy (died 1856), and was inserted by Hardman in 1861.

CARLISLE CATHEDRAL FROM THE SOUTH-EAST.

CARLISLE CATHEDRAL: THE GREAT EAST WINDOW.

The subjects include scenes from the Life of Christ, with the Crucifixion in the centre.

The organ, which quite fills up the eastern tower arch, is by Willis, and the case has been coloured by Hardman. Its unsymmetrical position, consequent on the narrowness of the tower arch, is unfortunate.

The third bay from the east in both choir aisles had Early English windows inserted, instead of the by no means beautiful Perpendicular insertions of Prior Gondibour.

The east end was almost entirely rebuilt, and a row of houses adjoining has been cleared away, so as to give a much better view. Each of the main massive buttresses contains two niches with rich canopies, and in them are inserted figures of St. Peter, St. Paul, St. James, and St. John. The series of pinnacles on the buttresses of aisles and east end is now very beautiful and rich.

A new bishop's throne was erected in 1880.

The architecture of Carlisle Cathedral may be summarised as follows: Norman, south transept, piers of tower, the portion of nave remaining. Early English; walls and windows of choir aisles, and St. Catherine's Chapel; part of the main arcade of the choir. Early Decorated: part of main arcade. Late Decorated: upper part of choir, east end and roof. Perpendicular: upper part of tower.

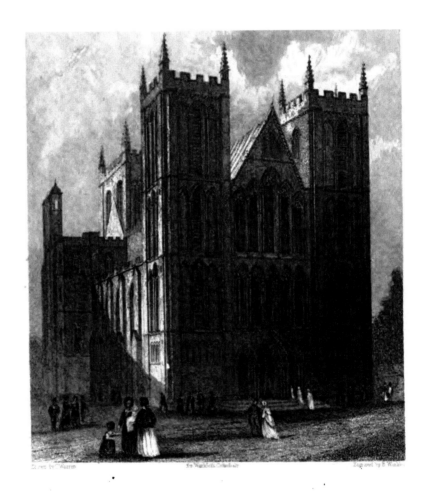

RIPON CATHEDRAL.
NORTH WEST VIEW

RIPON CATHEDRAL.

RIPON, formerly Inrhypum, Hripensis Ecclesia, or Ad Ripam, is a foundation which began as a Benedictine monastery, but was changed to a collegiate church about four hundred years after its first establishment. Bishop Tanner says, Alchfrid, king of the Northumbers, gave this place to Abbot Eata, to build a monastery; but, before that could be finished, he was sent away, and St. Wilfred made abbot here before A.D. 661.

This religious house was endowed with great privileges by King Athelstan, and continued in great repute till it was burnt down in the devastation which King Edred made in these parts, about A.D. 950. Archbishop Oswald, and his successors, archbishops of York, assisted in the rebuilding of the church; and Archbishop Aldred, about the time of the Conquest, endowed it with lands, and made it collegiate, which it continued to be, with one interruption only, till in 1836 it was erected into a see, when the collegiate was made the Cathedral church. It was first of all dedicated to St. Peter, but in some later writings it is called the Church of St. Wilfrid, and, as so many authors of repute make him the founder of it, some notice of so great an ecclesiastic will not be unacceptable to the general reader.

Godwin says "he was born of mean parentage, in the north of England, and untaught till he arrived at the age of fourteen years; that then, not enduring the frowardness of his stepmother, he went to seek his fortune, in which adventure, meeting with certain courtiers who had been obliged to his father for some courtesies, they presented him to the queen, whom for his wit and beauty he was not unfit to serve, who, finding his inclination to learning, sent him to Chad (formerly chamberlain to the king), then a monk at Lindisfarne, by whose dexterous instructions he became a great proficient in scholarship; where, affecting a monastic life, and being of a quick apprehension, he learned the Psalms and some other books, but was not shorne, though he much exceeded his ecclesiastical superiors in knowledge, being not a little taken notice of, and esteemed for his humility and obedience. Having served many years in that monastery, he resolved to go to Rome." Passing through Kent, says Bede, he became a pupil under Honorius, then archbishop of Canterbury, but did not remain long there; and when he resumed his journey towards Rome, the king of Kent associated with him a young man named Benedict Biscop, who had also a great desire to see Rome. When they reached Lyons, Wilfrid staid some time with the archbishop there, who was greatly pleased with him, and could hardly be persuaded to let him go. Benedict had pursued his journey after resting at Lyons, and when Wilfrid departed, it was not before the archbishop had extorted a promise from him to take Lyons in his way back to England. At Rome he learned the four books of the Gospel in order, as also the computation of Easter, with other matters of church discipline, and having spent some months in these studies, he returned to Lyons, and was received with great joy by Dulfin, the archbishop, with whom he staid three years, and then received from him the tonsure. Soon after this, Brunechild, the French queen, contrived the murder of the archbishop, when Wilfrid would have suffered death with him, but the soldiers sent on this bloody errand, perceiving him to be an Englishman and a stranger, spared his life. Wilfrid, much against his will, was appointed in the place of Dulfin, but soon quitted his post and returned to England, where he founded, with the king's assistance, the monastery of Ripon. It does not appear that Wilfrid was anything more than a priest when he was desired by the French queen to take care of the church of Lyons. Bede says he was consecrated bishop by Agilbert, bishop of the West Saxons, in the monastery of Ripon. He was soon after this sent into France by

King Alfrid, and while he continued there Chad was made bishop of York, by the command of King Oswi; but after presiding there for three years, he retired to his monastery of Lestingam, upon which Wilfrid returned to England, and undertook the charge of all the country from the Humber to Scotland, till he was driven thence by King Ecgfrid, and others were placed in his stead. Upon this he set out upon a second journey to Rome to lay his complaint before the Pope, but, by a strong easterly wind, was driven into Frizeland, where he was kindly received by the king and the inhabitants, to whom he preached the Gospel, and had the satisfaction to convert and baptize many thousands. He then went to Rome, where the Pope, having heard his cause, gave a decision in his favour. Godwin adds to this account many things not mentioned by Bede; 1st, that Wilfrid coming home, and finding another in his place, lived for some time in private, and was often pressed by Wulphere, king of Mercia, to accept the see of Lichfield, but he would not yield; that at length Chad was sent there, and Wilfrid got possession of York again, and repaired the Cathedral, which had become very ruinous. 2ndly, that Theodore, archbishop of Canterbury, thinking Wilfrid's diocese too large, and rich enough to maintain more bishops, went about to appoint two or three other bishops under him, which Wilfrid resisted, and again appealed to the Pope in person, who was then at the council of Constance, where, both by him and his council, it was ordered that the state of the bishoprick of York should not be altered without Wilfrid's own consent. 3rdly, that Ecgfrid, the king, so favoured Theodore's device, as that Wilfrid, on his return, perceived well he must either yield or forsake the country: he chose the latter, and lived in poverty and exile; and, arriving in Sussex, converted the people of that country, and became their bishop; laid the foundation of a Cathedral church at Selsey, though the see was afterwards removed to Chichester, where it continues to this day. 4thly, that after ten years banishment, Aldfrid (who succeeded Ecgfrid) sent for him, and he returned to his see of York; but after five years the king was displeased with him, which forced him to Rome again, where he again obtained a decision in his favour; and on his return (though with much difficulty) he was once more restored to his first charge, in which, after this his last restitution, he lived peaceably for the space of four years; that he died the 12th of October, 711, aged 76, and was buried in the monastery of Ripon, which he had built; but that church afterwards falling down for want of reparations, Odo, archbishop of Canterbury, removed his bones to his Cathedral, about the year 940, which is a little at variance with the account already quoted from Tanner, concerning the church being in good repair till it was burnt down in the year 950, by King Edred.

The chief benefactor to this church was King Athelstan, who made it a sanctuary, and extended the privileges of it to a mile from the town in all directions, so that whosoever violated the same should be liable to the loss of goods, and life itself.

By virtue of such charters, says Dugdale, and peaceful times, this religious house continued in prosperity many years, even till the Norman conquest, which at first was mixed with much rigour, and some broils, wherein this place ran the like fate with York, and several others in that county, which, by fine and spoil, suffered grievously. But when the public became somewhat settled, this church and town of Ripon recovered breath, and through the conqueror's favour, and kindness of succeeding kings, received confirmation of their liberties, as by the charters at this day extant are acknowledged. Through these, and other royal favours, this church continued in a flourishing state till the year 1318, when both the clergy and the townspeople were obliged to redeem themselves from plunder by payment of a thousand marks to the Scots, who, while the English were besieging Berwick, made an unexpected inroad into Yorkshire, by the way of Carlisle. Encouraged by the little opposition they met with, and the large booty they carried away with them, they came again the next year, and demanded again the same sum: but finding the impoverished inhabitants unable or unwilling to pay it, they not only set fire to the town, but to the church also, and put many people to death.

After this, Ripon for some years remained almost desolate, until Edward III., in the fourth year of his reign, entered Scotland with a powerful army, gave battle to the Scots at Gledesmore, and obtained a most decisive victory over them. This encouraged the archbishop of York, and other wealthy and influential persons in those parts, to contribute liberally to the rebuilding of the town

and minster, as the church is usually called, the which, says Dugdale, they raised anew, almost from its very foundation, erecting thereon three tall spire steeples, of more beauty and splendour than those before. It then flourished again, undisturbed by the civil wars between the houses of York and Lancaster, till the 38th of Henry VIII., when the collegiate churches, hospitals, and free chapels, were dissolved, as the monasteries had been some few years before. Ripon did not escape, but was dissolved by act of parliament, and the church made parochial, and so continued till the time of King James I., who again made it collegiate, but did not restore it to all its primitive rights and endowments. Upon the dissolution, the estates of this church, says Tanner, came to the crown, and were granted into lay hands, and so continued all Queen Elizabeth's reign. Of the abbots of Ripon nothing is known but the names of a very few of them. Botwine is stated in the Saxon chronicle to have died in 785; Simeon, of Durham, and the chronicle of Mailros, say in 786. He was succeeded by Alberht, who died in 787. Sigend was appointed the next abbot, but the time of his death is not known. After the church became collegiate, it appears to have been a religious society without a head; there were seven prebendaries, but no superior over them till the time of the restoration by James I., who added a dean to the seven prebendaries, about the year 1604.

With regard to the Minster or Cathedral, as it now appears, very little is known from authentic documents, as to when or by whom the several portions of it were erected. An historical and descriptive account of it was communicated to the Society of Antiquaries by Robert Darley Waddilove, D.D., the late dean, in 1810, and printed by them in their Archæologia, vol. xvii., p. 128—137. In this account, the architectural chronology of this church is discussed at considerable length. The whole of the west front, including its towers, the central tower, and the transept, with part of the choir and aisles, are ascribed to the time of Stephen, and are thought to have been raised by Thurston, archbishop of York. In 1317, the church and town of Ripon were burnt by the Scots; and the re-instalment of the former is said to have been entirely owing to the exertions of Archbishop Melton. He is said to have extended the church eastward to twice its former length. This was about 1331. The same author supposes the great window at the east end to be the work of the latter part of the fourteenth century.

EXTERIOR.

Although this Cathedral church is not one of the first magnitude and splendour, yet it is a stately structure, and greatly superior in all respects to many other English cathedrals, and to all the Welsh ones. Those of Carlisle, Chester, Oxford, Bristol, Rochester, and Chichester, are all inferior to Ripon, which rivals even those of Hereford, Exeter, and Worcester. As far as the west front alone is concerned, it is superior to most, and vies with all the rest, except York, Lincoln, Peterborough, and Wells, with which, in this respect, no others can come into competition. The plan is the ordinary one, of a gable between two square towers, but the height and breadth of the west wall of the nave, are unusually great, and the towers are in a continued line with it, and compose a part of this very uniform and elegant façade. The lowest part of the space between the towers is occupied by three pointed portals, side by side, the middle one higher and wider than those on each side, and all deeply recessed and decorated with many beautiful mouldings and slender shafts of early English workmanship. These portals have plain straight canopies, under each of which is a single quatrefoil panel. The division immediately above the portals is completely filled by five pointed windows of equal height and breadth, formerly divided by a mullion into two lights each, and a quatrefoil light at the top. These windows are also adorned with slender detached shafts, and the flower-like ornament filling up the hollow mouldings, so peculiar to this age and style. The next division contains five windows of the same description, with the outer ones lower than the next, and these again lower than the one in the middle, but they are all of equal breadth. Above these is the gable itself, in which are three pointed arches, the middle one pierced to light the roof. The gable has no parapet, but a feathered coping runs along it, and forms an elegant termination to the whole. The towers are exactly similar; they have good ornamented bases; the lowest division has an arcade of several trefoiled-headed arches, resting on slender detached columns; the next has three pointed arches, the middle one pierced for a window of one light only; the third division is similarly adorned; and in the fourth and last, which, together with the embattled parapet is nearly double the height of the one immediately below, the same arrangement is again repeated. The embattled parapet and pinnacles are modern additions, and though not in accordance with the architecture of the west front, have improved the effect of the whole, by taking off the low heavy appearance which the towers had before this was done. From what has been said of the detail of this front, it is evident that it could not have been erected as it now appears in the time of King Stephen; pointed architecture had not arrived to such a state of perfection as this front exhibits till a century after that monarch's reign. When, therefore, the late dean states that the whole of the west front, including the towers, was built in Stephen's time, his meaning must be restricted to the walls themselves, the arches, windows, and portals, with all their detail, having been altered when the church was restored after the fire. The south side is also uniform and stately. The aisle has pointed windows, with good early perpendicular tracery, projecting buttresses between each, terminated by crocketed pinnacles, which rise far above the embattled parapet. This aisle is lofty, as is also the clerestory above, whose windows, parapet, and buttresses are of the like description. The south wing of the transept is plain, exhibiting still, on all its three sides, much of the original Norman construction and detail, flat buttresses, round-headed windows, with some plain tracery inserted since. The clerestory windows in the east face of this wing of the transept are, however, pointed, divided into three lights, with good decorated tracery above the straight mullions. The parapet is plain and embattled, but the open spaces narrow and far between. On this side is an aisle, having a window to the south, and a double buttress at the outer angle. Very little of the east wall of this aisle is visible, as a building, called the vestry, adjoins it, and extends eastward almost the whole length of the choir. The south side of this building is embattled like that part of the transept just described. Beneath the parapet is a range of four flat-headed windows, divided into several lights, with decorated tracery above the dividing mullions; between some of these windows are buttresses which terminate a little under the parapet. Beneath the windows the wall is very plain, having only two parallel string courses and some small windows between. The east face of this building has a large flat-headed window under the parapet, divided into five lights, and having the same sort of tracery as the windows in the south side of it. Beneath this large window is a singular semicircular projection, terminated by a hemispherical roof, engaged in the wall. A string course divides this projection into two stories; in the upper a narrow round-headed window is seen, in the lower a door of the same form. Over this building is seen the clerestory of the choir; the windows, six in number, are pointed, divided into several lights, and have good decorated tracery. The buttresses between the windows are flat, and the parapet is quite plain. The south aisle of the choir is all concealed by the building before-mentioned, except the last compartment of it and its pointed window of two lights.

There is a simple grandeur about the east end of the choir and its aisles which is very pleasing. The latter are flanked with plain massive double buttresses, terminating in little gables, and above them rise octagonal turrets with conical roofs, like short spires. Each aisle has a pointed window to the east, of decorated character. The east wall of the choir itself is flanked with buttresses of the like kind, from which rise square pinnacles, enriched with panelling, and terminating in plain small pyramids. In this wall is a magnificent window of seven lights, sharply pointed, with excellent tracery in the head of it, composed principally of feathered circles. The large one at the top may indeed be called a rose or wheel, with six compartments or lights, which are worked into trefoils; in the smaller circles, six in number, the feathering is of five points, some of the intermediate spaces are trefoiled. This window is of excellent proportions, and one of the finest in England of this period of the pointed style. Above this, in the gable, is another window of the same character, but of very much smaller dimensions, and on each side of it the wall is adorned with a series of pointed arches, diminishing in correspondence with the slope of the gable, which has no parapet, but a plain bold coping, and on the gable point is set a plain cross.

The north side of the choir is clear of all adjuncts, and may be viewed perfectly well. The aisle has five pointed windows of two lights each, the clerestory six. The north wing of the transept is not unlike the south one, but the north face of it is flanked with thin Norman buttresses, ending in square open turrets, upon which are set something like Elizabethan domes. The west face of this wing has also some Norman buttresses and windows, with inserted tracery; one half of the parapet is embattled, and the other half plain. The original high-pitched roof of the transept is gone on both sides of the central tower, those of the nave and choir still remain. The north side of the nave is plain but grand. The aisle is lofty, has pointed windows of good proportions and perpendicular tracery, with slight buttresses between them of only one stage, and ending in small gables beneath the parapet, which is embattled. The clerestory is of the same character.

The central tower is by no means the best external feature of this Cathedral; it is broad and low, but like the towers at the west end has been improved in appearance in modern times, by the addition of an embattled parapet, and pinnacles at the four corners; that on the south-east angle rises higher than the others, and is indeed an octagonal turret, with a low spire-roof upon it. In each face of the tower are two pointed windows, with a thin buttress between them; they are divided into two lights each by a mullion, which, branching off to the sides of the arch, forms two smaller pointed arches, which are feathered; and the space between them and the point of the window is filled with a quatrefoil. This church is unusually lofty, and the towers rising but little above the roof-ridge, give it a lumpy look when seen altogether from a little distance, something like a tall man with high shoulders and short neck. In the west front there is nothing above the gable point of the nave but the parapet and pinnacles of the towers; but this, when viewed by itself, has a good effect, better than if the towers were higher, and better than if the wooden spires, covered with lead, were still to be seen upon them. They appear to want elevation only when seen at a distance, and in connection with the north or south side of the Cathedral. The central tower, however, from whatever point it is seen, and notwithstanding its modern additions, is still greatly deficient in respect of height. It is no higher than the western ones, and should be elevated considerably above them and every other part of the church. It would be very much improved by the addition of another story, equal in height to the upper story of the western towers, if the piers and arches upon which it is built would bear so great a superincumbent and additional weight. With this single defect, however, Ripon minster is a stately and interesting structure; and the lovers of the pointed style will congratulate themselves very much upon the continued preservation of such a valuable example of it.

INTERIOR.

The three portals, side by side, all lead into the nave; the aisles cannot be entered from the west: this is a very singular if not unique arrangement. On entering through any one of these portals into the nave of this Cathedral some disappointment will be felt. The exterior is so nearly perfect, that it raises an expectation of the same state of things with regard to the interior. But it is not so, as far at least as regards the nave, its aisles, and the transept. At once the eye detects certain defects, which every visitor of taste will regret. The nave has lost its original uniformity, and is now a piece of patchwork. It has no triforium, but the clerestory windows are large, and come down nearly to the point of the great arches, five in number, on each side of the nave. The last compartment eastward, on each side, shows what was intended at the time of the restoring of the church after the fire, though the nave arch is now walled up. The western arch and piers of the central tower have a very awkward appearance; the arch is semicircular, but was about to be made like the opposite one, into a pointed arch, when the work, for some reason or other, was stopped, and left as it now appears, with the pier on the south side carried up a long way above that on the left, and burying a considerable portion of the great arch. The ceiling of the nave is of arched oak groining, modelled after that of the transept at York. The great arches of the nave have many beautiful mouldings, springing from clustered pillars. The roofs of the aisles have received an excellent stone groined vaulting. The pavement, however, is well laid, and nearly new: and the proportions are excellent, approaching the just rules of architecture more nearly than any other structure of the middle ages in this country. In the transept some of the original Norman detail is yet visible, but the ceiling is no better than that of the nave and its aisles. The tower was raised on four semicircular arches; two of these now remain, but the intention to convert them into pointed, as the other two have been, is quite evident, from its having been partly accomplished on that towards the nave, as already noticed. The tower is open nearly to the top, showing all the windows, which admit a great body of light into the transept. The stone screen, separating the choir from the transept is a beautiful composition. In the centre is a large pointed arch of many mouldings, resting on as many slender shafts engaged, and having a flowing canopy, with a finial rising to the top of the screen; on each side of this arch are four niches with rich canopies, and intervening buttresses and pinnacles. The whole is crowned with a very rich cornice of exquisite tracery. The organ is large, and the case exhibits a good design, suiting very well with the screen on which it is placed.

Entering the choir through the archway in the screen, there is nothing to regret, except that the space beyond the stalls is too much encumbered with modern pews; every thing else is truly admirable. The original vaulting, which was destroyed by the falling of the great spire which once stood upon the central tower, has been replaced with an oaken roof richly decorated. The great arches on each side of the choir are lofty, consisting of many beautiful mouldings, and supported by clustered columns, with plain capitals. The triforium is lofty, having three pointed arches in each compartment, the middle one rising considerably higher than those on each side, but they have been filled with tracery of perpendicular character: the clerestory is also lofty, and the windows have been dealt with in the same manner. The great east window has a charming effect; the painted glass in it consists chiefly of the armorial bearings of various benefactors to the fabric, ancient and modern. The proportions of the choir are equally good with those of the nave: but the chief beauty of it is the carved wood work of the stalls, where the dean, subdean, and prebendaries sit. These stalls are allowed to exhibit a delicacy and lightness, superior even to that of those destroyed by the fire in the choir of York minster; or perhaps of those in any other Cathedral in the kingdom. On some of the wood work there is the date of 1494. A throne, at the end of the stalls on the south side of the choir, and of similar design, was erected by the late archbishop of York, for himself and his successors. This church being formerly under the jurisdiction of the archbishops of this province, who had a palace at or near Ripon, now destroyed. Since the erection of Ripon into a bishop's see, the archbishops will in future relinquish their seat in the choir of this Cathedral, which is now occupied by the bishop of the newly constituted diocese.

A descent of nine steps, down a passage about 45 feet long, leads to the crypt under the pavement of the great tower; it is a small vaulted room, only 11 feet 5 inches long, and 7 feet 8 inches wide, and 9 feet high. It was dedicated to the Holy and Undivided Trinity; and at the east end was placed an altar. On the north side is the hole, vulgarly called St. Wilfrid's needle, communicating with a passage, in which is a staircase, now walled up, leading to the choir.

The most remarkable monument in this Cathedral, is an altar tomb of grey marble in the south aisle of the nave, on which are sculptured a man and a lion in a grove of trees. No inscription remains, but tradition says this tomb covers the body of an Irish prince, who died at Ripon on his return home from the Holy Land. The other monuments worthy of notice, are those of Moses Fowler, first dean of Ripon after it was refounded by James I.; Hugh Ripley, thrice mayor, and last wakeman of this place, who died in 1637; Thomas Norton and his wife, recumbent on an altar tomb; Sir Edward Blacket, reclining, and his two wives standing over him; and a mural tablet to the memory of Sir John Mallory, who put to the sword a body of parliamentary forces under the command of Sir Thomas Mauleverer, whose main guard was stationed in the market place, and who had defaced the tombs and stained glass in the east window.

The dimensions of this Cathedral are as follows:—internally, whole length from east to west, 266 feet 5 inches; of the nave to the choir door, 167 feet 5 inches; of the choir, 101 feet: breadth

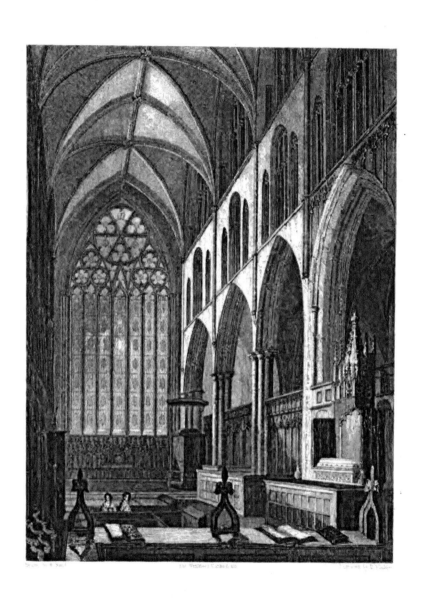

GROUND PLAN OF RIPON CATHEDRAL.

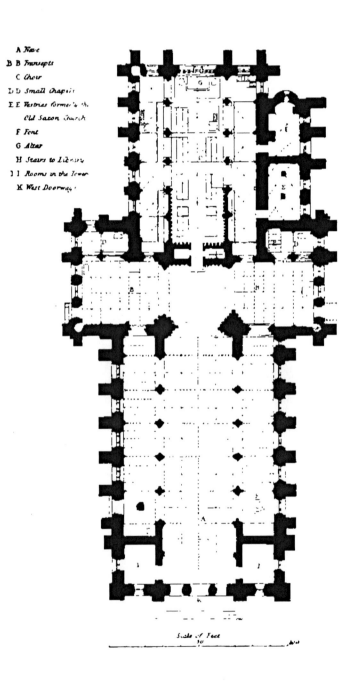

A Nave
B B Transepts
C Choir
D D Small Chapels
E E Vestries formerly the Old Saxon Church
F Font
G Altar
H Stairs to Library
I I Rooms in the Tower
K West Doorway

Scale of Feet

of nave and aisles, 87 feet; of the choir and ditto, 66 feet 8 inches. Height of nave, 88 feet 6 inches; height of choir, 79 feet. Length of the transept, 132 feet; breadth of ditto, at the north end, 35 feet 11 inches; at the south, 33 feet 3 inches. The height of all the towers is nearly the same, about 110 feet: they had all of them spires of wood, covered with lead, rising about 110 feet above the towers, but after the mischief done to the church by the fall of that on the central tower, called St. Wilfrid's, those on the two western towers were taken down to prevent similar accidents.

Of the cloisters nothing now remains. The chapter house is a small vaulted apartment, supported by two columns down the middle of it, and is entered from the south aisle of the choir, as is also the vestry beyond it, which has a semicircular termination at the east end. These two formed originally but one room, as did the vaults beneath. The room above the chapter house and vestry was formerly a chapel to the Virgin, yet denominated the Lady Loft, but which has, since the reformation of the church, been converted into a library, and now contains some manuscripts, divinity and classical books. Dr. Dibdin notices, in his Bibliographical Decameron, among the few scarce and curious old books an English Chronicle, Antwerp, 1493, and a Boetius of Caxton.

This Cathedral is dedicated to St. Peter and St. Wilfrid. The establishment, as settled by James I., consisted of a dean, subdean, six prebendaries, two vicars choral, six singing men, six choristers, an organist, and a verger, and the whole endowment amounted to £247 per annum. The dean and chapter returned it to the commissioners to be worth £804 gross, and £633 in the clear, per annum. The establishment now consists of a bishop, a dean, two archdeacons, and four canons.

At the same time that Ripon was made a bishop's see, it was enacted that the diocese of Ripon consist of that part of the county of York which was in the diocese of Chester, of the deanery of Craven, and of such parts of the deaneries of Ainsty and Pontefract, in the county and diocese of York, as lie to the westward of the following districts—viz., of the liberty of the Ainsty, and the wapentakes of Barkston, Ash, Osgoldcross, and Staincross; that the diocese should be included within the province of York; and that the collegiate church should be the Cathedral church.

The first bishop of Ripon was Charles Thomas Longley, D.D., who distinguished himself at Oxford, and was formerly one of the tutors of Christchurch, in that university and afterwards head master of Harrow School. He was consecrated in 1836, and has an income of £4,000 per annum made up from the funds which a recent arrangement created under the powers of the late Act. A palace has also been provided for him near the city of Ripon.

In the year 1856 Bishop Longley was translated to Durham, and the Rev. Robert Bickersteth installed in his place. He was succeeded in 1884 by William Boyd Carpenter.

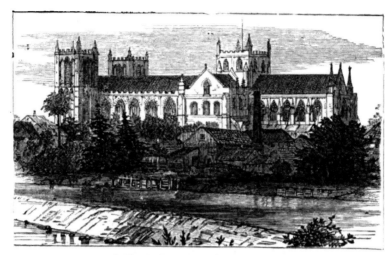

RIPON CATHEDRAL FROM THE SOUTH.

MODERN HISTORY OF RIPON CATHEDRAL.

In 1829, during the tenure of office of Dean Webber, and under the advice of Mr. Blore, architect, more than £3,000 was spent in putting a new roof and ceiling upon the nave, in groining the choir with lath and plaster, and adding a new altar-screen, replacing a large painting representing "an Ionic colonnade." Nearly all these have since been removed.

In 1842 the dilapidations of the Cathedral were such that it was declared to be very unsafe, and the Dean and Chapter said that they had done as much towards its repair as their resources allowed. The Ecclesiastical Commissioners were empowered by order in council to put the cathedral in a state of security, and effected some repairs, but they were very inadequate.

In 1854 the east window was filled with stained glass by Wailes, representing the Saviour and the apostles.

In 1861 Mr. (afterwards Sir) G. G. Scott was consulted about the condition of the building. He reported that the western towers were very insecure, owing to their faulty construction and history, the foundations never having been deep enough. There

RIPON CATHEDRAL FROM THE SOUTH-WEST.

were fissures of an alarming character on every side of each tower, from the base to the top of the walls. The west front also required extensive repair. The pinnacles, flying buttresses, and a considerable portion of the stonework of the choir was in a very bad state.

The work was commenced in 1862. The western tower and west front were first taken in hand. Much new stone was inserted, but all the old work that could be saved was preserved. The towers were underpinned and made secure. The mullions and tracery filling the lancets in the west front, later in date than the windows, were thoroughly unsound and were removed, restoring the windows to their original form. The three portals had originally gable points, which have been replaced; indeed, these portals are to a large extent new, and also the heads at the angles of the third arcade in the lower story. The pointed windows in the western towers, looking into the nave, previously closed, were opened. The roof has been raised, the flat panels being removed and an arched oak groining being substituted, constructed on the model of the transept roof at York. The nave aisles received an excellent stone groined vaulting. The exterior roof of the nave still remains of a low pitch.

The exterior low-pitched roof of the choir was removed, and a new one covered with lead was erected, at the original high pitch. The stonework of the whole exterior of the building was also repaired. The two large pinnacles at the east end were rebuilt.

Internally the galleries which disfigured the choir and to a great extent concealed the windows, were removed, as well as the closets beneath them, and the pews which filled the area. Several of the windows of the south aisle had been actually bricked up.

The plaster ceiling was replaced by a good oak roof, richly decorated in gold and colours. The fine stone groined roofs of the choir aisles were cleansed from the whitewash which had long covered them.

The plaster with which the canopies of the stalls had been repaired was removed, and were replaced by canopies of carved oak, corresponding with the stalls at the west end of the choir, and the beautifully-carved oak screens of the aisles were repaired. The ornamented stone sedilia were removed to the eastern bay (south arcade), and restored to their proper use. At the same time the original stone arcading was restored to the east end.

The entire choir, with the aisles, was refloored, and suitable oak

RIPON CATHEDRAL: THE NAVE.

seats were placed in them. A pavement of variously coloured marbles was laid within the communion rails.

A beautifully carved oaken pulpit, a brass eagle lectern, and a litany desk were also added to the choir.

The southern chapel or chapter-house received considerable repairs both externally and internally, as well as the library above the chapter-house. The crypt also was carefully repaired.

The central tower and the transepts were thoroughly repaired. Powerful iron girders added to the security of the tower. Carved oak ceilings replaced the sham groining in the transepts; and the lantern roof was enriched by a painted ceiling bearing the emblems of the four Evangelists, with the "Agnus Dei," which forms part of the armorial bearings of the see of Ripon, in the centre.

The total cost of the restoration was £42,000, of which £15,000 was contributed by the Ecclesiastical Commissioners. The work was not finally completed till October, 1872; but meanwhile the choir was finished, in 1868, and reopened on January 27, 1869.

A new organ was erected in 1878 by Messrs. Lewis and Co., of London, and includes part of the old organ built by Father Schmidt. It stands partly on the rood screen and partly in the choir aisles, these portions being connected with the central portion by pneumatic apparatus.

At the north-east corner of the east aisle of the south transept, in altering the steps leading to the library, a fresco painting was discovered on the slope of the head of the transition Norman window, through which the entrance was made. The subject is "Christ coming to Judgment;" and on the north wall of the aisle another was discovered, "The offerings of the Magi."

A considerable number of new stained windows have been inserted. One in the north aisle of the choir, of two lights, in memory of Mr. J. Robinson of Ripon (died 1869) represents Job and his friends in one light, and St. Paul and Ananias in another. Two others in the same aisle, nearest the east end, were given by the Marquis of Ripon and Lady Mary Vyner in memory of two sons of the latter, Mr. F. G. Vyner, murdered by Greek brigands in 1870; and Mr. Reginald Vyner, M.P. for Ripon, who died in 1870. They are very fine work, by Heaton, Butler, and Bayne.

In 1886 the lancet windows of the west front were filled with stained glass in memory of the first two bishops of the diocese, Bishops Longley and Bickersteth. They fill the two tiers of five lights, and represent in the lower tier the parable of the ten virgins; while in the higher tier scenes relative to the future state of the blessed and of the unfaithful are represented, with Christ in majesty in the centre, and surrounded by angels.

RIPON CATHEDRAL: THE CHOIR.

The glass in the west window of the south nave aisle was taken from the east window about 1853.

St. Walburg's Cathedral

MANCHESTER CATHEDRAL.

THE diocese of Manchester dates no farther back than 1847. It includes the greater part of the county of Lancashire, including besides Manchester and Salford, Ashton-under-Lyne, Bolton, Bury, Oldham, Blackburn, Rochdale, Lancaster, Preston, Blackpool, Burnley, and many other populous towns. The income of the Bishop is £4,200 per annum. There are three archdeaconries, of Manchester, Lancaster, and Blackburn.

The first bishop of the new diocese was James Prince Lee, who died into 1870. His successor was James Fraser, whose name, previously noted chiefly for work in promoting education, became widely known as that of the most catholic of bishops, the most genial in his recognition of Nonconformity, the most manly in his attitude to all parties, the most welcome and most happy in his ministrations to working men in the open air, in shed and factory. His death in 1886 was followed by the appointment of James Moorhouse, Bishop of Melbourne, Australia, from 1876 to 1886.

Of a see that has been erected little more than thirty years the ecclesiastical historian can have little or nothing to record. Happily, however, the religious establishment over which the Bishop of Manchester presides has existed for some centuries, as well as the fabric which now forms his Cathedral Church. Some account of the origin of that establishment, together with the history and description of that church, it is now intended to lay before the reader.

Bishop Tanner, in his work, entitled, "Notitia Monastica,"

states, that the Collegiate Church of Manchester owes its origin to the munificence of Thomas de la Ware, or Warre, as it was afterwards written, some time rector of the parish there, who had the barony and estate of his family by the death of his brother John, Lord de la Ware without heirs. Some time after he had thus obtained possession of the honours and estates of his family, he sought and obtained leave of the king (9 Hen. V.) to make his parish church collegiate, to consist of a warden and a certain number of priests. In the 26 Hen. VIII., that number was eight, as appears by a manuscript in the First Fruits' Office, in which they are called vicars. This collegiate foundation was dedicated to the Blessed Virgin Mary, and endowed with revenues to the yearly value of £200, or, as they were returned into the First Fruits' Office (26 Hen. VIII.), £226 12s. 5d. in the whole, and £213 10s. 11d. clear. This religious establishment was dissolved in 1547 by King Edward VI., but refounded, first, by Queen Mary, and afterwards by Queen Elizabeth, A. D. 1578, and again by King Charles I., A. D. 1636, for a warden, four fellows, two chaplains, four singing men, and four choristers, being incorporated as they were before, by the name of the warden and fellows of Christ's Church in Manchester.

In Strype's Annals, Manchester College is called that noble and useful foundation for learning and propagation of religion in those northern parts. The reader will find a very full and perfect account of this collegiate establishment in a work drawn up by Dr. Hibbert, from a variety of original and some scarce documents, and published at Manchester in 1830. The same work contains also an historical and descriptive account of the present fabric, now the Cathedral Church of Manchester, by Mr. Palmer, architect. From this source the following information has been principally derived.

Of Thomas de la Ware, the founder, it is therein stated that he was in holy orders in 1380, and then collated to the Grindale prebend in York Cathedral; that he was the brother of John de la Ware, Baron of Manchester. Soon after 1380, he became the parson of Manchester. He was presented, says Hollingworth, and admitted rector, and had a licence granted him to be non-resident. He was also the last parson or rector of this church.

In 1399, his elder brother, the said baron, died without issue, when the rector, being then forty years of age, succeeded to his honours and estates. The said Thomas, observes Hollingworth, being the next heir, and indeed the only heir male of that family, came by inheritance to be Lord de la Warre. Notwithstanding his licence of non-residence, his favourite abode was in Manchester, where he assiduously presided over the extensive deanery of which this town was the centre, and officiated as rector of St. Mary's Church. The names of two of his chaplains are recorded in an old deed, bearing the date of the year 1405. These were John Fawkes and Roger de Haywood. On the 29th of September in that year, the founder was collated to the prebend of Riccal, belonging to the see of Lincoln. For a period of many years, however, nothing whatever is known of this distinguished priest and baron. His title was Decanus Decanatus de Mancestre, and "this regular use of the decanal for the rectorial appellation," observes Mr. Whitaker, "shows the deanery to have been united to the rectory."

When Thomas de la Warre had been twenty years in possession of the Lordship of Manchester, he took into consideration its thriving state, and the inefficiency of the existing church to accommodate a greatly increased neighbourhood. The old town of Manchester, named Aldport, situated in the immediate vicinity of the ruins of Mancastle, had been forsaken for the new site, near the confluence of the Irk and the Irwell. St. Michael's Church in Aldport had long ceased to exist, and all memory of it would have faded away, but for the annual fair which survived the decay of the fabric, its celebration still taking place on the site of the original churchyard, and the day of the feast deviating but little from the period on which the tutelar saint was in very early times commemorated.

St. Mary's Church, built of timber, erected in Aca's field, during a later period of the Anglo-Saxon times, was old and much decayed. The tenement of the parsonage afforded but very inadequate accommodation to the more luxurious priests of later times, whom the Norman conquest introduced in succession to the rich endowment of the parsonage and deanery of Manchester, a ready pretext was, therefore, afforded them for their frequent absence from their post, to the neglect of the pastoral duties which they owed to a populous district. These were the considerations which urged the pious De la Warre, who possessed the patronage of the living of Manchester, to attempt the foundation of a new and capacious church, commensurate with the increased extent of the town, as well as a set of buildings capable of accommodating the additional number of clergy, who would be required for the administration of its sacred rites. His plan was soon carried into effect, and his foundation amply endowed. This being accomplished, the munificent and pious founder presented to William, Bishop of Coventry and Lichfield, John Huntington, B.D., and Rector of Ashton-under-Line, to be the first keeper or warden. The eight fellows associated with the first warden, were two parish priests, two canons, and four deacons, to whom were attached four clerks and six choristers. The whole was then acknowledged as a body corporate, under the title of the Guild or Company of the Blessed Virgin Mary in Manchester.

The first warden entered upon his sacred functions in the year 1422. He was a man who, in the words of Hollingworth, was allowed to possess a considerable share of the learning most in request during the times in which he lived. The quaint Fuller, who allows a place to Thomas de la Warre among his worthies, gives another and very different account of the origin of this religious house. He states, without giving any authority for it, that the founder, when he succeeded to the barony on the death of his elder brother, obtained the Pope's permission to marry, for the continuance of so honourable a family, on condition that he would build a college for such a number of priests (fellows under a warden) as the Bishops of Durham and Lichfield should think fit, which he did accordingly in Manchester.

To return to the first warden, this excellent man, as Dr. Hibbert calls him, died on the 11th of November, 1458, having held his office thirty-seven years; he was buried in the vault of the choir, which he himself had constructed under the high altar as it then stood. Upon that part of the floor of the vault, under which his remains were interred, was placed a stone with a brass inlaid, representing him in sacerdotal vestments, with a label issuing from his mouth, bearing this inscription, " Domine dilexi

MANCHESTER CATHEDRAL.
NORTH EAST VIEW

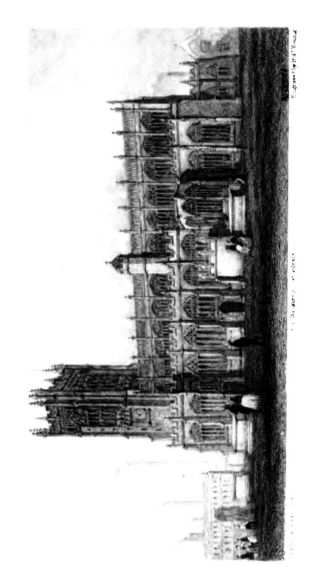

SANDWICH CHURCH.

decorem domus tuæ;" on a narrow border of brass round the stone is this inscription, "Hic jacet Johannes Huntington Baccalaureus in decretis, primus Magister vel Custos hujus Collegii, qui obiit 11 Nov., 1453." It appears that the first collegiate church was only of timber, and built on the site of the present cathedral, but the domestic portions of the college were of stone, and probably completed in the lifetime of the first warden.

John Both was the second warden; he was deprived by Edward IV., in 1465, for the active part he took in the wars between the houses of York and Lancaster, and was succeeded by Ralph Langley, who resigned in 1481, when James Stanley, D.D., the first of that name, was appointed, and died in 1485. To him succeeded James Stanley the second: in his time great additions were made to the Collegiate Church. But " who contributed most to the building," says Hollingworth, " is not certainly known;" but the names and arms of the Stanleys, Wests, Radclyffs, Byrons, and others, in the windows, before they were destroyed, witnessed their assistance to it. In 1506 this warden was raised to the see of Ely, but he did not resign his wardenship till 1509; he died in 1515, and was buried in the small elegant chapel erected by himself, to the north of a more spacious one dedicated to St. John the Baptist, which is said to have been the joint work of himself and his natural son, John Stanley. Robert Cliffe then succeeded, but nothing is recorded of him or his successor,—Alday George West was the next warden, the third son of Sir T. West, Lord de la Warre, which title came to this family by the death of the founder of the college without issue. In 1535 he was succeeded by George Collyer, the year in which Henry VIII. assumed the title of Temporal Head of the Church of England, but being a zealous Romanist, he refused to acknowledge the king's supremacy, but continued in his office notwithstanding till the first year of Edward VI., when an act of parliament was passed dissolving the college, and Warden Collyer retired into Staffordshire, but on the accession of Queen Mary he was recalled. The queen then refounded the college for a master or keeper, eight fellows, chaplains, four clerks and six choristers, and did also confirm and re-establish the statutes of the first foundation. Only two fellows were nominated by the queen, Lawrence Vaux, afterwards warden, and John Coppages. George Collyer continued warden till he died in 1557, and was buried in the Lady Chapel. Although a rigid Romanist, he was no persecutor, and accounted the most bountiful and generous warden that had ever presided over this religious foundation. His successor, the aforenamed Lawrence Vaux, upon the accession of Queen Elizabeth, refusing to take the oaths, was deprived, having held the office only three years. The college at this time, by a statute made in the first year of her reign, was deemed by some to be quite dissolved, and fallen into the queen's hands, and was thereupon refounded by her, and William Birch appointed warden, who was succeeded by Thomas Herle, and he by John Wolton; of these wardens nothing is recorded. To the last-mentioned succeeded William Chadderton, in 1579; he was promoted to the see of Chester, and afterwards translated to that of Lincoln, in 1595, when he resigned his wardenship. He was succeeded by John Dee, who held the office about thirteen years, and was in his turn succeeded by Richard Murray, in 1608, who retired or was rather driven out by the virulent attacks of his political and religious opponents in 1636. The year before this, the college was refounded by Charles I. Richard Heyrick was the next warden, a great enemy to the restoration of Romanism, attempted in his time; he died in 1667, and was buried in the choir of the Collegiate Church. His successor was Nicholas Stratford, D.D., who was also Dean of St. Asaph, and Prebendary of Lincoln; he resigned the wardenship in 1684, on account of the strife which raged in Manchester between the Royalists and the Dissenters, and was consecrated Bishop of Chester in 1689. On his resignation, Richard Wroe was appointed to succeed him, who, from his eloquent preaching, obtained the epithet of the Silver-tongued; he died January 1st, 1718: he was also Prebendary of Chester. To him succeeded Samuel Peploe, who in 1726 was consecrated Bishop of Chester, and resigned the wardenship in 1738, in favour of his son, Samuel Peploe, the younger, LL.D., who held at the same time several other ecclesiastical preferments, and died in 1781, at the age of eighty-two. Richard Asheton, D.D., was the next warden, who dying in 1800, was succeeded by Thomas Blackburn, LL.D. He died in 1823, and was succeeded by Thomas Calvert, D.D., who had previously been Fellow and Tutor of St. John's College, Cambridge, and Norrisian Professor of Divinity in that University. In his time the style of this religious foundation was changed from that of Warden and Fellows to that of Dean and Canons. He died in 1840, when the Hon. and Very Rev. William Herbert, D.C.L., was appointed, who dying in 1847, was succeeded by the Very Rev. George Hull Bowers, B.D.

Before a detailed description of the fabric of the present Cathedral Church is attempted, it may be acceptable to the reader to be made acquainted with its architectural history. It has been already stated that the first warden found a church of wood in a state of decay, and too small for the new foundation. He began to the east of it a chancel of stone, which he lived to see completed. His work was equal in extent to the present choir, with a north and south aisle, and there is reason to believe that a small vestry was added to the latter. His choir, however, was carried up only a little above the arches separating it from the side aisles. The church remained in this state till 1465, when Ralph Langley entered on the office of warden, who took down the wooden fabric which remained between the stone chancel and the lower part of the present tower, which had been erected perhaps soon after the chancel, for the purpose of receiving one or more bells. Finding the tower in good condition and sufficiently strong, the warden joined his new building of stone to it. He built also the present nave, with north and south aisles, together with the Chapel of St. James on the north, and that of St. Nicholas on the south, thus giving the church a cruciform plan. Some think he took down the choir of the first warden, but he probably only added the clerestory with the octagonal turrets on each side, and certainly he replaced the timber-roof of that warden. He also took down the old vestry, and built on its site the present chapter-house. He gave also the stalls of the south side, those on the north being the gift of the family of Bexwith. About the same time, the wall of the south aisle of the nave was taken down, and the Chapel of St. George added by W. Galley, merchant of Manchester. In 1506 Jesus Chapel was added to the south aisle of the choir by Richard Bexwith, and some benefactors, now unknown, added a second north aisle to the nave. In 1513 the chapel on the north side of the chancel was finished, and dedicated to our Saviour and St. John the Baptist, by Bishop Stanley and his natural son, James Stanley. To the north of this, a small sepulchral chapel was built by the same bishop, in which also he was afterwards buried, under the arch of entrance, and a tomb erected to his memory, which still exists. It is an altar tomb of freestone, and of very simple design. The slab at the top bears a brass, representing Bishop Stanley, in his full episcopal costume, but the figure has lost some of its ornamental details, and the indents of shields serve to show that such things have been. On a brass plate beneath the feet of the prelate is the following inscription, in the character and spelling of the times:—

Off yir charite pray for the soule of James Stanley su'tyme bushup of Ely and Warden of this Colege of Manchestur whih decessed out of this transitere worlb the xxii day of March the yer of our Lord God mccccc and xv upon whose soul and all christen soules Jhesu had mercy.

> Vibe Deo gratus toto mu'do tumulatus
> Crimine mu'dat' semp' transire paratus
> Filii homi' usque quo grabi corde ut quid
> Diligit banitate' et querit' mendaciu'
> Utinam saperent et intelligere't ac
> Nobissimo probidere't.

The elegant screens which still remain in various parts of the church, as well as those which have been removed from the front of the Chapel of St. Nicholas and St. George, were all put up in this warden's time. Warden West is said to have built the Lady Chapel, but it is more probable that he only repaired the original one: however this may be, the greater part was rebuilt some time in the 17th century. He is thought to have erected the clerestory of the nave, and to have given the present roof of it. About this time (1520) the upper part of the tower was added, but by what benefactor is not known. By what has been already said, the reader will perceive that this Cathedral Church must have lost all its cruciform character and appearance, both externally and internally. Much of it has been rebuilt in modern times, by which it has lost a great deal of its primeval character and beauty; in some cases no attempt has been made to restore correctly the decayed details, and in others they have been replaced by unsuccessful imitations or details totally incongruous. In 1812, the remains of Bishop Stanley were exhumed. The ground on the north side of the tomb was excavated, and about four feet beneath the surface of the floor, the remains of the bishop were discovered, with his arms crossed and folded on his breast. The skeleton measured six feet four inches in length, which verifies the description given of him by the old rhyming biographer of the house of Stanley—

> "A goodlie tall man as was in all England,
> And spedd well all matters that he took in hand."

The body was not enclosed in lead; nothing was found but the dust of decayed timber lying on each side of the skeleton, no remains even of any vestments or episcopal ornaments; the bones were in a good state of preservation, and were again restored to their former place, with a notice that they had been disturbed in 1812.

EXTERIOR.

The situation of this Cathedral is not happily chosen; it stands low, and the churchyard being paved entirely with flat stones, memorials of those whose remains are buried beneath, does anything but contribute to its attractions. The best points of view are from the south-west and south-east, especially the latter, which shows the Lady Chapel, the south aisle of the choir, the chapter-house, the whole length of the clerestory, both of choir and nave, with its octagonal turret, pinnacles, and open parapet, together with the upper story of the great western tower, which is rich and elegant, flanked at the angles with octangular turrets engaged, adorned with large belfry windows of good design, terminated by an embattled parapet and crocketted pinnacles. The great defect of this church is a want of elevation. The various chapels which have been added by various benefactors at different times, since the original foundation of this religious establishment, have together contributed to destroy the cruciform character which, for a short time, it must have assumed; nor have these additions added anything to the interest or comeliness of its external form. Had it retained, however, its transeptal form, it could not have been accounted a regularly cruciform church, there being no central tower. The Cathedral Church of Bangor, although it has transepts, loses much of its cruciform effect by having the tower at the west end, instead of being placed at the intersection of the cross. The clerestory of the nave and choir being continued in one long line, interrupted only by an octangular turret on each side, marking the place of the choir arch within, together with the chapter-house on the south side, give to this church a certain effect and dignity which no simply parish church, however large, is found to possess.

INTERIOR.

The want of elevation is, perhaps, still more felt on first entering this Cathedral, than it is externally; but that which has destroyed its cruciform appearance, both externally and internally, has, perhaps, added to its imposing effect within. There is a sort of mysterious intricacy of plan formed by the pillars and arches of the subsequently added aisles and chapels, by which they communicate with each other, which is very striking, and adds much to the interest of the whole interior.

The principal entrance, which was through the tower, is now by the south porch, which adjoins Brown's Chapel, and is said to have been built by a person of the name of Bibby; the principal entrance used to be through the tower. The roof of the nave is formed into compartments by longitudinal and transverse moulded beams, the intersections of which are enriched with sculptured bosses, consisting of a great variety of foliage, of beautiful design, and the same plan is observed throughout the aisles of the nave. The west end of the middle aisle, where once the old font stood, is fitted up with stalls, seats, and pews, for the convenience of the municipal officers and their attendants; over these seats is what is called the Chetham gallery, set apart for the use of the governor, the boys, and the domestics of the hospital of that name. Hollingworth, after informing his readers that St. George of England was one of the patron saints of this church, observes, "the statues of the Virgin Mary and St. Dyonise, the other patron saints, were upon the two highest pillars next to the quire, unto them usually men did bow at their coming into the church." On the removal of the old gallery, on the south side of the nave, a demi-angel was discovered issuing from the front of the last pillar, adjoining to the choir; it supported in its hands a plain shield, and above its head a moulded bracket was placed, for the reception, doubtless, of a statue, and being protected by the projecting gallery, it was saved from destruction; it was found in rather a mutilated condition, and has been, alas! restored, or patched up rather with Roman cement. Undoubtedly a similar figure once adorned the opposite pillar, but that was hacked away to make room for the old pulpit, or, being more exposed, was perhaps destroyed by some very zealous Iconoclast. These angels, with their brackets, are supposed to have once supported the effigies of the patron saints mentioned by Hollingworth, and to whom the church was originally dedicated. In describing the interior of this Cathedral Church, it may be expected that some further account of the several appended chantry chapels should be added to what has been already stated. St. George's Chantry is the first on the south side, and adjoins the ancient porch. It was built, according to Hollingworth, by one William Galley, some time merchant of Manchester, who died in 1508, and whom he states to have been buried in the midst of it, under a small stone. But, observes Dr. Hibbert, "this chantry is evidently the one stated, in the great ecclesiastical inquisition taken by order of Henry VIII., in the twenty-seventh year of his reign, to have been founded by William Radcliff, and at that time was worth £3 per annum, clear of all reprisals, arising from burbages within the vill of Manchester, and that Hugh Bryddoke was the chantry priest there officiating. On the dissolution of the chantries, under the regency of Edward VI., a pension of £4 12s. 8d. per annum was granted to Edward Smyth, priest of St. George's Chantry. In Hollingworth's time, this chantry was used for the purpose of preaching the early sermon on Sunday mornings; and he adds, that its chiefest ornament was a statue of St. George on horseback.

The Chantry of St. Nicholas adjoins to and is situated on the east end of the last-mentioned chantry. Hollingworth observes, that Thomas del Booth, son and heir of Thomas Booth, Knight, the founder of it, gave to Hugh Scoles, chaplain, a certain place in Bexwith, together with the advowson of the chantry of St. Nicholas, in St. Marie's Church, in Manchester; and the said Hugh Scoles gave the said premises to John Trafford, Knight. But Dr. Hibbert thinks this chantry is the one mentioned in the ecclesiastical survey as the foundation of Robert Chetham, and that Robert Byron was then chaplain and chantry priest thereof.

The Chantry of St. James is the smallest within this Cathedral Church, and is situated on the north side, immediately opposite that of St. Nicholas, and in the original plan, formed the north transept of the collegiate church. Hollingworth says, "it was probably builded by one of the Strangeways, and that in his time it was the property of John Hartley of Strangeways, Esq.;" in it, he further adds, "there is a pardon under the picture of the Resurrection of Christ from the Sepulchre. The pardon for V Pater nr, V Aves, and a Crede, is XXVI thousand and XVI dayes of pardon." "But," observes Dr. Hibbert, "the picture and the soothing consolation have long since disappeared."

There are other chantries surrounding the choir, but before any description of them is commenced, some account of the choir itself should be given. It is entered from the nave by an arch in the middle of a good carved oak screen. This portion, which is in fact the Cathedral (for the nave and its aisles, and surrounding chapels, belong to the parish), is eminently beautiful, and equals in everything (except dimensions) many of the choirs of our cathedral or collegiate churches, and surpasses some. Like the nave, it has six arches on each side, but the stalls, with their canopies, are the chief ornament of this choir, and deserve particular notice; they display some of the best examples of oak carving in the kingdom, rich, elaborate, and delicate in the extreme. The roof is in its plan very similar to that of the nave, but here the square panels are subdivided into smaller ones by other and more slender beams, and each space is filled up with such delicate tracery that it resembles lace-work. The east window occupies nearly the whole of the

MANCHESTER CATHEDRAL.
VIEW FROM THE WEST END OF NAVE

upper part of the east end of the choir. In the splay of each joint is a bracket and niche, with rich canopy, terminating in a crocketted spire, which rises to the springing of the arch, and from which the whole soffit of the arch is worked into paneled tracery: the tracery of the window is of good perpendicular design. In the windows of the choir, and its aisles and chapels, are still to be seen some fragments of the original stained glass.

Of the chantries which adjoin the choir aisles, that called the Chantry of Jesus is on the south side, and communicates with the south aisle by two pointed arches, and is enclosed by an oak screen of rich design and most exquisite workmanship. Between the solid and the open part of the screen, a small horizontal panel occupies the spaces between the buttresses, and continues along the whole length of it. In this panel has been an inscription, but all that is remaining of it, at present, is a capital H at the beginning, and a little distance from it a capital M, in the character of the period, but here and there occur the marks where letters have been painted on a vermilion ground. This chantry Dr. Hibbert supposes to be the one mentioned in the ecclesiastical survey of the foundation of Ralph Hulme, the certified value of which was returned at £5 3s. 6d. per annum, clear of all reprisals, and that John Bexwyke was the officiating chantry priest. And this supposition is, he adds, strengthened by the fact, that the small cemetery appendant on the south side of it is yet remaining in the possession of his descendants.

The Chantry of St. John the Baptist is on the north side of the chancel, and its length is co-extensive with the north aisle, into which it opens with five pointed arches, and is enclosed by an open screen of carved oak, similar in design and workmanship to others about the church, but far inferior to that of the Jesus Chantry. From this chantry a small sepulchral chapel juts out to the north, and opens into it by one large arch, whose piers are worked into niches, with rich canopies, which rise nearly to the moulded capitals. Beneath this arch repose the remains of the founder of both, the Warden Stanley, and from this circumstance they are now generally known by the name of Stanley's Chapels. An account of this warden's tomb, and discovery of his remains, has been already given. It may be here mentioned, that in the sepulchral chapel, near the east end of the bishop's tomb, on each side of the east window, is a demi-angel, forming the bracket of a niche on both sides of it; these figures support shields, the one on the south side bears the arms of the see of Ely, viz. three ducal crowns, and the other on the north is charged in the dexter chief with a roundle, on which is sculptured the letter S; and in the sinister chief, an eagle's leg erased, with an ibex couchant in base, which appears to have been a favourite device of either the bishop or his natural son, Sir John Stanley.

The Chantry of St. Mary, or the Lady Chapel, is at the eastern extremity of the choir, and opens into the area behind the communion screen, by an arch of many bold mouldings, which, with its piers, are remnants of Warden Huntingdon's structure. The screen, which separates this chapel from the area before it, deserves particular notice, because, says Dr. Hibbert, it has been the most splendid of all in the whole sacred edifice, but together with the stone niches which flank each side of it, has suffered much from the misplaced zeal of the Puritan soldiers, and now exhibits to the spectator a melancholy picture of magnificence in decay. Along the upper part of the screen has been a series of pierced canopies, but nothing now remains of them, except the back part of each. Over the door, which is in the centre of the screen, are the fragments of St. George in combat with the dragon, and on each side have been three statues, but one is wanting. Those on each door jamb are female figures, with crowns on their heads; under the pedestal which supports the one on the south side is the representation of a subdued evil spirit, and under the other is a lamb, on the back of which a man is seated, his arms elevated, and in the attitude of ascending. The remaining figures are so mutilated, that it cannot now be ascertained with probability even what they were intended to represent.

The small octagonal chapter-house at the east end of the south choir aisle has in four of its sides Perpendicular windows of five lights each.

The cathedral establishment consists of a dean, four canons, twenty-four honorary canons, and two minor canons.

GROUND PLAN OF MANCHESTER CATHEDRAL.

A — St Marys or Lady Chapel
B — St John the Baptists or Darby Chapel
C — Chapter House
D — Jesus Chantry
E — Hulmes Chantry
F — St Nicolas Chantry
G — St Georges Chantry
H — St James Chantry

I —
K —
L —
M —
N —
O —
P —

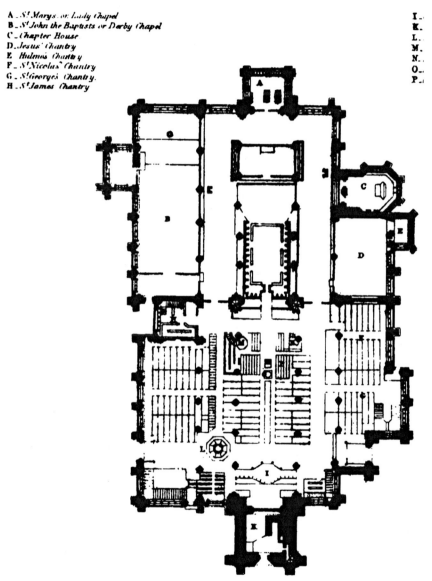

MANCHESTER CATHEDRAL: THE CHOIR

MODERN HISTORY OF MANCHESTER CATHEDRAL.

Since the foundation of the see of Manchester in 1848, a great part of the cathedral has been restored, and some portions rebuilt, Mr. J. P. Holden being the superintending architect. The outside was refaced in 1862-8, with millstone grit from Ramsbottom. The battlements, pinnacles, and turrets have been

MANCHESTER CATHEDRAL: FROM THE SOUTH.

considerably altered in design, though still retaining the same general style.

The western tower was entirely rebuilt in 1868, the former Perpendicular one being unsafe. The new tower, 137 feet high, is highly ornamental and of good design, but only partially reproduces the original. Each face of the upper storey has a lofty window of four lights in two tiers, with tracery and crocketed work in the head. Above these the space is panelled, and the whole is surmounted by an open embattled parapet. At the angles are double buttresses, terminating in crocketed pinnacles, and between these at each angle, is a third similar pinnacle, rising higher. Thus there are three pinnacles grouped at each angle of the tower. In the tower the old clock and ten bells are replaced. The nave roof was formerly coloured in red, blue, white, and gold, but is now restored to the natural colour of the wood. That of the choir is white, affording a striking contrast. The floor of the nave is tiled in lozenge patterns. The nave has been fitted throughout with open benches.

The font, at the west end of the outer north aisle of the nave, is a modern erection, octagonal in shape, and of Perpendicular design. It is a memorial of Mr. and Mrs. Edward Frere. The beautiful canopied cover of the font was given in memory of Mr. George Lings.

The Derby or Stanley Chapel on the north side of the north choir aisle was entirely rebuilt in 1861, the sculptures being re-worked according to the former design. This cost was borne by the Stanley family.

The Jesus Chapel on the south side of the cathedral has also been rebuilt, and supplied with a flat panelled wooden ceiling. The chapter-house has been supplied with a high conical roof instead of the flat one it had received.

The St. Nicholas or Trafford's Chapel (south of south nave aisle) which was rebuilt in a florid style in the beginning of the present century, when many of its characteristic features—screens, reredos, tombs, etc., were removed, has been further restored and repaired, in 1885-6, by Mr. J. Crowther, architect. St. George's Chapel, adjacent, was at the same time repaired.

MANCHESTER CATHEDRAL: THE CHOIR SCREEN AND ORGAN.

The canopied episcopal throne was erected in 1853.

An extensive Caen stone reredos extends quite across the choir; it is of Perpendicular design, with large niches; but the design is by no means first class. It was given by the Burley family.

The choir paving, of tiles, was the gift of Mr. William Andrew in 1859.

New flat panelled roofs have been erected in both the north and south choir aisles.

The organ is a new one, placed above the choir screen as before, the gift of Mr. W. H. Houldsworth, M.P., in 1872.

In the south nave aisle is a monument to Mr. Dauntsey Hulme (died 1828) by Westmacott, junr. It is an excellent work, representing the story of the Good Samaritan.

At the east end of the north choir aisle is a fine statue by Theed of Humphrey Chetham (died 1653), a great benefactor to Manchester, founder of the Chetham Hospital and the very fine Chetham Library. The statue was given by Mr. George Pilkington of Manchester in 1853.

In the south choir aisle is a statue of Thomas Fleming, one of Manchester's benefactors (died 1848), a good piece of sculpture by Bailey.

At the west end of the south nave aisle new stained glass windows have been inserted, as elsewhere in the cathedral. The east window of the choir, of seven lights, contains good stained glass by Hardman. In the centre the crucifixion is depicted; in the northern lights are events preceding, in the southern, events following it. The west window of the north choir aisle contains stained glass by Wailes.

The restorations were completed in 1867: since 1848 they have cost £35,000.

SOUTHWELL CATHEDRAL: BEFORE RESTORATION.
(*From a sketch by Mr. W. Livesay, Sadbury, Derby.*)

SOUTHWELL CATHEDRAL.

THE diocese of Southwell is one of the latest formed in this country, having been created in 1884, on fulfilment of the conditions prescribed in the Bishoprics' Act of 1878. The first bishop, Dr. George Ridding, was educated at Winchester College, and at Balliol College, Oxford, and was subsequently Tutor of Exeter College, 1852-63, and head master of Winchester College, 1868-84. The new diocese was fortunate in having assigned to it as a Cathedral the ancient collegiate church of Southwell, seven miles west of Newark and fourteen north east of Nottingham. This, which was also the parish church, had for many years been under restoration, and was reopened on February 2nd, 1888. bishop presides over the counties of Derby and No n fro ioceses of Lichfield and Lincoln ach c itutes an archdeaconry. At preno de thedral chapter. The rector of sub- hop's stipend is £3,500. wa d "Suwelle" and "Sudwell," and derives its name from four wells, anciently reputed to possess almost miraculous healing virtues. The collegiate church of St. Mary was founded by Paulinus, first archbishop of York, about the year 630, but nothing is known of the building then erected. No doubt there was an important church here long before the Conquest, and it was apparently rebuilt about 1050. Probably some fragments of this church still exist in the shape of small capitals, and various mouldings of a rougher type than those of the existing church, found during repairs of the south wall of the nave and in the piers of the central tower. The present church dates from the reign of Henry I., when the Norman portions of the building were erected, namely, the nave with its aisles, the north porch, the transepts, and the three towers. It appears that Archbishop Thomas of York (1109-1114) besought the aid of the people of Nottinghamshire " for the building of the church of St. Mary of Suwell." Further than this there is no precise information about the Norman building, except that it had a choir as well as a nave, the former only 59 feet long, and having aisles extending little more than half its length. The east end was a square one, with turrets at the corners; all this was ascertained in the early modern restorations, and it was seen that the whole building was designed in one style.

The Norman choir was allowed to remain for little more than a hundred years. It began to be replaced by the present Early English choir, and its aisles and small eastern transepts about 1230-40; perhaps the work was not completed till later in the century. The chapter-house was completed about 1290. In the fourteenth century the decorated organ-screen was built, and pinnacles and flying buttresses were added to and over the choir aisles. After this period the fabric of the church was not greatly altered till the present century. The roofs and gables, originally high-pitched, were lowered, certainly before 1672; the lowering of the roofs of the small eastern transepts reduced them externally to mere projections from the aisles. The cloisters were built later than the library, which itself is of somewhat later date than the choir. At some time in the Late Decorated period three-light windows were inserted in the lower story of the west face of the western towers.

The windows of the nave aisles had the original Norman windows replaced by Early Perpendicular ones of three lights, all but the western in the north aisle; that adjacent to it is a late restoration. The western bays of the south aisle have been made to correspond with these in modern times. The large west window of the nave is a Late Perpendicular insertion. It is not known how the lights of the west front were arranged in the Norman design. The lofty leaden spires which originally surmounted the western towers were removed in 1801, in consequence of their dangerous condition; and a few years afterwards the old high-pitched roof of the chapter-house was removed, and a lower one substituted. New stalls, pews, and galleries, were about the same time inserted in the choir.[1]

For about forty years the ecclesiastical commissioners have been charged with the duty of repairing the building, and before 1851 the western towers were repaired and underpinned under Mr. Railton, and a good deal of repair was effected under the direction of Archdeacon Wilkins by John Gregory, mason. At this time the western windows of the nave aisles, before referred to, were reconstructed to their original Norman forms, and were filled with stained glass.

In 1851 Mr. Ewan Christian made a complete examination of the building, and he advised a process of gradual repair, which was carried out by John Gregory and his labourer John Cook, with great skill and devotion to their work. This went on till 1875, when a further report on the building advised the restoration of the roofs to their original pitch, excepting that of the choir, as well as the rebuilding of the western spires and of the roof of the chapter-house. Those works were accordingly carried out by contract. The nave and transepts were refloored in stone and marble. The plaster-screens placed between the choir and its aisles early in the century were removed, and new oaken ones were substituted, designed in accordance with remains found in the roof of the chapter-house. Much has still to be done before the building can be considered completed and fitted. The ex-

[1] A full account of the history of Southwell Minster, as far as known, was given by the Rev. J. F. Dimock in the Journal of the British Archæological Association for January 1853.

tensive graveyard surrounding the church also requires beautifying; at present it is covered with unsightly tombstones, and is quite destitute of the aspect generally associated with the precincts of a stately cathedral.

Returning to the history of the church as a collegiate body, in the time of William I., there were ten prebends, to whom six were afterwards added. The college dates from the year 1216, when Walter de Grey, Archbishop of York, founded it and drew up statutes for it. There were then sixteen prebends, each of whom appointed his own vicar-choral. In 1397 the members of the college had residential buildings on the east side of Greet Brook, and at a later date in the churchyard. These dwellings were rebuilt in 1780, but in the process many oriel windows, porches, and projecting oratories disappeared. In 1540 the foundation was surrendered to Henry VIII., who contemplated founding a new bishopric of Southwell, and actually appointed Richard Cox (afterwards bishop of Ely) in 1543, refounding at the same time the old chapter and re-endowing it with most of its estates. Edward VI. again dissolved the chapter, and granted the estates to the Earl of Warwick, afterwards Duke of Northumberland. On the execution of the latter by Queen Mary, the estates were restored to the church, and a charter was subsequently granted by Queen Elizabeth and confirmed by James I. These details were formerly to be found (dated 1608) inscribed on a pillar in the nave, called Lee's pillar, from the name of the inscriber. The recent foundation of the bishopric of Southwell, with this church as its cathedral, has already been recounted. We now proceed to describe its

EXTERIOR.

There is nothing to interfere with the predominance of the Cathedral, so well known as Southwell Minster, in the small town of three thousand inhabitants by which it is surrounded, and as the town is itself situated on elevated ground near the western bank of the little river Greet, a tributary of the Trent, it is well seen from an extensive district. Although its towers are not

SOUTHWELL CATHEDRAL FROM THE NORTH WEST.
(From a Sketch by Mr. W. Livesay, Sudbury, Derby.)

very lofty, their massiveness, their being three in number, and being of Norman date give impressiveness to the building; and inasmuch as its main features are Norman and Early English of excellent design, it cannot fail to strike the visitor as one of the most interesting of English architectural monuments.

The church, built mainly of Bolsover magnesian limestone, consists of a nave with two west towers, a choir, main transepts, a central tower, a chapter house on the north east, and small eastern transepts. The west front, if not quite so impressive as those of some cathedrals, has a perennial interest from its fine Norman towers and central portal. The towers, which are engaged in the nave aisles, and form their termination, consist of seven stages separated by string-courses. The buttresses at each corner are broad and project but slightly. The west windows in the lower stage (filled with stained glass) are modern insertions, copied from the Norman windows in the nave-aisles and transepts, replacing the three-light Decorated windows inserted in the fourteenth century. The upper part of the tower is much more ornamented than the lower, chiefly with arcading in the upper three storeys. In the north tower the second stage from the top has an arcade of interlacing round-headed arches. The corresponding arcade in the south tower has lancet arches. The former plain parapets and corner pinnacles have been removed, and the erection of spires, reconstructed after the style of the former ones, has restored to the west front one element of its dignity which most people will think an improvement.

The greater part of the space between the western towers is occupied by a large Perpendicular window of seven lights, surrounded by a battlemented parapet. Beneath the window is a very fine central Norman portal, of five orders, the inner richly ornamented with zigzag moulding, the other four decorated alternately with edge-rolls flanked by hollows, and with zigzag. The whole portal is finished externally by double-billet moulding. The wooden doors probably date from the fourteenth century, and are covered with elaborate iron scroll work.

The south side of the nave shows the comparatively low aisle backed by the clerestory of the nave with its series of seven plain circular windows, perhaps unique in England, especially as there is nothing to mark the divisions between the bays. This is surmounted by a plain parapet and by the roof, now restored to its proper high pitch. The windows of the aisle are two modern Norman and five Early Perpendicular, larger than those they displaced. Between the upper string-course and the parapet of the aisle is a row of small windows giving light to the triforium.

The north side of the nave is similar in all respects to the south, except that the western window is original Norman, and that the line is broken at the third bay by a very fine original Norman porch. The plain north wall of the porch is hollowed by a broad massive arch of two orders. The walls of the interior of the porch have arcades of intersecting arches, above which runs a string-course of zigzag, also forming the abacus of the capitals of the shafts of the outer arch. The inner portal leading into the north nave aisle is very elaborate, of six orders, the inner being continuous to the ground, and all enriched with zigzag and other Norman mouldings. The roof is a plain waggon vault. A chamber over the doorway is lighted by three elaborate Norman windows in the gable. Cylindrical pinnacles finish off the corners of the porch, and the western one is a chimney shaft, pierced with holes to emit smoke.

The transepts occupy three bays each, and consequently project two bays beyond the nave aisles. There are three tiers of windows, the two lower being of the usual Norman type, the upper circular, like those in the clerestory of the nave. There was formerly an eastern apse or chapel in the south transept. The recent restoration of the high pitch to the transept roof has greatly improved the general effect. The lofty unbroken gables of the transepts are ornamented all over with zigzag of a different character on each face. The mouldings of all the windows deserve careful study by the archæologist. There are no aisles in the transepts. In the south face is a Norman doorway of three orders, richly ornamented with zigzag. Almost adjacent to this transept are the ruins of the old palace of the Archbishop of York.

Between the arms of the transept rises the massive central tower in two stages, with a plain parapet, four small cylindrical

SOUTHWELL CATHEDRAL; THE CENTRAL TOWER AND NORTH TRANSEPT.

Norman (not in their original position)* pinnacles at the corners, and a nondescript projection in the middle of each side. The lower stage has an arcade of intersecting arches, the upper has an arcade of seven round-headed arches, the three middle ones pierced for windows and divided by shafts for two lights. This tower contains a fine peal of eight bells, the tenor weighing one ton thirteen hundredweight.

No complete view of the choir from the northern side is obtainable, as the chapter house, library, cloister, etc., occupy that side. The chapel on the east side of the north transept was, till lately, the library. Its north front projects a little beyond the north front of the transept, and rises to nearly the same height (excepting the gable). On the south it abuts against the north choir aisle. It is only a little later in date than the choir, and its north face is Early English with Decorated details. The lower stage has a large window of three lights, with Late Decorated tracery. The second stage has a beautiful arcade of lancets, some pierced for windows. Above is a depressed Early English arch with dog-tooth moulding, enclosing inferior Perpendicular mullions and tracery.

The chapter-house with its vestibule projects to the east and north of this last building, the vestibule having two windows facing north and west, harmonising with the chapter-house. The latter is a very fine octagonal building, in Early Decorated or Geometrical style. At each angle is a prominent massive buttress in two main stages, the lower terminated above by a shallow niche, which once contained a statue; above this is an acute crocketed gable. Behind this a square pedestal with rounded edges and hollowed faces rises through the parapet, carrying a crocketed pinnacle. Between each buttress is a large three-light Geometrical window. The restoration of the high-pitched roof to this chapter-house, in 1882, renders it again one of the most beautiful of chapter-houses, with its quatrefoils and trefoils, its niches, gargoyles, and crocketed pinnacles, and its elaborate parapet. We must not omit to notice the circular stair-turret engaged on its south-west face.

* Mr. Dimock thinks these pinnacles originally belonged to the corners of the transepts, whence much stone was formerly taken for the parapet of the tower. They are much too small for their present situation.

SOUTHWELL CATHEDRAL: THE CHAPTER HOUSE.

The choir can scarcely be seen from the north, so we pass at once to view the east end, one of the first rank in Early English architecture. The east end projects two bays beyond the aisles, and includes, above the basement, two tiers each of four large lancets. The sides of this projecting portion have heavy buttresses carried up to acute triangular heads far above the parapet, while the corner buttresses have massive octagonal pinnacles. The windows in these bays are separate lancets, deeply set in the wall. The eastern gable is still far lower than it formerly was, the roof of the choir not having yet been raised to its old high pitch; but it is hoped that this may be done at some future time. From the shortness of the choir aisles, and the projection of the eastern transeptal chapel from their second bay, the choir has rather an unusual appearance on the north side, especially as the transeptal chapel has lost its original high gable and lofty roof. At this point, where the old roof is indicated, the choir clerestory is without windows. The proper restoration of these transepts would be a great improvement. The aisle buttresses, the two flying buttresses with crocketed pinnacles, west of the transeptal chapel, the lancet windows in aisle and in clerestory, the parapet with its grotesques beneath, all combine to make up a fine Early English picture, with the Norman tower and transept abutting against them on the west. The eastern part of the choir was built before the western part, and before the earlier and shorter Norman choir was taken down.

INTERIOR.

Entering by the western door, we are at once impressed by the massiveness and simplicity of the building. The massive cylindrical piers of the nave, the main Norman arches, and the great ones on which the tower stand, and the Norman waggon roof, now fortunately restored instead of the flat one formerly existing, present us with an aspect surpassed by but few Norman interiors. The nave is seven bays in length in addition to the engaged western towers.

The main pillars of the nave are nearly five feet in diameter, although only nine and a half feet from base to capital. The

SOUTHWELL CATHEDRAL: THE NAVE.

capitals are variously ornamented with zig-zag, billet, and other mouldings. The arches are ornamented chiefly by edge-rolls and filleted hollows, with the double billet externally. The triforium arches, large proportionately, are interesting because of the variations in their treatment from those below, while having the same width of arch. Before 1851 these were blocked up by plaster partitions; their removal, and that of the whitewash on the whole surface, has been a great improvement. The clerestory, low relatively, has in each bay a plain arch opening into a passage in the thickness of the wall, and abutting upon the circular windows noticed outside.

The nave aisles are finely vaulted and groined in stone, but otherwise have no special interest. West of the north doorway there is a sepulchral recess in the wall with a semi-circular arch. Beneath it is a raised cross on a coffin-shaped slab of Purbeck marble, probably of thirteenth century date. The roof of this bay had been formerly painted, and it was probably a chantry chapel.

The massive tower piers, of clustered columns, project inwardly much beyond the line of the nave piers, the distance between them being only 19 feet, while that between the nave piers is 28 feet. The span of the transept arches is greater. There are several orders in these arches, and a prominent feature is the cable moulding. Above the arches are now to be seen the pierced Norman window arches looking into the tower. The former flat ceiling under the tower has long since been removed, and a gallery substituted for the ringers, so that the next stage is visible from below—namely, the clock-chamber floor. Originally the tower was almost entirely open as a lantern, and it is probable that its being again opened would have an extremely good effect. Throughout the Norman portion of the building the masonry is excellent and fine-jointed.

The view across the transepts is peculiarly Norman, with the exception of the Decorated screen. The three stages into which the interior is divided have each their peculiarities. On the west side there are the round-arched openings into the nave-aisles, and triforium gallery, and two Norman windows deep in the wall and with enriched arches. The two windows on the south side in the lower stage differ in height, the western one being cut short so as to allow of the doorway beneath it. Projecting about two feet from the wall are two ornamental Norman arches, which span the transept, resting on a cylindrical central shaft; they carry an open gallery leading into the gallery in the thickness of the wall in the second stage of the east and west sides. A pair of handsome Norman arches communicates with the windows of the second stage, and shorter slightly-ornamented arches above open to the circular exterior windows of the third stage. On the east side of the south transept, the south half of the lower stage is occupied by a large circular arch blocked up, formerly opening into an apse or eastern chapel. In this wall is inserted an arch or closed doorway, constructed probably from one of the windows of the destroyed chapel. Adjacent to the tower pier is a lofty arch which leads into the choir aisle. The same is the case in the north transept. The broad south eastern arch is surmounted by three contiguous round-headed arches, and these by two small clerestory arches. There are no windows in the south transept in either of the two lower stages.

In reflooring the south transept recently a portion of the mosaic floor of the early church was discovered, formed of rough tesseræ of various colours. This interesting fragment, which could not be exposed, was left *in situ.*

The north transept closely resembles the southern arm. It has in its east wall, besides the large Norman arch (with two Early English arches within it), which leads into the adjoining chapel, and that into the choir aisle, a smaller arch, with a modern doorway inserted beneath, opening to the space under the staircase which leads up to the library. The restoration of the waggon roofs of the transepts in the last few years has been a great improvement. The foundations of the north transept apsidal chapel remain, and are now marked by lines in the floor of the later chapel.

The eastern tower arch resembles the western very closely, though the lower part is much blocked up by the screen. The arches opening into the transepts differ considerably from these, massive plain semi-cylindrical shafts bearing all the orders of

SOUTHWELL CATHEDRAL: THE CHOIR, LOOKING EAST.

the arches; they have also a larger span than the others. The eastern shafts do not project so far into the transept as the western, and consequently the centres of the arches are not over the centre of the transepts. The capitals of the eastern arch are enriched with interesting sculptured groups in low relief. The other capitals are plain.

The stone organ screen, formerly the Rood-screen (dating about 1337), has three canopied arches having free foliations. The foliage of the capitals clings closely round them; the parapet is pierced in a continuous undulation, with the openings foliated. The flat stone roof is supported by flying ribs, with trefoiled circles in the open spandrils above. On the choir side the central doorway is flanked on either side by return stalls; above which is a stage of blank arcading, and the whole is beautifully enriched. The organ above was erected by Father Schmidt.

Passing now into the choir, we find it to be one of the most beautiful of Early English choirs. There are six bays opening into the aisles, the arches being much higher than those of the nave, in three orders, supported on clustered shafts; they have several peculiarities showing a late period of Early English style. Large corbels between the arches carry the vaulting shafts, the fine roof of stone being vaulted on a quadripartite plan, with fine bosses of foliage at the intersections. The two bays beyond the aisles may be regarded as a Lady Chapel.

The triforium and clerestory have an arrangement very unusual at this period: there is only one stage looking inwards, each bay having a pair of fine lancet arches rising high towards the roof, while at the other side of the triforium gallery are two lancets below, looking into the space between the aisle-vault and roof, with two clerestory lancets above. The lancets at the east end present much the same appearance as on the outside.

In the south wall, just beyond the easternmost arch, are very fine fourteenth-century canopied sedilia and piscina, inserted when the Rood-screen was erected.

The choir aisles present no very unusual features in their style. There are stone sedilia and piscinas in the eastern bay of the south aisle and in the small eastern transepts. There are modern doors into these transepts. The vaulting is quadripartite, with additional ribs.

In the centre of the choir is a fine brazen eagle lectern, given by Prebendary Sir Richard Kaye, in 1805, said to have been fished up out of the lake at Newstead Abbey.

The canopied stalls in the two western bays of the choir, executed in plaster and composition by Bernasconi early in this century, have been removed and replaced by handsomely carved oak stalls and screens. In the latter have been re-used some portions of the old thirteenth-century screens.

The choir has been refloored with Hopton Wood stone in patterns, and the space within the communion-rail chiefly with coloured marbles.

There are few monuments of any note in the Cathedral. Six Archbishops of York were buried here: Geoffrey de Ludeham, 1264; Thomas de Corbridge, 1303; William Booth, 1464; Laurence Booth, 1480; Robert Holgate, 1545; Edwin Sandys, 1588. The tomb of the latter was at one time on the north side of the choir, but was removed towards the end of the last century to the north transept. It is an alabaster altar tomb, with the archbishop's recumbent effigy, and having figures of his wife, two sons, and six daughters on the sides, together with a Latin inscription. The effigy is, according to Bloxam, the only effigy of this period wearing a vestment or chasuble. More than one of the archbishops' tombs and brasses have disappeared.

The chapel, formerly used as a library, adjoining the east side of the north transept, is entered by two acute arches within an older Norman arch. The chapel is in two bays, each with an east window, and has quadripartite vaulting. The shafts are all keeled. There was formerly an altar in each bay; the top stones of these altars were found in the paving, and have been laid down under their former positions. The room above is now occupied by the library, and is entered by a staircase from the north choir aisle. The "White Book of Southwell" is one of the treasures of the library, being an old register of the church, containing grants from the Conquest down to the end of Henry VIII.'s reign.

The chapter-house is entered from the north choir aisle by

a beautiful arched doorway opening into a short cloister adjacent to the foregoing chapel, and abutting on the east on a small open court, enclosed between it, the choir aisle, the chapter-house, and the small eastern transept. This cloister passage has on one side a blank arcading, on the other a small doorway, and what once was an open arcade, now partially blocked up, the wall above it raised, and square-headed Perpendicular windows added, with a nearly flat roof of the same date, covered with lead.

Farther north the passage becomes the vestibule of the chapter-house, and, in fact, is one with it, built in the same style. The wall arcading is of beautiful cusped trefoil. The windows have geometrical tracery of similar character to that in the chapter-house windows, and the stone vaulting is quadripartite. The doorway into the chapter-house is very beautiful. It is double, a slender clustered shaft in the middle carrying two subordinate arches, with a quatrefoiled arch above. The upper arch has five orders, ornamented largely with foliage beautifully sculptured, like the capitals.

The interior of the chapter-house has an exquisite arcading running round the wall, forming five stalls in each of seven sides, the doorway forming the eighth. The window arches are of two orders, the capitals with beautiful foliage. The west side above the door has a blank arch, with mullions and tracery, like that of the windows. The adjoining side to the south is also blank, having the staircase to the roof outside it. There is much that is Early English in this beautiful chapter-house, with much that is characteristic of Early Decorated. The foliage, unlike that of the Early English period, is everywhere natural, representing oak, vine, hop, ivy, maple, and other leaves, no two capitals or bosses being alike. Figures are frequently introduced among the foliage, heads of kids or other animals. The roof vaulting is of stone, without a central pillar.

The windows contain some fragments of early painted glass, dating from Edward I.'s time, occupying portions of the tracery lights; one of these represents a knight on horseback tilting, with a long spear under his arm. Of Perpendicular date are a few shields of arms and other fragments in the west window of the nave. The four lower eastern windows of the choir contain sixteenth-century glass paintings of the French school, presented by Mr. Gally Knight, in 1818. They represent the Baptism of Christ, the Raising of Lazarus, the Triumphal Entry into Jerusalem, and the Mocking of Christ.

The following are the principal dimensions of Southwell Cathedral: internal length, 313 feet; nave, 143 feet 6 inches long, 60 feet broad; transept, 126 feet; central tower, 116 feet high, base, about 40 feet square; height of western towers and spires, 149 feet. The height from floor of nave up to the ridge of the open roof is 60 feet, and the internal height of the choir from the floor to the point of the groining is 50 feet.

There are three old gateways to the Cathedral precincts—on the west, north-east, and south. The partially ruined palace of the Archbishops of York, near to the south of the Cathedral, was built by Archbishop Kempe, 1435-1452, and his successors, and was a favourite residence of Wolsey. The Bishop of Nottingham (suffragan) purchased the remains, and in 1882 restored the great chamber, or smaller hall, which adjoined the great hall. It is a fine room, panelled in oak, and with a fine open wooden roof. The windows have been filled with royal and other shields, which were formerly in the great hall.

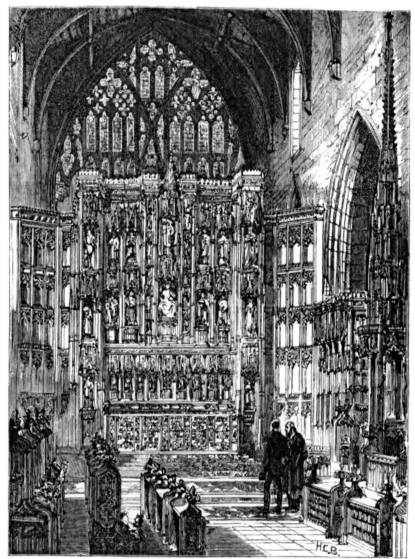

NEW REREDOS: NEWCASTLE CATHEDRAL.

NEWCASTLE CATHEDRAL.

The diocese of Newcastle is the late representative of the very ancient Northumbrian see dating from A.D. 635, when St. Aidan, a missionary from Iona, set up his "bishop's stool" on the island of Lindisfarne. Some details of the successive changes which the Northumbrian see underwent, and its final transfer to Durham, have been given under Durham Cathedral. In Henry VIII.'s reign the need for a subdivision of the diocese was recognised by the appointment of a suffragan bishop of Berwick, but only one appointment was made. In Edward VI.'s reign the establishment of a see of Newcastle was proposed, but was not carried out, and it was not till 1878 that provision was made for its foundation, by the Bishoprics' Act of that year, as soon as an endowment of £3,500 per annum should have been provided, including £1,000 given up by the Bishop of Durham. The see was definitely founded in 1882, the diocese consisting of the county of Northumberland, with the parish of Alston in Cumberland. The first Bishop, Dr. E. R. Wilberforce, son of the late Bishop of Winchester, was consecrated in Durham Cathedral on July 25th, 1882, and enthroned in the parish church of St. Nicholas, Newcastle, which had been appointed as the cathedral of the diocese. His palace is Benwell Tower, the gift of Mr. J. W. Pease, of Newcastle. There is no dean, but there are fifteen honorary canons. The diocese is divided into two archdeaconries, of Northumberland and of Lindisfarne. The vicar of Newcastle is one of the canons.

Newcastle Cathedral, though its dimensions and architectural features do not place it high among English Cathedrals, has many features of interest. A Norman church formerly existed on the same site, having been consecrated in 1091. It was burnt down in 1216. In the present church there remains but little of the early rebuilding. The nave dates from about 1350, being of Late Decorated style. The transepts were built in 1368. The choir, Early Perpendicular, followed, the east window being the gift of Roger Thornton, who died in 1429. The completion of the tower and construction of the steeple is due to Robert Rhodes, who died in 1474. In 1784-7 the church was repaired and largely "restored"—that is, in this case, injured. The carved oak pews in the nave were removed, and it was devoted to burials only; the reading desk and pulpit, with its pinnacled canopy, the font and organ gallery (occupying the space at the crossing) being all removed.

The large Corporation pew with its canopy was taken away, as also the arched screen with its tracery. A large number of ancient monuments, brasses and tombstones were removed. A shameful auction got rid of the old brasses and tombstones that were not claimed by the representatives of families. In 1832 the tower was found to be inclining dangerously to the south, and consequently buttresses were added to the south porch. The north porch was added in 1834. The east window was renewed in 1861, and consequently its structure, like its glass, is entirely modern. The principal window in the north transept is likewise a modern restoration. In 1866-71 the tower, which had again become endangered, was repaired and strengthened at a cost of £8,500. In 1873-7 a considerable restoration was effected under Sir G. G. Scott, when the screen surrounding the choir was removed, and the nave, previously neither seated nor used, was brought into the area occupied for service.

All the plaster and whitewash which had defaced the church was removed. The organ loft was taken away, and the organ placed over the crypt in St. George's Porch.

During this restoration some remains of the previous Norman Church were discovered, including some moulded shafts and caps in St. Mary's Chapel (the south transept), and a pillar enclosed in the north-west pillar of the transept crossing.

It may be noted that the reformer, John Knox, preached in this church for two years (circ. 1550), having been asked to do so by the Government of Edward VI.

The new reredos and other additions and improvements in the choir are noticed later.

EXTERIOR.

The Cathedral, situated on somewhat elevated ground near the approach to the High Level bridge, is a full-scale parish church, with a fine west tower, which renders it a very conspicuous object in the city. The tower is engaged in the nave, and forms the main feature of the west front. Excepting the tower, the whole building has no striking feature, except some of the windows, whose tracery will be best studied from the interior. It is much hemmed in by buildings, and the roof being low-pitched, only the tower is seen at any distance. It consequently is the chief part of the exterior demanding special description.

The tower is an Early Perpendicular building in three stages, crowned by a beautiful steeple. The lower stage contains a doorway and plain Perpendicular windows on three faces. The second has much smaller windows lighting the belfry, and shows a clockface both north and south. The third stage is built slightly within the lower ones, and encloses the bell-chamber. It is taller than the stage below, and on each face are two double-light windows (unglazed), separated by a median flat buttress rising from the pediment of the second stage, and continued beyond the battlements as an octagonal turret terminated by a graceful pinnacle. At the four corners of the tower are flat and massive buttresses, also continued above the battlements, and terminated by carved figures. At the north-west is Adam conveying an apple to his mouth; Eve is on the north-east offering an apple to Adam; Aaron, mitred, and carrying an open book, occupies the south-west; and David, crowned, and striking a harp, is at the south-east. From just within the battlements rise large octagonal turrets at each corner, turning by crocketed pinnacles, each ending in a vane ornamented with *fleur-de-lis*.

The steeple is carried upon four elegant flying buttresses or segments of arches. Where they intersect, twenty feet above the battlements, there rises a lofty square lantern with an open window on each side, small buttresses at the angles supporting pinnacles, and these connected by smaller flying buttresses with a central crocketed pinnacle, hollow internally. Rickman says: "This steeple is as fine a combination as any of its date, and the lightness and boldness of the upper part can hardly be exceeded." Its total height is 193 feet 6 inches; at the base it measures 36 feet 9 inches by 35 feet.

The bells are now nine in number, and with the exception of the largest, are of good quality. Until 1717 there were only five bells, of which the first, dedicated to St. Nicholas, bears the following legend, in black letter:—

"Cunctis modulamina Promans
Sum Nicholaius Ovans;"

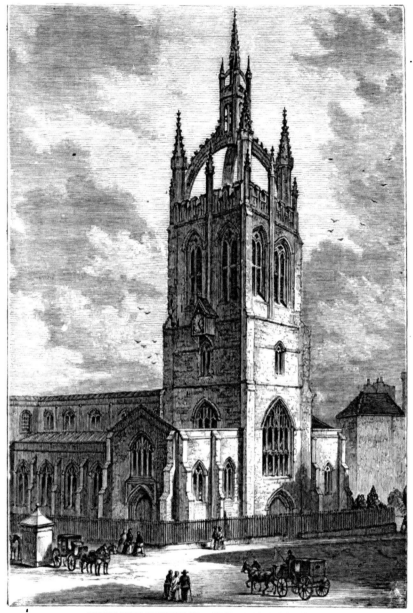

NEWCASTLE CATHEDRAL: FROM THE NORTH-WEST.

which may be translated, "Giving out modulations to all, I am Nicholas rejoicing." The second and third bells are dedicated to the Virgin and to St. Michael. The fourth, or common bell, was tolled for municipal business, and is also known as the thief and reiver bell, from its having been tolled on the eve of the great annual fairs, to let thieves and horse, cattle and sheep-stealers know that they might attend it without any question. The fifth bell bears the arms of Newcastle. Three other bells were added by the Corporation, in 1717, and some of these have been recast. In 1833 a big bell, bequeathed by Major Anderson, was added, and the clock strikes the hours upon it. Its weight is three tons twelve hundredweight.

The west front and part of the north side of the cathedral front an open space. On the south side the choir is concealed by a large library and vestry of classical design, dating from 1736, and very incongruous with the church. It contains Dr. Tomlinson's Theological Library, which he left to the parish. Sir Walter Blackett erected the building, and gave an endowment to pay a librarian.

INTERIOR.

On entering the church by the western door the general impression is good, as the tower arches of clustered columns rise to an imposing height and the groined roof is characteristically beautiful. The nave is divided from the aisles by acute arches supported on octagonal piers. The arches at the crossing of the transepts are bold and lofty. There is not much else of beauty to note about the nave. The clerestory is very inferior.

The choir has four very broad arches on either side. The east window is a large Perpendicular one, with characteristic tracery, the lower part blocked by the new reredos, which separates the eastern chapel from the rest of the choir. It was rebuilt in 1860, in memory of Dr. Ions, formerly organist of the church (died 1857), and has been filled with stained glass by Wailes. The Crucifixion is illustrated in the five middle compartments, and beneath is a representation of the Last Supper. The tracery depicts the archangels and prophets. The east window of the north and south choir aisles respectively are also memorial windows, the former representing the Resurrection, the latter the Ascension. There are several other modern stained-glass windows in the church. The large window in St. Mary's Chapel is a memorial to the Rev. Clement Moody, vicar of the church from 1853 to 1871.

Since the constitution of the new diocese extensive works have been carried out in the choir under the direction of Mr. Johnson, of Newcastle, to provide for the Cathedral use of the church. They include a lofty reredos of alabaster with side wings of stone, and adjacent sedilia also of stone, bishop's throne, stalls for the canons and choir, side screens and canopies, and a western screen with gates to the choir. The reredos represents Our Lord enthroned and surrounded by saints, viz., St. Oswald, the Venerable Bede, St. Nicholas, St. Cuthbert, St. Benedict Biscop, St. Aidan, St. Edwin, the Four Evangelists, St. Wilfrid, and St. Paulinus. There are also the archangel Gabriel and the Virgin Mary. The reredos with all the surrounding stonework was the gift of Mr. Percy Westmacott.

Eastward of the reredos, and occupying the last bay of the structural choir, a chapel has been formed called the Chapel of the Incarnation, which is used for smaller services. The reredos in the chapel is of wood painted and gilded, with a large picture of the Nativity and smaller ones of the prophets who prophesied of it. The new woodwork throughout is very richly carved, and is designed on the Northern types of which beautiful fragments remain at Hexham, Carlisle, and Brancepeth.

At the back of the new reredos is placed a large oil-painting said to be by Tintoretto, presented by Sir Matthew White Ridley in 1813. The subject is Christ Washing the Disciples Feet. Hung at the east end are paintings of the Flight into Egypt and the Adoration of the Magi, presented in 1879 by Mr. Hugh Taylor.

The north transept window, a large Decorated one, was renewed a few years ago, as closely as possible like its former self. The windows near it on the east side (flowing Decorated) retain their old tracery.

The (nine) mortuary chapels or chantries attached to the church call for no special notice. The font standing under the tower should be examined; it dates from Rhodes's time. The basin is an octagonal one of marble, the eight faces sculptured with shields of arms, six being those of Rhodes. Above it rises an elegant pinnacled canopy.

There still remain a considerable number of interesting monuments in the nave. The Maddison monument is the most noteworthy. Formerly fixed to a pillar in the south-choir aisle, it was removed during the late restoration to the south transept which was formerly St. Mary's Chapel, and fixed against the west wall. It has been carefully cleaned of paint and dirt, and now presents something of its original appearance. It is an elaborate Jacobean work, representing six of the Maddison family, male and female, in the sixteenth and seventeenth centuries, all kneeling; below are sixteen smaller figures, representing the children of one family. Above are figures of Faith, Hope, and Charity, with emblems.

Another less elaborate monument, belonging to the same period, is that to William Hall and his mother. Several of the figures are modern restorations (1877).

The Askew monument, by Henry Webber (1801), is in the south-nave aisle. The Ridley monuments are (1) in the south-choir wall, to Matthew Ridley (who died 1778), by Bacon; (2) in the nave, to Sir Matthew White Ridley (died 1813), by Flaxman. Another of Flaxman's works is the monument to Rev. Hugh Moises, for many years head-master of Newcastle Grammar School (died 1806). The cenotaph to Admiral Lord Collingwood (died 1819) is by Rossi. The monument in memory of Colonel Bewicke is by Bailey, after a design by Theed.

In the south transept is a recumbent figure, perhaps the most ancient now remaining in the church. It is cross-legged, wearing a hauberk of chain-mail and surcoat, with a sword and shield; at its feet is a lion. This has been conjectured to be the monument of Peter de Mauley, a baron of Richard II.'s time.

The dimensions of the church are—greatest internal length, 243 feet; length of nave, 110 feet; width of nave, 74 feet; length of transept, 127 feet; width of transept, 25 feet; internal height, 47 feet; length of choir, 110 feet.

WAKEFIELD CATHEDRAL: THE CHOIR, LOOKING EAST.

WAKEFIELD CATHEDRAL.

The diocese of Wakefield, taken out of Ripon, was founded in 1887, in pursuance of the Bishoprics Act, 1878 It includes the rural deaneries of Birstal, Dewsbury, Halifax, Huddersfield, Silkstone, and Wakefield. The first bishop is Dr. Walsham How, previously Suffragan Bishop of Bedford.

The parish church of All Saints, in Northgate, near the centre of the city, which was assigned as the cathedral of the new diocese, is a good parish church, with western tower and spire, almost entirely Perpendicular; but it has few claims to architectural eminence, and has been so much refaced and rebuilt that it may be best regarded as a modern edifice upon Early English and Perpendicular lines. It appears to stand on the site of a Norman church, which lasted till early in the 14th century. A new and larger church was then built, and consecrated in 1329. This, again, was rebuilt in 1470, with the exception, it is said, of the tower and spire. In 1715 the vane and one-third of the spire were blown down, and it was then partly rebuilt, but not to its original height. In 1724 the south side of the church was recased, and about the end of the same century the north side and east end were also rebuilt, and a vestry stuck right against the east window; and it cannot be said that these rebuildings reproduced faithfully the original designs. In 1802 the spire was again found to be seriously injured, and again repaired and strengthened with iron bands. In 1823 it again underwent partial rebuilding, and was carried up to its original height. At some period, rather uncertain, a Perpendicular window to the belfry was inserted in the west face, with a doorway beneath. The tower was again recased in 1858, and the spire rebuilt. The restoration continued in progress from that year till 1874, during which many necessary alterations and valuable improvements were made. The plaster and coloured wash which had defaced the walls were removed. The lofty arch of the tower at the west end was opened up and forms a principal entrance, and a groined roof was inserted below the belfry. A new door was made in the north aisle, and the old north porch was removed. The vestry beneath the east window was removed, and its place was taken by a new building added to the north choir aisle. The organ was also removed to the north choir aisle. The north, south, and west galleries in the nave aisles were removed, making the view much more open and the general aspect much more beautiful. The floor of the whole church was relaid. A new reredos and new stained-glass windows were inserted. The roofs throughout were cleansed and decorated. The whole of the windows were renewed. In

WAKEFIELD CATHEDRAL FROM THE SOUTH-EAST.

fact, one may say that nearly everything in the church is either new, or newly decorated, or cleaned, which no one who knew the church previously, in modern times, will regret.

EXTERIOR.

The good position of Wakefield Cathedral, near the Market-place, at the junction of the three principal streets, and with a considerable churchyard and open space surrounding it, allows full justice to be done to its merits, which are not inconsiderable, regarding it as a parish church. Viewed from the south, we see the long, continuous line of nave and choir, with their aisles, flat roofs, and Perpendicular windows in both aisles and clerestory, somewhat interesting southern porch, and, at the west end, clear of the aisle, the substantial tower and lofty crocketed spire, rising to a height of 247 feet, including the vane. The view of the tower from the west is less satisfactory, presenting the inferior doorway and Perpendicular window below the bell-chamber. The tower contains a fine peal of ten bells, which in 1817 replaced one of eight, and has also a clock and chimes; the Cambridge chimes were added during the last restoration, by Mr. J. C. Charlesworth, of Chapelthorpe Hall. The east end, with its window, has been rebuilt, and the buttresses on the east and south renewed. The clerestory windows, formerly very plain, have been replaced by others in Perpendicular style, more suitable to the general design.

INTERIOR.

Entering beneath the tower, a comparatively plain interior is seen, with the exception of the long row of Decorated arches of nave and choir, the boundary between which is marked by a larger arch of the same character and a handsome screen. The ceilings are almost flat, but rise slightly to the centre; they are panelled in wood, with elaborated bosses at the intersections. These are now decorated in gilt and colour. The Early English arches, with their series of mouldings, are handsome in themselves, but are somewhat detracted from by the much inferior Perpendicular arches and windows of the clerestory. The piers are also varied, having been built at different times. Some are circular, some octagonal, some clustered. There is one more on the south side than on

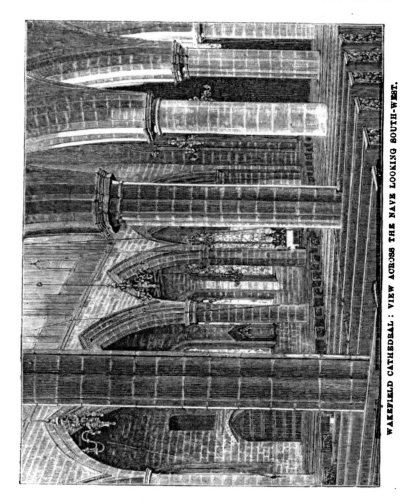

WAKEFIELD CATHEDRAL: VIEW ACROSS THE NAVE LOOKING SOUTH-WEST.

the north. The whole view has been much improved by the removal of the galleries. The organ, which is a powerful and melodious one, has been re-erected in the north-choir aisle. The removal of the old, unsightly pews, and their substitution by open oak seats with elaborately carved ends, extending entirely across both nave and aisles, is also a great improvement.

The upper part of the screen, of post-Reformation date, is elaborately carved; it was extended in the late restoration. The choir stalls have been increased in number, and the old ones repaired and cleaned. The floor has been relaid with stone and black marble in diamond patterns. The sanctuary has been laid with encaustic tiles. A handsome reredos of Caen stone and white marble, partly gilt, has been erected after the designs of Sir G. G. Scott, at the cost of the Rev. H. Dawson, of Wakefield.

Of the new stained-glass windows we may note especially that at the east end, by Lavers and Barraud, of London, inserted at the cost of the executors of Mr. R. Ingram. It represents the Crucifixion, and Christ seated as King over the Church. The south-west, or baptistry window represents the Baptism of Christ, the Descent of the Holy Ghost upon Him, and Christ Blessing Little Children. The west window under the tower, like the preceding, is by Hardman.

The Pilkington chantry, on the south side of the choir, has been restored by Sir L. Pilkington, Bart., of Chevet Park, containing the monument to Sir Lyon Pilkington (died 1714). There are no monuments of early date, but a crowd of last-century memorials and stones of no special interest.

The total length of the church is 182 feet 8 inches by 67 feet 3 inches broad at the west end, and 71 feet 5 inches at the east end.

ST. DAVID'S CATHEDRAL.

As this was once an archbishopric, it is proper in writing the history of the Welsh Sees to give it the precedence; the others, Llandaff, Bangor, and St. Asaph, having been suffragans to it. When it lost its metropolitan rank, it became together with the other three suffragan to the see of Canterbury, and the whole of Wales is still included within that province. St. David's is in South Wales, and in a remote corner of the County of Pembroke, within a short distance from the sea coast.

This see is of very remote antiquity, the origin of it given by Browne Willis, who collected his account from Godwin, Leland, and Wharton, is as follows:—It was from the first a metropolitan see, but began at a place called Caerleon on Usk in Monmouthshire; a bishop named Elveus, is said to have baptized St. David, who was nursed at a place called Vetus Menevia, in Welsh, Henenemew. Gistilianus, another bishop of Caerleon, was St. David's uncle. The transferring of the see from Caerleon to Menevia, was owing to St. David's great veneration and love for St. Patrick, who founded it, and an equal veneration and love for St. David himself on the part of his successors in the see, caused them to call the place after his name, the Latin appellation however still prevails, and the bishops of St. David's are styled *Episcopi Menevenses.*

St. Patrick died in 472, in the 111th year of his age, many years before St. David governed this see. Dubritius presided over Wales as archbishop of Caerleon, and in his extreme old age resigned his see to St. David. Some say Dubritius died in 522, but others with more probability in 612: that he was buried in the isle of Bardsey, from whence his bones were carried to Llandaff. His successor, David, was royally descended, being son of Xantus, a Prince of Wales, and uncle to King Arthur. He was a very learned and eloquent man, and of incredible austerity. Many miracles are said to be wrought by him. Godwin says, he governed this church sixty-five years, and died March 1, 642, aged 146 years. Other historians give a very different account of the time of his death, some placing it in the year 546, and others a little after the year 609. In some of these accounts, it is stated that he became bishop in 519, which if true, and he continued till after 609, he must have held the see ninety years at least, instead of sixty-five, which might be, considering his great age. However this may be, it is certain he removed the see from Caerleon to the place where it still continues to be, not only for the reason before mentioned, but probably also from having been brought up here, although the reason given by some authors, is, that the barren and desolate situation attracted him, being extremely fond of retirement, and that Caerleon was distasteful to him on account of its large population, which withdrew him too much from contemplation. He was therefore the first archbishop of Menevia, or St. David's. Of those who succeeded him, little is known but their names, and not even these correctly, being so variously spelt. Lendivord, the ninth archbishop, had the misfortune to see his cathedral burnt by the West Saxons in 712, in the reign of King Ina. Asser, the twenty-third, was a famous writer, and died in 906. Sampson, the twenty-fifth archbishop, is famous in history, on account of his retiring to Dol, in Bretagne, during a contagious sickness in his diocese. He there either founded a see, or finding one vacant, contrived to possess himself of it, and to the great discontent of the archbishop of Tours, began to exercise archiepiscopal authority within that province. His successors at Dol for a long time claimed the same honour and power, till one of the Popes settled the dispute in favour of the archbishops of Tours: but the bishops of Dol have still the cross carried before them in processions, and take precedence of all other bishops in the province of Tours. On this prelate's abdication, his see lost its metropolitan rank, and his successors were only bishops of St. David's, though all the Welsh bishops received their consecration from them till the time of Henry I., when Bishop Bernard, a Norman, not chosen by the clergy of Wales according to custom, but forced upon them by the king, yielded submission to the see of Canterbury.

Sampson, who may be looked upon as the author of this (once called) misfortune to the Welsh church, died at Dol, and was there buried, though his relics were afterwards taken to Middleton, in the county of Dorset, where a magnificent abbey, built by King Athelstan, was dedicated to his honour, which, however, is not a little stained if it be true that he deserted his post and his flock on account of the danger to himself of remaining amongst them during a time of pestilence, when his presence was most needed. His death is supposed to have happened about the beginning of the tenth century.

As to the Cathedrals before the present, nothing is recorded. Browne Willis states that "in the year 1176, when Peter de Leia became bishop of the see, the Cathedral had been so much ruined by the incursions of the Danes and other pirates that it was thought right to take it down and rebuild it," which this bishop accordingly did. In 1220 the tower fell, destroying the choir and transepts. The Cathedral was again completed in the Early English period; but many alterations were made by Bishop Gower (1328-47), in the Decorated style.

The situation of this Cathedral is most extraordinary, for besides the barren and desolate appearance of the whole country around it, as far as the eye can reach, it is placed so that approaching it from the main road (on either side of which the humble dwellings of the citizens of St. David's are irregularly placed), nothing of it can be seen but the top of the central tower, till the visitor begins to descend into the huge pit in which it is set. Then not only the Cathedral, but the magnificent ruins of the episcopal palace break upon the view, together with those of many other ecclesiastical edifices.

EXTERIOR.

The Cathedral church stands in a close, nearly a mile in compass, open only towards the sea, surrounded by a stone wall, having on the west a rivulet called Alan, and to the north the College.

The west front was modelled by Nash towards the end of the last century. His very inferior work has since been displaced by Sir G. G. Scott, so as to make the west front something like what it was originally.

The south side of the nave and its aisle are very plain. The first window in the aisle from the west has been walled up, and two small loop-holes inserted in the wall to admit a little light. The next compartment is occupied by a much improved porch with a small pointed window over the arch of entrance, pointed also, lighting a chamber above the porch. Beyond the porch are four other windows, some having Decorated, and some Perpendicular tracery. Slight buttresses are placed between the windows, and their pinnacles, either formerly destroyed or worn away by the keen sea breezes, have now been restored. The parapet of this aisle is quite plain, as is also that of the clerestory above, in which are twelve round-headed windows, two in each bay. The parapet projects a little from the wall, and rests on corbels; the buttresses between the windows are flat, and project no more from the wall than the parapet. The south wing of the transept is very plain; its west wall has one round-headed window in it of no great merit, one buttress, and a plain parapet. The south face is flanked with square buttresses or turrets, terminating octagonally with a low spire; the eastern one contains a stair leading to the triforium. Within a lofty semi-circular arch are four pointed windows, two below and two over them, with Perpendicular tracery. In the gable point is a small pointed window of one light. Against the east wall of this wing of the transept is a chapel, formerly, like the south choir aisle and the Lady Chapel, unroofed. The east wall of the choir had a large Perpendicular window; the clerestory is quite plain; the parapet is embattled. The north aisle of the choir also was unroofed. Against the east wall of the north wing of the transept is the Chapel of St. Thomas of Canterbury, with a roof of stone vaulting. Above is a chamber formerly a school-room, now a library. In the north face of the transept is a large Perpendicular window. The west wall is perfectly plain. The north side of the nave and its aisle have a very rude appearance, owing chiefly to some massive buttresses against the wall of the aisle. The clerestory windows are round-headed, and two have wooden casements inserted; there is a pointed window in the aisle, now nearly all walled up, and an entrance into the aisle under a semicircular arch of ordinary Norman work. The parapets of the aisle and clerestory are quite plain. The central tower is lofty, having two stages above the roof of the nave, but is not well

Kirkwall Cathedral.

proportioned—its height is too great, and the upper stage projects a little over the tower, giving it the look of being top-heavy. In the lower stage there is a Decorated window in each of the four sides, flanked on either hand by an ornamental shallow canopy. The upper stage has two very small pointed windows side by side in each side of it, set in a great expanse of plain wall. The parapet is open, but not rich, and both at the four corners and the centre of each side are pinnacles, which, as well as the whole of the towers, have been carefully restored.

The ruins of St. Mary's College are still standing on the north side of this Cathedral, and the more extensive ones of the once magnificent palace of the prelates are still to be seen a little to the south-west of it. The whole scene is one of departed grandeur.

INTERIOR.

The usual way of entering this Cathedral is through the south porch. Not having been led to expect much within, from its external appearance, the visitor is agreeably surprised, for there are a spaciousness and dignity about the nave and its aisles, and even a richness of effect, which connect it at once with the ancient importance of this see and its former splendour and ecclesiastical magnificence. The nave is broad; the arches, six in number on each side, are semicircular, with many bold mouldings, and among them the zigzag, all excellently well cut, and resting upon columns composed of one large and several smaller cylindrical shafts around them. Above the arches of the nave runs a plain horizontal string-course; the windows of the clerestory are deeply recessed within semicircular arches, richly decorated with late Norman mouldings delicately carved, which extend through the triforium and rest upon the string-course before mentioned. The triforium has not a good effect, and appears more like the walling up of the lower part of the clerestory arches. Thus far all is original, the work of Peter de Leia, about the latter end of the twelfth century. The roof of the nave does not accord with the rest of it, although in itself exceedingly rich and curious; it is flat, of Irish oak, arranged in square compartments, with pendants on each side, connected with each other by a series of small Tudor arches, all very well and elaborately carved.

The rood-loft projects a little into the nave; it is a very rich example of the Decorated style, and is topped by a row of small arches filled with Perpendicular tracery and with groining rising to a cornice of carved oak. This rood-loft shuts out the transept from the nave; in the centre of it is the entrance into the choir, under a pointed archway, which is elegantly vaulted. The arch towards the choir is now restored, parts of the original bay behind having been discovered and replaced. The choir is very small, occupying only the space beneath the central tower, and is tolerably well furnished with stalls and seats. The organ was under the north arch of the tower, which is pointed and richly adorned with mouldings; the piers from which they spring are not so massive as usual, and have been strengthened with additional masonry. There is a good open screen of late Decorated character, dividing the choir from the space beyond, in the eastern wall of which there are some very rich Norman arches, under the great east window. To the east of the space beyond the choir is Bishop Vaughan's Chapel, a very rich and elegant example of the latest period of the pure pointed style. The vaulting, of delicate fan tracery, resembles that of King's College Chapel, at Cambridge. Beyond this is the avenue leading to the Lady Chapel, which is vaulted in a less elaborate style, but is very good of its kind.

The dimensions of the Cathedral are as follows: Length from east to west, 290 feet; of the nave, 124; of choir and space beyond it, 80; transept, 120; breadth of body and aisles together, 76 feet; height of body, 46; of the central tower, 127 feet.

There are several ancient monuments of bishops and other dignitaries of this Cathedral, one cross-legged knight, the shrine of St. David (as it is called), and the tomb of the Earl of Richmond, father of Henry VII. There are no modern monuments deserving of notice.

The cloisters were on the north side of the Cathedral; trace of them remain on the south wall of the crypt of the Chapel of St. Mary's College.

The Cathedral is dedicated to St. David and St. Andrew. It had no dean, till in 1840 that title was conferred upon the precentor. The bishop has a stall assigned him on the right hand,

at the entrance into the choir. It has also a chancellor, treasurer, four archdeacons—viz., of St. David's, Brecknock, Caermarthen, and Cardigan—and twenty-two prebendaries, though the chapter consists of only five members, a dean and four canons. There are three priest vicars and two lay vicars.

The old diocese was of vast extent, comprehending the entire counties of Pembroke, Caermarthen, Cardigan, and Radnor, except five parishes, which belonged to the see of Hereford. It had also eight parishes in Herefordshire, twenty-two in Glamorganshire, two in Montgomeryshire, and two in Monmouthshire; but the Act of 1839-40 has altered it by the transfer of all the parishes in the three last-mentioned counties to the other Welsh dioceses.

The bishopric of St. David's is charged in the King's books at £426 2s. 1d. per annum; and it was afterwards declared to be worth, annually, £2,490 in the gross and £1,897 in the clear.

The more eminent bishops before the Reformation are—

Thomas Beck, elected in 1280, who founded two colleges—one at Abergwilly, for twenty-two prebendaries, and one at Llandewybrevy, for thirteen.

Henry Gower, who was also Chancellor of England, and built the great palace at St. David's.

Adam Houghton founded St. Mary's College, near the Cathedral, for seven Fellows, and was Chancellor of England; he was consecrated in 1361, and died in 1388.

Henry Chicheley held this see from 1408 to 1414, when he was translated to Canterbury, and is called the most worthy prelate of his time; he founded two colleges—one at Higham Ferrers, in Northamptonshire, his native county; and one at Oxford, viz., All Souls.

Among the eminent prelates of this see since the Reformation should be mentioned—

William Laud, afterwards Archbishop of Canterbury.

George Bull, D.D., who, after a vacancy of nearly six years, was elected bishop of this see in 1704, and died in 1709, and was buried in the collegiate church of Brecon. He was the greatest divine of his day; and what is said in his epitaph is strictly true—viz., that he was excellently learned, pious, and charitable. Robert Nelson has published an account of his life and writings.

Thomas Burgess, D.D., was consecrated Bishop of St. David's in the year 1803, and having been eminently useful to this diocese for twenty-two years, was translated to Salisbury in 1825.

Connop Thirlwall, Bishop of St. David's from 1840 to 1878, is noted as the historian of Greece and as one of the keenest intellects that ever adorned the episcopal bench. His charges were the most brilliant and thoughtful of modern times.

His successor, Dr. William Basil Jones, is joint author with Prof. Freeman of an invaluable work, "The History and Antiquities of St. David's," published in 1856.

ST. DAVID'S CATHEDRAL: NORTH-EAST VIEW.

MODERN HISTORY OF ST. DAVID'S CATHEDRAL.

IN 1843 the south transept was adapted as a parish church, and the vestry added to its eastern side during the seventeenth century was converted into an eastern aisle. In 1846 the rood-screen was partly restored, and the large window of the north transept was replaced by a Decorated one designed by Mr. Butterfield. In 1849 several of the Perpendicular windows in the south-nave aisle having been blown in, they were replaced by Decorated ones; also the north aisle of the presbytery was roofed over.

In 1862 it was determined to carry out a complete restoration, as far as possible. Mr. (afterwards Sir) G. G. Scott was called in, and found almost every part in need of restoration, but the central tower was in great danger. It was necessary to rebuild from the foundations the two western piers, each bearing a weight of 1,150 tons. These had to be temporarily shored with timber and braced with iron ties. The stone employed in this work was the purple stone of the neighbouring cliffs, somewhat harder than the original stone of the tower. Mr. Scott considered this the most difficult and hazardous work of tower-rebuilding on which he had been engaged. During this work it was necessary to reopen the tombs of three bishops. This was done with great care, and several objects taken from them are now preserved in the chapter-house. Among them are the bronze-gilt head of a pastoral staff, of Early Decorated style, two chalices, etc.

Bishop Gower, in building the middle or Decorated stage of the tower, formed it into a beautiful lantern, but when, at the end of the fifteenth or beginning of the sixteenth century, wooden groining was inserted, it cut Gower's lantern windows in two, hiding their heads altogether. Mr. Scott, in his restoration, raised the groining to the top of the stage, so as to include the whole of the windows, thus adding greatly to the efficiency and beauty of the lantern.

In the choir proper (under the tower) the wall which formerly filled up the south arch has been removed. The organ, which formerly stood beneath the northern arch, has been presented to the church of St. Martin, Haverfordwest, and was replaced in 1883 by a powerful instrument by Willis, erected chiefly on the screen, portions being placed in the transepts. The stalls, open screen, and Bishop's throne, necessarily removed during the rebuilding of the tower, were carefully repaired, all ancient work being touched as little as possible. The floor has been laid with encaustic tiles. The presbytery underwent a thorough restoration at Sir G. G. Scott's hands. The aisles, so long unroofed and walled off, have been again connected with the main presbytery, roofed in oak, and restored. Instead of the upper Perpendicular window, the original four lancets have been rebuilt, enough of the original mouldings having been found built up in the raised sidewalls of the presbytery, to go far towards completing them. Externally they form a continuous arcade of twelve, four being windows and eight niches. The lower tier of windows is still blocked by Bishop Vaughan's chapel; the stonework, however, has been repaired, and the spaces filled with beautiful Venetian mosaics by Salviati, designed by Powel, of Birmingham, and given, like

ST. DAVID'S CATHEDRAL: THE NAVE.

the stained glass which now fills the upper windows, by the late Rev. John Lucy.

The colour in the old roof of the presbytery, after its repair, was carefully reproduced. It contains many ancient shields of arms; in those affixed to the corbels have been inserted those of the members of the cathedral body at the time of restoration. The old wooden sedilia, dating from the fifteenth century, were found in one of the walled-up arches, and were restored. Three of the arches on the north side were occupied by ancient tombs, including the substructure of St. David's shrine. These also have been restored.

The present altar, recently constructed, consists of a fine slab of grey sandstone, upon an oaken frame; behind it, in the floor, are inserted some old altar-slabs, found used as paving in another part of the presbytery.

The base of the shrine of St. David is the most important monument in the presbytery, and one of the few shrines extant in this country; it is in the third bay from the east, on the north side. On a massive base are three low, pointed arches, with quatrefoils in the spandrils between. The flat top rests on three Early English arches backed by a wall panelled behind. The shafts are restorations. The arches formerly contained paintings, and the whole was covered with a wooden canopy. The shrine, replacing a previous one, was made in 1275; in 1284 Edward I. and his Queen Eleanor made a pilgrimage thither. The tomb of Edmund Tudor, father of Henry VII., is near this, in the centre of the presbytery. It is an altar tomb of Purbeck marble, and was removed, after the Dissolution, with the Earl's remains from the Church of the Grey Friars, at Carmarthen, where he was originally buried.

In the third bay from the east of the arcade separating the presbytery from its south aisle, are two effigies of bishops. In the north choir aisle are canopied recesses, recently restored, which formerly contained effigies, which have disappeared. In one of them has been placed the effigy of a knight in armour of the fourteenth century, similar to an effigy opposite to it in the south aisle. In the south choir aisle are several other effigies of unidentified persons.

The monument or shrine of St. Caradoc (died 1124) is on the south side of the north transept. Two pointed arches in a low wall support a flat table, at the back of which is a round arch. The most important of the monuments in the rood-screen is that of Bishop Gower (died 1347).

The remodelling of the west front was completed in 1883, and is believed to reproduce the essential features of the original plan. Above a Norman doorway with enriched mouldings are first a niche containing a sitting statue of Bishop Thirlwall, and then two tiers of windows. The lower tier has three fine Norman windows richly moulded, while the upper consists of five lancets. A circular window is inserted at the end of each nave aisle. On either side of the doorway is a massive quadrangular turret-buttress, modified from Nash's design; similar buttresses are at the corners of the north and south aisles. The whole of this west front is a memorial to Bishop Thirlwall (died 1878).

The cost of the restoration and repairs, including those of the tower, has exceeded £39,000. Bequests by Mr. and Mrs. J. Montgomery Traherne, amounting to £4,000, have provided for the restoration of the south transept, of the paving of the nave and its aisles, the oak ceiling of the north aisle, and the organ-case.

For a full account of the history and antiquities of St. David's Professor Freeman and Bishop Basil Jones's elaborate work should be consulted.

LLANDAFF CATHEDRAL.

LLANDAFF CATHEDRAL has undergone more change in recent years than any English cathedral. It is now transformed, so that the plates we give of its former condition are of especial value as historic representations. The see is no doubt of great antiquity, although there is no evidence in favour of the tradition that the British King Lucius built a church here in A.D. 180. At Augustine's conferences with British bishops (A.D. 603) there were present seven Welsh bishops, according to Bede, including a Bishop of Llandaff; and the British or Welsh Church remained practically apart from the English till after the Norman conquest. During the Roman period there was a see of Caerleon, or Usk, which had authority over all Wales. Later, probably in the sixth century, this see was subdivided into five—one for each of the principalities of Gwynedd (Bangor), Powys (St. Asaph's), Dyfed (St. David's), Cardigan (Llanbadarn), and Gwent (Llandaff). Llanbadarn was absorbed in St. David's, but the other four remain.

Dyfryg, or Dubricius, is the first Bishop of Llandaff of whom we hear, and he probably founded the first church there, as well as a school for priests. It is said that he died in 612, after some years' retirement in the island of Bardsey, whence his relics were removed to Llandaff by Bishop Urban in 1120. Many miracles and wonders are related in connection with Dyfryg and his successor, St. Teilo, also called Eliud. His reputation for sanctity was so great that many churches in his diocese were dedicated to his memory after his death.

Urban (1107—1134) was the first Bishop appointed under Norman influence, instead of by the Welsh princes, and in 1120 he began the construction of a new cathedral, in place of the one he found at Llandaff, which was not more than forty feet long. It was not till the Early English period that the nave reached its present westward extension. The Lady Chapel was added in the

Early Decorated period, while the presbytery was largely rebuilt in the Later Decorated time. Later still the aisle walls were rebuilt. The north-west tower (Perpendicular) was built by Jasper Tudor, Earl of Pembroke, Henry VIII.'s uncle.

About the middle of the sixteenth century decay overtook this cathedral, and in 1575 it was almost a ruin. Gradually the services were discontinued or maimed, the residentiary canons ceased to reside, and their houses served for stables and pigsties. In 1595 the Cathedral was "digged and delved pits and unpaved, being more like a desolate and profane place than a house of prayer and holy exercises." In 1649 the Commonwealth seized the Cathedral revenues, and the chapter library was dispersed and many of the books burnt. Dilapidation and decay continued, and the removal of the see to Cardiff was even proposed; roofs fell in, and gradually the western half of the nave became a ruin. Service, no longer choral, was only held in the Lady Chapel till 1849.

From a print and description of Llandaff Cathedral given by Browne Willis, taken in 1717, the south tower was then in a ruinous state, and part of the parapet and two of the pinnacles of the north tower, which had been thrown down by a storm on the 27th of November, 1503, had not been replaced.

In 1732 a new broom was called in, in the person of Mr. Ward, of Bath, and on his advice and design a kind of Italian church was erected within the old cathedral. A new west front was erected, crossing the old nave at the eastern side of the fourth bay. Beyond this all the beautiful Gothic work was hidden by new walls and plaster, and reduced, as Mr. Freeman says, to the likeness of a conventicle or a third-rate town-hall. Even the windows were despoiled, and made little better than round-headed staircase windows. The altar was placed within a sort of portico at the east end of this structure, with two rows of four columns each. In 1756 the south-west tower had become so dilapidated that the greater part was taken down. The Lady Chapel retained most nearly its old aspect, but it had received a new east window, round-headed and of no merit, in 1740.

When the drawings were made for Winkles' Cathedrals the west front and western part of the nave were a beautiful ruin. The base of the south-west tower was almost concealed by a mass of ivy,

which spread over nearly half the west end. The north-west tower had in the lowest stage an Early English window walled up; a mean modern battlement replaced the original parapet and pinnacles, and unsightly buttresses of several stages supported the outer angles.

The east window of the Lady Chapel was the first modern restoration, the original form being restored by the Rev. H. Douglas (1835-6). In 1843, at a meeting to present a testimonial to Dean Knight Bruce, it was resolved to restore the Cathedral. The work was begun with the Lady Chapel, which was made fit for service; then, under Dean Conybeare, the Italian temple was entirely taken down, and the presbytery, choir, and eastern portion of the nave reopened for service on 16th April, 1857. The repair of the nave followed, and a new south-west tower was begun; and finally, the nave, west front, and towers were reconstructed as at present seen, being completed and reopened in 1869. In 1880 a fine peal of eight bells was placed in the north-west tower by public subscription, as a memorial to Dean Williams (died 1877); the tenor, of twenty-three and a half hundredweight, is the old bell. In 1881 a clock and carillon were added. The cost of the restorations and new buildings has been more than £30,000. The excellent architect has been Mr. John Prichard, of Llandaff.

EXTERIOR.

A striking view of the west front is obtained on approaching the Cathedral by the steep descent from the village-like city. The Cathedral is well open to view on the other sides, and is especially well seen from the south, but from the west only the top of the spire is visible till the brow of the descent is reached. The Cathedral consists of a long unbroken body, including nave, choir, presbytery, and aisles, and an eastern Lady Chapel reaching a smaller height. The west end has two towers terminating the aisles, the south-western topped by a handsome spire. The only appendage of the building is the square chapter-house, projecting from the south aisle of the presbytery. The lack of transepts, central tower, and subsidiary chapels makes this a marked exception to most English cathedrals.

The central part of the west front had remained comparatively uninjured, and required but moderate repair. It is pure and beautiful Early English, although the portal in the lowest stage (flanked by plain walls) is round-headed, but yet of Early English date. It is of peculiar structure, inasmuch as the actual doorway is formed of two narrow, round-headed arches, to which a central vaulting-shaft was never affixed. In the spandril is a sculptured figure, probably representing one of the founders. The second stage has three fine lancet-windows, with a very acute arch between each. The gable has a large central window with its arch nearly round, and on either side are three imperfect round-headed trefoil arches, diminishing to the outer ones. The central window has a trefoil arch, containing a figure of our Lord in majesty. The summit of the gable is occupied by a stone cross.

The north-western tower (of Jasper Tudor) is of Perpendicular style and date, resting on the arches of its Early English predecessor. It is of three stages, massive and plain, with buttresses not rising to the top, an elaborate parapet, and large open-work pinnacles somewhat overhanging at the corners. The large windows in the upper stage are filled with ornamental stonework between the mullions. The parapet and pinnacles had to be renewed in the late restoration; the stair turret in the north angle terminates in a larger pinnacle, or small spire. This enrichment, though too elaborate for the rest of the tower, is in itself of good design.

The south-western tower is new and designed by Mr. Prichard. Although the architect has been criticised for not rebuilding an Early English tower of which scarcely anything remained, and also for building one with a somewhat Continental aspect, it is an eminently successful work, and has elevated Llandaff markedly among our national cathedrals. The lower stage is groined, and is supported by massive buttresses terminating in open canopies opposite the gable windows of the west front. Under these canopies are statues of St. Peter and St. Paul, to whom Bishop Urban appears to have dedicated the Cathedral, and of Bishop Ollivant. Above the aisle roof, where the tower abuts against it, is an arcade of four arches, including seated figures of the Evangelists. The second stage (the ringers' floor) has plain two-light windows, while the belfry stage

LLANDAFF CATHEDRAL: FROM THE SOUTH-WEST.

above has large lancets of two lights, in style corresponding with the lancets of the nave front, flanked by niches under lancet arches, containing figures representing the various nations of the world. Above the arches of the windows project heads of the great mission apostles and preachers. The cornice above is machicolated and the parapet open. The octagonal spire rises effectively from the tower, with which it is well connected by pointed arches and pinnacles. The oolitic stone of which the whole is built has a very pleasing effect.

It is not necessary to dilate much on the remaining features of the exterior. The new octagonal roof of the chapter-house, the base of a flèche, as an external mark of division between the choir and presbytery, buttresses strengthening the aisle walls, the buttresses of the Lady Chapel with their new pinnacles, the new parapets of the aisle wall, and the new Decorated portal in the south aisle of the presbytery, all do something to take away the unbroken and uniform appearance which the exterior formerly had. The chapter-house is much improved in appearance by the rebuilding of the second stage, which formerly had square walls, and the substitution of the octagonal roof. The Norman portals near the west end of both aisles are worthy of remark, being elaborately decorated; they are later than the Norman work of the presbytery. Each aisle has another doorway farther east, of Decorated style.

INTERIOR.

The view presented from the west end now gives a better idea of the original design than was obtainable for centuries previous. The graceful arcades, the east window, the remarkable Norman arch above the altar, and seen through this the stone roof and east window of the Lady Chapel, certainly combine in a dignified and beautiful view. The nave has six bays, the choir proper two, and the presbytery two. Between the former there is no partition, except a low wooden screen, the difference being marked by low walls extending between the choir arches and by slight differences in the piers. Otherwise the nave and choir proper are similar, of Early English style. The capitals of the main arches are beautifully sculptured, but the orders of the arches are plain.

There is no triforium, the clerestory immediately surmounting the string-course and having a passage cut through it. Between the massive piers, with clusters of three shafts on the principal faces, rise triple clustered vaulting-shafts. The clerestory has been rebuilt from the model of the single bay (on the south side) which remained; it has a pair of lancets in each bay. At the west end of the nave the three great lancets with their mouldings occupy the entire width, for the outer narrow arches are not repeated within. A group of shafts from the windows is brought to the ground on either side of the portal, which descends several steps to the floor, thus greatly enhancing the general effect of the west end.

In the choir the stalls occupy two bays, the new organ (by Gray and Davison) being placed in the north-eastern arch, the trumpet pipes projecting very ungracefully forward. The stalls are admirably designed by Mr. Prichard and executed by Llandaff workmen; like the Bishop's throne and the base of the screen, they are inlaid with coloured woods, small figures of the Apostles being inserted between the sub-stalls. The Bishop's throne is placed at the south-east of the choir, and has an enriched canopy, including figures of Latin Doctors and Anglican Reformers. The eastern panel depicts St. Paul Preaching at Athens, the western one Christ's command to Peter, "Feed My sheep." On the front of the desk is a panel representing the Dispersal of the Apostles.

The pulpit is on the north side, and is built of Caen stone, with shafts of coloured marbles. The panels contain striking figures of Moses with the Law, David, John the Baptist, and St. Paul, after Mr. Woolner's designs. The font, designed by Mr. Seddon, was given by Dean Williams; sculptured round the bowl are scenes from the life of Noah.

The aisles, rebuilt in the Decorated period, need only be mentioned for their windows with ogee heads and reticulated tracery. The roofs, as well as those of the nave and choir, are modern open wooden ones, although a flat one was evidently intended by the original builders. Stone arches cross each bay of the aisles, in connection with the external buttresses already mentioned.

The choir is divided from the presbytery by a modern acute

arch. The presbytery itself has many characters due to the Decorated period in which it was rebuilt, but the Norman arch at the east end, the Norman south wall, and parts of Norman windows were retained. The north side is Early Decorated; the

LLANDAFF CATHEDRAL: THE CHOIR.

clerestory and gable were destroyed in the Italian remodelling of Mr. Wood, and are recent reconstructions. The clerestory is a Decorated development of that of the nave. In the eastern gable a Decorated window of three lights is introduced, resting on a small blind arcade, and flanked by a large blind arch on either side.

Above this window is a central circular window, with quatrefoiled tracery. The modern roof is constructed as an enrichment of the plan of the nave and choir roofs. On the south side of the presbytery are some interesting Norman remains of windows and walls joining the Decorated work very peculiarly.

The Norman arch at the east end is shorn of its proper dimensions, for the shafts extend several feet deeper. It has four orders, characteristically ornamented, and the exterior one has a series of little circles, each studded with points and having eight leaves within; this is almost unique. The floor of the presbytery is inlaid with various marbles in diamond. The old reredos, dating from the end of the 14th century, having an arcade of niches, was happily recovered, having been plastered over in the Italian temple. It was, however, so damaged that it was not thought advisable to restore it, and it was removed to the north choir aisle. The new reredos, of Caen stone, with shafts of polished marble, has three arches with foiled heads, with gables rising above; the whole enriched with leafage. The arches have been filled with beautiful pictures by Mr. Dante Gabriel Rossetti; the central one represents the Nativity, that on the north side David as a Shepherd, that on the south side David as a King. The ideas of the side pictures are connected with the central thus: An angel has just entered the stable where Christ is newly born, and leads by the hand a king and a shepherd, who bow themselves before the manger on which the Virgin Mother kneels, holding the infant Saviour.

In the easternmost bay on the south side are four sedilia, under four equal canopied arches. At the ends and in the canopies are excellent figures of angels and Evangelists, and in the spandrils are emblematic buds with leafage. Mr. Prichard's design and the local workmen's execution are alike excellent.

The south aisle of the presbytery has one bay vaulted, leading to the chapter-house. Beyond, the windows are Decorated, but the western one is flat-headed, with five lights. The tracery is nearly all modern, as in the north aisle.

The presbytery aisles open into the Lady Chapel by Early English arches. The Lady Chapel is of five bays, and has a stone vaulted roof, carried on Purbeck shafts, and with carved bosses at the intersections. - The structure is very early Decorated. The east window, designed by Mr. Prichard, is of five lights.- The wall at the back of the altar has a deep recess in the centre, and an arcade of six arches on either side in two tiers. It remains to note that the chapter-house, of Early English date, is peculiar in being square, with a central round pillar; its new roof, enclosing an upper room where the archives of the Cathedral are preserved, has already been referred to.

All the stained glass is modern, but not designed quite consistently or harmoniously. Messrs. Morris and Marshall have inserted some windows of excellent character, the figures being set in exquisite grisaille. Note those in the south aisle of the presbytery. Others of the stained windows are by Lavers and Barraud, Clayton and Bell, O'Connor, Willement, and Morris.

The monuments include, in the north nave aisle, the altar-tomb of Sir W. Mathew and his wife (died 1528 and 1530), the effigy of an unknown bishop, and a marble slab supported by two arches, having the Judgment of Solomon and Moses with the Law sculptured at the back (by Armstead), erected to Henry Thomas, Esq. (died 1807). In the south nave aisle is the recumbent figure of an unknown bishop.

In the north aisle of the presbytery and choir we find, in order from the west, the effigy attributed to Dyfryg or Dubricius, placed now in the recess where is Bishop Bromfield's tomb (died 1393), a woman's figure in a winding-sheet (fifteenth century), and the altar-tomb of Sir D. Mathew (died 1461). In the south aisle of the presbytery is the effigy perhaps of a Lady Audley.

On the south side of the presbytery is the tomb ascribed to St. Teilo. It is in an original recess, but has received modern ornamentation, of Early Decorated style, the diaper of the canopy being the gift of a son of Edward Clarke, stonemason, who executed the sedilia, reredos, etc. There is also an ancient effigy of a bishop which had been immured here, and may have been intended for St. Teilo.

On the north side of the presbytery is the tomb of Bishop Marshall (died 1496), erected by himself in his lifetime; his figure is fully vested, and carries a mitre and staff.

In the Lady Chapel is the altar-tomb of Christopher Mathew,

in armour (died 1500), and his wife. The effigy of Bishop William de Bruce (died 1287), the reputed builder of this chapel, is also here, and by its side is a brass showing the burial-place of Bishop Copleston (died 1849.)

The principal dimensions of the Cathedral are as follows: Length, including Lady Chapel, 245 feet; width, 70 feet; height, 65 feet; north-west tower, 105 feet high; south-west tower, 195 feet 7 inches; Lady Chapel, 54 feet long by 25 feet wide and 30 feet high.

The diocese of Llandaff extends over all Monmouthshire, and Glamorganshire east of the river Neath. The chapter consists of a dean, two archdeacons (of Monmouth and Llandaff), a chancellor, precentor and four canons, and five prebendaries; there are also two minor canons, an organist, verger, and bell-ringer, ten lay clerks, and twenty choir-boys.

The Bishops of the diocese include Urban (1107-1134), who removed the relics of Dyfryg from Bardsey to Llandaff, and began to rebuild the Cathedral. Another Urban, or Nicholas ap Gwrgant (1181-1183), however, seems to have had a great share in this building. Henry, Prior of Abergavenny (1193-1218), first organised the chapter. William of Radnor (1257-1266) is an example of a bishop elected in defiance of the Crown; he was ultimately consecrated at St. Paul's by Archbishop Boniface. William de Bruce, or Bruys (1266-1287), was probably the builder of the Lady Chapel. George de Athequa, a Spanish Dominican, chaplain to Queen Catharine of Aragon, held the see from 1517 to 1537. Holgate, afterwards Archbishop of York, was Bishop of Llandaff from 1537 to 1545. Anthony Kitchin (1545-1563) was the only bishop who took the oath concerning the Royal supremacy on Queen Elizabeth's accession, and consequently retained his see; he is responsible for a great impoverishment of the see. Bishop Blethin (1575-90) is noted for his having proposed to diminish the number of persons on the foundation, a process which culminated early this century in its reduction to one vicar-choral. William Morgan (1595-1601) was the first translator of the Bible into Welsh; he was in 1601 translated to St. Asaph.

Francis Godwin (1601-1617), translated in 1617 to Hereford, is the well-known author of the "Lives of the English Bishops."

In the bishopric of William Beaw (1679-1706) the choir service was given up. In his time the gross value of the bishopric was £230 per annum, which, after deductions, only sufficed to provide him with firing and with vinegar, pepper, and salt. Shute Barrington began here (1769-1782) his long episcopate of fifty-six years, continued at Salisbury, completed at Durham.

Richard Watson (1782-1816) was at one time Professor of Chemistry, and afterwards Regius Professor of Divinity, in Cambridge University. During his episcopate he lived chiefly at Windermere, and became known as an agriculturist and planter, as well as by controversial works, including an "Apology for Christianity," an answer to Gibbon; and an "Apology for the Bible," which is credited with having produced a great effect on Thomas Paine. Edward Copleston, a notable Fellow of Oriel College, was Bishop from 1828 to 1849. Alfred Ollivant succeeded him, and did very much for the Cathedral and diocese. The present Bishop, Dr. Richard Lewis, was appointed in 1883.

BIVOUAC CAMP KETTLE.

BEARWARD IN THE DISTANCE

BANGOR CATHEDRAL.

TANNER says, "a bishopric was probably erected here before the middle of the sixth century, by Malgwyn, or Malgo Conan, prince of North Wales; and Deiniel or Daniel, son of Dinothus, abbot of Bangor, in Flintshire, who had before founded a college or monastery here, was made the first bishop;" and then adds, "we have very little or no account of the monastery afterwards, and but a slender one of the bishops, till A.D. 1039, after which time there seems to have been a regular succession of prelates in this see, though by reason of the wars they had not all of them a quiet enjoyment." Willis says that Daniel was consecrated by Dubritius, archbishop of Caerleon, about the year 550, four years after which he died, and was buried in the Isle of Bardsey, where holy men in those days were frequently interred. But the learned Usher and other writers place Daniel's coming to Bangor in the year 516, and his death in 554 (December 10), and say that the same year in which he died Prince Maglocunus erected Bangor into a city, which took its name from its fine situation, or beauty of its choir, as some of them surmise; in which notion they have been followed by other writers, who pretend to derive Bangor from *Bonus Chorus*. Godwin allows of no bishop of Bangor before the Norman conquest; his words are, "What time a cathedral church was first erected at Bangor, or who was the first bishop there, I think it hard to define; for my part, I scarcely find any mention of any bishop of Bangor before the Conquest, except happily of one Marclois, that died, as the chronicle of Wales reporteth, in the year 943; but I assure myself upon many presumptions, he is mistaken for Marchlrith, bishop of Llandaff. The first bishop of Bangor was Herveus, who being violently thrust out of his bishoprick, accepted gladly of Ely, in the year 1109, the year after his consecration, becoming a a Bangor, so there also, the first bishop."

Le Neve follows Godwin, and has placed the coming of Hervey to Bangor in the year 1107; but Willis asserts, that he was consecrated bishop of this see in or before the year 1093, by Thomas, archbishop of York, in the vacancy of the see of Canterbury, which continued from 1089 till 1093, as particular notice is taken, by the author of *Decem Scriptores*, of his confirmation in this see during that time. It is recorded in the Monasticon, that he was witness to the foundation charter of Chester Abbey, in 1095, and was present at the consecration of that of Gloucester in 1100. Moreover, that in 1102 he sat at the synod held at London, and therefore he must have continued bishop of this see at least fifteen or sixteen years, and, as Willis observes, "might have done much longer, but that being very rigid in his discipline, and ill-treating the Welsh, they thereby grew refractory, and having murdered his brother, threatened to treat him in like manner, whereupon he fled to King Henry I. for protection, who assigned him, in 1107, the abbey of Ely for his support, which being converted into a bishopric in 1109, he quitted Bangor, and accepted the see of Ely, which he held till his death, which happened in 1131. Wharton supposes him to have been by birth a Scotchman, and that he was also bishop of Lisieux, in Normandy. Dempster mentions him to have been Henry I.'s confessor.

There is no account of the Cathedral in these early times, and few vestiges even of late Norman work remain in the present edifice. Towards the middle of the thirteenth century the Cathedral was burnt down, and the whole diocese laid waste by the English. It was rebuilt about the close of that century by Bishop Anian and his successors, but was most certainly destroyed again in the year 1404, by Owen Glendower, who set fire to it, and burned it down to the ground, because the bishop, Richard Younge, was in the interest of the king, Henry IV. From this time till 1496 the Cathedral lay in ruins, when it was begun to be rebuilt by Henry Dean, elected bishop of this see that same year. He built only the present choir, for, being translated to Salisbury, and afterwards to Canterbury, he had no time to do more here, but left his crozier and mitre, both of great value, to his successor at Bangor, on condition that he would go on with the good work. His successor was Thomas Pigot, who lived entirely at Chertsey, being at the same time abbot of the monastery there, and held this see but little more than three years; it is not recorded that he did anything towards the completion of the Cathedral. His successor was John Penny, who, being soon after translated to Carlisle, did nothing to advance the rebuilding of this church, the completion of which, as it now appears, is to be attributed entirely to the munificence and zeal of Thomas Skeffington, consecrated bishop of this see June 17, 1509. He was also abbot of Beaulieu, in Hampshire, and almost constantly resided there instead of at Bangor. "However," says Willis, "being a man of a generous spirit, and to atone for his neglect at Bangor, he became a most magnificent benefactor thereto, by building the steeple and entire body of the church, from the choir downwards to the west end." He also gave four bells, to be placed in the tower he had built. His body was buried at Beaulieu, and his heart in this Cathedral, by his own particular desire. The bells were afterwards sold by Bishop Bulkely, who was consecrated in 1541, and who has been stigmatized as the waster and dilapidator of this church's goods, though Willis thinks without sufficient ground for it. However this may be, Henry Rowlands, D.D., consecrated in 1598, gave four new bells, and put a new roof upon the body of the Cathedral. The Cathedral suffered, like all others, in the great rebellion; and was restored, together with the old form of worship by Bishop Roberts, who suffered much for his loyalty, and was deprived for a time not only of this see, but of all he had besides. In his will he left £100 towards beautifying the choir, and died in 1665. Bishop Morgan, also, was a great benefactor to the fabric of the Cathedral between the years 1666 and 1673, the date of his translation to this see, and his death. But his successor, Humphrey Lloyd, D.D., was a greater benefactor still, by procuring land for the continual support of the fabric, endowment of the choir, and augmentation of the bishoprick. He also recast the four bells given by Bishop Rowlands, and added a fifth, much larger than any of the former, and at his own expense.

EXTERIOR.

This Cathedral is a larger edifice than that of St. Asaph, and is more imposing and cathedral-like. Still it is outwardly one of the plainest fabrics enjoying that title which the Established Church possesses. It is particularly wanting in elevation, and though in the form of a cross, aspires to little more in appearance than a good-sized and ordinary parish church. The many calamities already detailed and the extreme poverty of the see, in former times, are together sufficient to account for its limited dimensions and the plainness of its architecture. At the west end stands the plain square tower of Bishop Skeffington; it consists of three stories; the lowest contains a pointed door under a square head, the next a pointed window of three lights, with perpendicular tracery, and the highest another pointed window of the same number of lights, without tracery; above this is an embattled parapet, and at each of the four corners a crocketted pinnacle is placed. The tower is built out from the gable end of the nave, and at the angles of it are plain buttresses of several stages, which terminate a little above the second storey of it. Just above the door already described is the following inscription in ancient characters:—"Thomas Skevyngton, Episcopus Bangorie, hoc Campanile et Ecclesiam fieri fecit Ao. Partus Virginei mcccccxxxii." The west ends of the aisles on both sides are quite plain.

The south side of the Cathedral is regular and uniform, and though simple and plain, wants nothing but elevation to give it some importance. The aisle has six rather acutely pointed windows of three lights, and good proportion, with plain buttresses between, of two stages, which terminate a little below the parapet, which is quite plain. The windows have tracery, which does not partake of the character of the age and style when the Cathedral was rebuilt, and must be either imitations of the Decorated windows or the windows themselves, repaired after the second destruction of the Cathedral by fire. At the second compartment from the west end is an obtusely pointed door, evidently of the time of Bishop Skeffington, and over it a small niche. The clerestory windows are also of the same form and character with the south door. The south wing of the transept has an embattled parapet; the east and west walls of it are quite plain, but the south front had a large Perpendicular window of five lights, now replaced by two two-light windows of Early Decorated character. At the angles are large and remark-

able buttresses. They appear to be as old as the time of Edward I.

The choir has no aisles on either side of it. The south side has two small Perpendicular windows towards the upper part and western extremity, and a short, plain buttress underneath, and a large window of the same form, with five lights and Perpendicular tracery, nearer to the east end. The choir has an embattled parapet all round. The east end itself has a low gable point, and beneath it a large window, more sharply pointed, of five lights, Perpendicular tracery, and good proportion; it is divided by a transom, beneath which are small pointed arches, feathered. This end is flanked with a plain, heavy buttress, of two stages, at each angle. In a line with the east end of the choir, and of nearly equal height with it, is the east end of a building, the upper storey of which has been added in modern times, the lower being of the age of the rest of the Cathedral, or rather of the choir: it has a sloping embattled parapet, and a window of monstrous design, composed of five lancet-looking lights, under a wide and much depressed ogee arch: beneath this is an obtusely pointed window, of only three lights. At the north-east angle is a double buttress. The north side of this building has three pointed windows in the upper part, and a door beneath, by which the chapter house is entered; a few steps lead up to the door, and there is a low buttress on each side of it.

The east face of the north wing of the transept is concealed by the building last described. At the north-east angle of it is a round turret engaged, which takes an octagonal form when it reaches the bottom of the embattled parapet, and rises a little above it. This turret may probably be another small portion of the former Cathedral. The north front of this wing of the transept is flanked with double buttresses at the corners, and contains a large obtusely pointed window, of five lights, and perpendicular tracery. The north side of the nave, with its aisle, is so nearly like the south side, that the description of the latter, already given, will serve for the former also.

The reconstruction of the north-eastern range of buildings, including the chapter-house, is described at page 209. It has been thought best to leave this description of their former state unaltered.

INTERIOR.

Entering the nave by the south door, the scene which presents itself to the spectator is now much more pleasing than it had been before the recent restoration. Six Perpendicular arches on each side, with a few simple mouldings, resting on columns as simple, of octangular form, with plain capitals and bases, divide the aisles from the nave. Here is no triforium, but all above the arches is plain wall, with short windows of triple lights in the clerestory, one over each arch. There is an octagonal font, of Perpendicular character. In the time of Bishop Cleaver, at the beginning of this century, the flat roof of the nave and its aisles was ascertained to be in a state of dangerous decay, and was then restored in plain deal. The carved work and escutcheons of which Browne Willis speaks no longer exist. The roof has recently been renewed in oak. The transept within is quite plain, and was formerly shut out from view by the heavy organ-loft, stretching across at the fourth bay. The four pointed arches at the crossing seem to have been designed to support a central tower, as usual, which was never erected, but this lack has now been partially remedied. The ceiling of the choir was flat till the late restoration, which restored it to its original high pitch. The fittings, stalls, decoration, and pavement are all new. The building on the north side of the choir had till the late restoration no communication with it internally. It consists of two stories, and is divided into several apartments, which are put to the following uses: chapter-house, library, vestry, and registrar's office.

The dimensions of this Cathedral are as follows: length from east to west, including the tower, 233 feet; length of nave, excluding tower, 114 feet; breadth of nave and side aisles, 60 feet; length of transept, from north to south, 96 feet; height of the nave to the highest point of the roof, only 34 feet; of the tower only, 60 feet; the square of the tower, 24 feet. It should be mentioned that the nave of this Cathedral is made use of as the parish church of Bangor, in which Divine service is performed in the Welsh language.

The bishop is a member of the chapter, as being archdeacon both of Bangor and Anglesea; the other members are, the dean, two archdeacons, of Merioneth and Bangor, who, with two others, are canons residentiary, the treasurer, precentor, chancellor, and six canons non-residentiary. There are also belonging to this Cathedral, which is dedicated to St. Daniel, two minor canons, five lay vicars, twelve choristers, and organist, with other inferior officers.

The diocese of Bangor comprises the whole of Anglesea, the whole of Caernarvonshire, except three parishes, more than half the county of Merioneth, and seven parishes in the county of Montgomery.

The annual value of this bishopric, in the king's books, is £151 3s. 0d. in the whole, and £131 16s. 4d. clear. It was afterwards returned to the Commissioners as being worth £6,580 in the whole, and £4,464 clear, per annum.

Among the more eminent prelates of modern times, the names of Hoadley and Sherlock are most conspicuous. The former was consecrated March 18, 1715, and while bishop of this see preached a sermon in London on this text, "My kingdom is not of this world," which caused the famous Bangorian Controversy, and employed the press for many years. Bishop Hoadley was a learned man and great writer, though his periods are too long. He was amiable, witty, easy, and good-tempered, happy everywhere, but peculiarly so in his own family, where he took every opportunity of instructing by his influence and example. He was successively translated to Hereford, Salisbury, and Winchester, of which last see he continued bishop for nearly twenty-seven years, and died April 17, 1761, at the age of eighty-five years.

The latter, Thomas Sherlock, D.D., was eldest son of William Sherlock, D.D., dean of St. Paul's, and born in 1678. He was master of the Temple, in London, and of Catherine Hall, in Cambridge; dean of Chichester in 1716, and soon after his promotion appeared as an author for the first time in the Bangorian Controversy. He was consecrated bishop of Bangor in 1728, translated to Salisbury in 1734, in both which stations his abilities were so conspicuous that on the death of Archbishop Potter in 1747, the see of Canterbury was offered him, but he declined to accept it on account of the state of his health. The following year, however, he was so much recovered that he accepted a translation to the see of London, which he held thirteen years, and died July 18, 1761, in the 84th year of his age. Dr. Nichols, who succeeded him in the mastership of the Temple, gives the following character of him:—"His learning was very extensive; he had a great and an understanding mind; a quick, comprehensive, and a solid judgment; these advantages he improved by much industry and application; in piety, constant and exemplary; in preaching the duties and maintaining the doctrines of Christianity, warm and zealous; and in his charities diffusive and munificent." In Bishop Sherlock's sermons are some passages of uncommon animation. Dr. Blair, in his "Lectures on Rhetoric," quotes one in particular which occurs in a sermon on John xx. 30, 31, towards the conclusion, wherein a contrast is drawn between the Mahometan and Christian religions, and says "this is more than elegant, it is truly sublime." It is said that the Lord Chancellor Hardwicke was so deeply impressed with admiration of this passage that he never forgot it, and often repeated it *verbatim*.

Zachary Pearce, bishop of Bangor from 1747 to 1756, when he was translated to Rochester, is the most notable bishop since Sherlock. His classical works, as well as his commentaries and sermons, suffice to perpetuate his memory.

BANGOR CATHEDRAL: THE NAVE AND CHOIR.

MODERN HISTORY OF BANGOR CATHEDRAL.

BANGOR Cathedral, though but a moderate building after all, has undergone striking changes in the present century. During Bishop Cleaver's reign (1800-6) the roof of the nave being found decayed, it was repaired in plain deal, and all the carved work destroyed. In the course of repairs undertaken in 1824-7 the old stalls were removed, and according to Sir G. G. Scott, "the most execrable gimcrack substituted that ever disgraced a church." A eavy organ screen and loft were built across the fourth bay of the nave from the west, and the choir so separated was reserved for services in English, while the Welsh services were held in the remaining portion of the nave. At this time the arches of the crossing were replaced by Perpendicular ones reaching only to the clerestory and supported on corbels.

In 1866 Sir G. G. Scott found the Cathedral in a very degenerate state; but having examined the remains which indicated what Bishop Anian's and the Early Decorated Cathedral had been, he recommended its partial restoration to that state and the building of a central Decorated tower and spire at the crossing. The restoration of the north and south transepts and the raising of the central tower to the roof ridge were then undertaken. Consequently, more of the Perpendicular additions and alterations in the transepts have disappeared. The walls and their fittings were carefully examined for remnants of the ancient work, and they furnished a large quantity of early stonework, which has been replaced where it was conjectured to have been before.

During the restoration much light was thrown on the structure of the Norman Cathedral. A small Norman window was distinguishable walled-up in the south wall of the choir, and farther east was a narrow Norman buttress, which continued into the wall, so as to show that it was the eastern limit of the Norman church. From this was traceable the base of a semicircular Norman apse. Moreover, the Norman base of the south transept was made out, twelve feet shorter than the present one; there were also traces of the bases of the four Norman piers at the crossing.

In the large south window of the south transept two windows, each of two lights, with circles in their heads, have replaced the five-light Perpendicular window, and surmounting them is a large circular window with nine cusps, rescued from the ruins. The north aspect of the north transept has recovered its one window of four lights, and the circles above each pair of lights and at the crown of the whole window have each nine cusps. Both these windows are in beautiful Early Decorated style, and contain a considerable proportion of the original mouldings.

On careful examination it was evident that the piers at the crossing had been designed to support a tower, and it was resolved to erect one. The mouldings of the arches destroyed in 1824 were used as far as they were available, and the arches restored with some additional strength. The north and south piers on the eastern side had clustered shafts, and these have been rebuilt; those on the western side had semicircular shafts, which have been also rebuilt. Above these tower arches has been built a blank arcade of acute arches with Decorated capitals. It was ceiled over with woodwork, and covered with a temporary roof. Some cracks in the piers are due to the expansion of the cement in setting. The tower remains unfinished owing to want of funds.

The choir was restored without disturbing the main lines of its existing condition, showing, as it does, " evidences of the three-fold history of the church—its reconstruction after early Norman devastation early in the twelfth century, its enlargement in the thirteenth century, and its restoration in the time of Henry VII." The arrangement of the stalls, just east of the crossing, by Bishop Deane, is retained, and the organ-loft and screen have been removed entirely. The organ is now placed in a suitable chamber, built on the north side of the choir. The Perpendicular windows remain untransformed. The roof is raised, however, to a high pitch, and is of open woodwork, richly decorated with gold and colour. The pavement is new, but designed in accordance with ancient tiles found *in situ* in the choir. Further, the wall at the east end has been decorated and painted, Christ in Glory occupying the centre above, and saints being represented below.

The range of buildings north of the choir has been reconstructed, so as to bring them back to the Early Decorated style. From the organ chamber, entered through the eastern arch of the transept, the vestibule of the muniment-room is entered, and from this the chapter-room above is approached by steps. In it is now placed the chapter library, including some rare Aldine and Stephen's editions and the notable Pontifical of Bishop Anian, 1291, or so-called " Bangor Use," or service-book.

On the exterior of the south transept the remarkable but-

BANGOR CATHEDRAL: SOUTH VIEW (1886).

tresses, which were in ruins, have been restored. The principal ones are gabled, and have mouldings and shafts at the corners. A small one reaches to the middle of the base of the large south window. Some fragments of other buttresses have been built up at the east end of the choir.

The monuments in Bangor Cathedral are few. In the south transept is an inscription on the wall, recording that a body buried in the wall, in a stone coffin, is supposed to be that of Owen Gwynedh, sovereign Prince of Wales (died 1169). His brother, Cadwallader, and their father, Gryffydh ap Cynan, last King of Wales, were also buried in this Cathedral. Gryffydh is said to have been buried near the great altar. In the north transept is a tablet to the Rev. Gronovil Owen, a notable Welsh bard, who died in 1831.

The choir contains two tombs of the Decorated period (fourteenth century); they are close to the tower piers, and pass through the wall. One of them is probably that of the second Bishop Anian (died 1328). The tomb on the right side is that of Tudor ap Grono ap Tudor (died 1365).

The restoration of the nave was not completed till 1880. Both nave and aisles were repaved, the plaster and whitewash were removed from the walls, and the stonework was repaired. The roof, which was too substantial to be removed, and too ugly to be allowed to remain visible, was skilfully covered with a richly panelled oak ceiling; but no new works of importance were undertaken.

Externally a battlement has recently been placed upon the nave, the tombstones in the churchyard have been laid down, and the railings have been lowered and put back.

During the restoration in 1879 there was discovered under the floor of the chapter-house an effigy, in low relief, of a lady in a square head-dress and peculiar gown, with a long string of beads in one hand, and both palms outwards and raised in prayer. This rare effigy, apparently dating from the fourteenth or fifteenth century, is now placed in the west wall of the north aisle.

Recently Mrs. Symes, of Gorphyswfa, has presented Bangor Cathedral with a new reredos, as a memorial of her brother, Lieutenant-Colonel Holt. The same lady has also given a stained glass window as a memorial to the late Dean Edwards. The daughters of the late dean have presented a new baptismal font, and Lady Penrhyn has given a new altar frontal.

ST. ASAPH CATHEDRAL.

ALL authors agree that Kentigern, bishop of Glasgow, was the founder of this see, upon occasion of his being driven out of Scotland, about the middle of the sixth century, and became the first bishop of it. After remaining here a few years he returned to Scotland, and made Asaph, one of his disciples, his successor in this see, who was an eminently holy and good man; and from him both the church and place have ever since been called St. Asaph. He was remarkable, says Collier, for frequently repeating this sentence,—"they who hinder the progress of God's Word, envy the happiness of mankind." He died A.D. 596, and from that time till the year 1143 there is no account of this church, nor of any of the bishops; and though, says Tanner, "there hath been a constant and regular succession from the first, yet, by reason of the wars between the English and the Welch, and Owen Glendower's rebellion, the Cathedral Church, with the bishop's and canons' houses, were more than once destroyed, and remained for many years in ruins. Upon one of these devastations, or the fear of it, Bishop Anian the Second endeavoured, A.D. 1278, to remove the see to Ruddlan, two miles northward; and King Edward I. granted his licence for it, A.D. 1284, and promised both ground for the church, &c., and one thousand marks towards the building, but this did not take effect.

Kentigern is said to have fled to St. David first of all, at Menevia, and after staying some time with him, Cathwallian, Prince of Wales, assigned him a place for a monastery near the river Elwy, where he gathered together 965 brethren, who lived together in monastic discipline; of this number, 300, who were illiterate, he appointed to till the ground, and look after the cattle belonging to the society; 300 more he employed in preparing food and other necessaries; and to the remaining 365, who were learned, he committed the performance of divine service, and divided them in such sort as that when one set had done another immediately began, so that service was continually going on without a moment's intermission. The first foundation of this church is said to have been of timber, and afterwards of stone, when the settling of it was confirmed by Malgo or Maglocunus, a British king of these parts, who much opposed it at first, but became afterwards so well appeased as not only to allow it to be an episcopal see, but to bestow upon it lands, immunities, and privileges. Gilbert is the first name preserved in the catalogue of the bishops of this see after that of St. Asaph; he was consecrated by Theobald, archbishop of Canterbury, in 1143, and was present at the consecration of St. Augustin's Abbey Church, at Bristol, on Easter-day, A.D. 1148, and died 1151. There is no account existing of the Cathedral Church in his time; it was burnt down, together with the houses of the dean and canons, in 1282, in the wars between England and Wales, when Anian II. was bishop of this see, who was persuaded by the archbishop of Canterbury to rebuild it on the same spot, rather than remove the see to Ruddlan. The greater part of the present fabric is the work of this bishop, the walls of which, says Willis, have stood ever since the year 1284, but the roof or upper part was again burnt down about the year 1404, by Owen Glendower, and not rebuilt till the year 1490, having remained above eighty years in ruins, with only the principal walls standing, till Bishop Redman began to repair and rebuild some parts, for he raised the walls to the present height, and put on a new roof; he also made the east window and stalls of the choir, and erected a throne, since destroyed by Bishop John Owen, who is said to have made in the Cathedral a neat wainscot pulpit in 1631, and at the same time to have fixed seats and forms for the accommodation of persons coming to hear divine service, and to have rebuilt or beautified his episcopal throne, and to have given a large new organ. He also repaired the steeple and belfry. The Cathedral suffered very much after this in the great rebellion, when one Milles, who had the post-office, possessed himself of the bishop's

palace, and sold, says Willis, wine and other liquors there, and kept his horses and oxen in the body of the church, tied up and fed his calves in the bishop's throne and other parts of the choir, removed the font into his yard, set it in the ground, and made use of it for a hog trough. After the restoration of the church and monarchy the Cathedral was repaired by George Griffith, D.D., who was consecrated in 1660 and died in 1666. Isaac Barrow, D.D., elected in 1669, repaired several parts of the Cathedral, especially the north and south aisles, and put new leads upon them; he also wainscoted the east parts of the choir. William Fleetwood, D.D., elected in 1708, was also a benefactor to this Cathedral by paving great part of it, at his own expense, with broad stone, and adorning and painting the choir. John Wynne, D.D., principal of Jesus College, Oxford, elected in 1714, was also a great benefactor to this Cathedral in repairing the mischief done to it by a violent storm which happened on the 2nd of February, 1714-15, when the top of the tower was blown down and fell into the choir, by which great damage was done to the roof, organ, and seats The choir was, about 1780, spoiled by a plaster ceiling and modern tracery. Bishop Cleaver (1806-15) lowered the nave roof so as to conceal the clerestory. The recent restorations are referred to later.

The situation of this Cathedral is very pleasing; it stands on a rising ground within a large church yard, between the rivers Elwy to the west and Clwyd to the east, at the lower end of the Vale of Clwyd, not far from the sea coast, and in the county of Flint.

EXTERIOR.

A very few words will be sufficient to describe, both externally and internally, this very small and plain Cathedral. It is more uniformly built than most other Cathedrals are; is in the form of a cross; but the nave only has side aisles, and there are no chapels. The west front is simple and unpretending. The west wall of the nave has a gable, and in it is a pointed door rather deeply recessed, which leads into the nave, and over it is a large, well proportioned, and pointed window of late decorated architecture. It is flanked with a plain square buttress on each side, upon which panelled and crocketed pinnacles are set. The west walls of the nave aisles have sloping tops, with a small pointed window of two lights in each, and flanked externally with double buttresses, plain, short, and without pinnacles. Throughout the whole west front there is no parapet, but only a plain coping. Of late a plain cross has been set upon the gable point with good effect. The south side of the nave and its aisle present little else but plain walls with small windows, similar to those already described. The aisle has a plain parapet, the clerestory an embattled one, the windows of which, five in number, are Tudor-arched. The west wall of the south wing of the transept is entirely plain; its south face has a well proportioned window pointed and of late decorated character; it is flanked with double buttresses without pinnacles, the wall about the window is plain, the gable has no parapet, but on the gable point is a small plain cross; the east wall of this wing has two good pointed windows and a plain buttress between them. In the south wall of the choir are two windows of like kind, pointed and late decorated, but not so large nor so well proportioned. Between these windows are two buttresses which terminate in small gables under the cornice, and are panelled. There is no clerestory or parapet. The east end of the choir has a large window, an imitation of one at Tintern Abbey; it is flanked with double buttresses of several stages, and terminated with panelled and crocketed pinnacles. On the gable point is a cross. The north side of the choir is in all respects like the south, except that it has an embattled parapet resting on a trefoiled cornice. The east wall of the north wing of the transept has one good pointed window of the decorated style, one plain buttress, and no parapet. The north face of it has one large window in the same style, a plain gable and coping, no cross on the point, and flanked with plain double buttresses of two stages. The west face is a plain wall with a plain parapet. The north side of the nave and its aisle differs somewhat from the south side; the aisle has small buttresses between the windows, the clerestory is embattled and has new windows in it. The central tower is broad, square, and of no great elevation. There is a pointed and late decorated window in each face of it, and it is crowned with an embattled parapet. Up the north-east angle of it runs a square turret, engaged with long loops to light the staircase constructed within it. The turret rises a little above the tower, and is finished with an embattled parapet.

INTERIOR.

Entering by the west door, the nave and its aisles are plain almost to meanness. The arches are pointed, and the columns without capitals, only a continuation of the arch mouldings; here is no triforium, and the clerestory is very plain, the windows square-headed. The original style of oak vaulting has recently been restored in the nave. The pavement is good, and with the great west window helps to take off a little from the plain appearance of this portion of the Cathedral.

The tower rests upon four pointed arches, and instead of the plaster ceiling oak vaulting has been introduced. The transept has been cut up and divided into several small apartments. The south end is enclosed for a chapter-house, the north has two small vestries and a larger room. The choir has been nearly rebuilt. The vaulting now reveals the original carved and cradled timber roof. Portions of the canopies of the stalls are exceedingly rich tabernacle work, erected by Bishop Redman; these have escaped the general destruction of the original choir. To the east of the stalls on the south side is the bishop's throne; on the north, opposite the throne is the pulpit; both these are modern productions, and are made to correspond a little with the stalls. In front of the stalls on both sides are open seats, which are continued across the transept under the tower. The east window is filled with modern stained glass.

There is no crypt, no Lady Chapel, no cloister, no chapter-house, and there are few monuments deserving of any particular notice or description.

The dimensions of this Cathedral are as follows: Length, from east to west, 179 feet; of the transept, from north to south, 108 feet; breadth of the nave and aisles, 68 feet; of the choir, 32 feet; height of nave from the pavement to the highest point of the timber roof, 60 feet; height of the central tower, 93 feet.

Besides the bishop, the establishment of this Cathedral, which is dedicated to St. Asaph, consists of a dean, nine prebendaries, four canons, four vicars choral, four singing men, four choristers, and an organist. The chapter at present consists of a dean and four canons. There are two archdeacons, of St. Asaph and Montgomery.

The old diocese comprises the whole of Flintshire; all Denbighshire; nearly half the county of Merioneth; thirty-seven parishes in Montgomeryshire; several parishes in Shropshire and Caernarvonshire.

The annual value of this bishopric in the king's books is £187 11s. 8d.; and it was afterwards returned to the commissioners to be worth £7408 per annum in the gross, and £6301 in the clear. It is now of the value of £4200 a year.

Small and inconsiderable as this Cathedral and its establishment may be, it is far otherwise with the bishops who have presided over this diocese. The see of St. Asaph can boast of some of the most eminent prelates that the English church ever produced. Bishops Anian II. and Redman, the rebuilders of the Cathedral, have been already mentioned.

Reginald Peacock, born in Wales, once a scholar of Oriel College, Oxford, was consecrated bishop of this see in 1444, and was translated to Chichester in 1449, but was deprived of that see in 1457 for some opinions which were in those times condemned as heretical. He was afterwards ordered by Thomas Bouchier, archbishop of Canterbury, into close confinement at Thorney Abbey, in Cambridgeshire, where he died about a year afterwards.

John Owen, D.D., fellow of Jesus College, Cambridge, although an Englishman, made himself perfect master of Welsh, preached in that language, and ordered sermons to be preached in it, all over his diocese, to which he proved himself to be indeed a spiritual father. He was consecrated in 1629, was an extraordinary sufferer in the great rebellion, and died in 1651.

Isaac Barrow, D.D., after having suffered much in the great rebellion, was, in 1662, nominated bishop of Sodor and Man, where the good that he did is felt to this day. He was translated to St. Asaph, in 1669, where he devoted all his substance to works of charity, till his death, which happened at Shrewsbury, to the grief of all good men, June 24th, 1630, and was buried outside the Cathedral, near the west door.

William Beveridge, D.D., a very eminent and learned divine, was consecrated bishop of this see, July 16, 1704—being then sixty-seven years of age,—and held it till his death, which happened March 5, 1707-8, at his lodgings in the cloisters at Westminster, in the seventy-first year of his age, and was buried in St. Paul's Cathedral. He left the greatest part of his estate to the Societies for Propagating the Gospel in Foreign Parts, and Promoting Christian Knowledge. Bishop Beveridge was a man of extensive and almost universal learning, particularly ready in the Scriptures, which he had so thoroughly studied that he was able to produce suitable passages on all occasions, and happy in explaining them to others. He was also a person of the strictest integrity, of true and sincere piety, exemplary charity, great zeal for religion, and so highly esteemed on all these accounts, that when he was dying, one of his own order said of him: "There goes one of the greatest, and of the best men, that ever England bred."

Thomas Tanner, D.D., an excellent antiquary and prelate, whose virtues and learning are acknowledged by all his contemporaries, was consecrated January 23, 1732. He is the author of a work called Notitia Monastica, full of very valuable information, and now also very scarce. He died at Christ Church, Oxford, December 14, 1735, aged sixty-one, and was buried in the nave of that Cathedral, of which he was also a canon, without any funeral pomp, according to his own direction.

Samuel Horsley, LL.D., was consecrated bishop of St. David's in 1788, and translated to the see of Rochester in 1793, when he also held the deanery of Westminster in commendam, but resigned it on his translation to this see in 1802. He died October 4, 1806, in his seventy-third year, and was buried in the parish church of St. Mary, Newington. The inscription on his monument was written by himself. He was of Trinity Hall, Cambridge, where he applied himself much to the study of mathematics, and stored his mind with the writings of the ancient and modern divines and logicians. He published a complete edition of Sir Isaac Newton's works; and was a most successful controversialist against Priestly. Throughout life he was a most indefatigable student, and one of the most powerful champions of the Christian faith which the church has seen in modern times. That he was an original thinker, strong minded, warm, and uncompromising, his writings, especially his sermons and charges, are a sufficient proof. His style is nervous and authoritative. He had a roughness of temper, but not unqualified with much kindness of heart, benevolence, and charity. As a speaker, he was deservedly considered in the first class; and his opposers found it easier to find fault with his manner than his matter: but he would not speak unless he had something original to produce, and was on that account listened to with eagerness, even by those who could not act with him.

William Cleaver, D.D., succeeded him. He was first of Magdalen College, Oxford, but removed to Brasenose, of which he was afterwards elected principal. He was consecrated bishop of Chester, translated to Bangor in 1799, and to this see in 1806. He died the 15th May, 1815, aged seventy-three, and was buried in the Chapel of Brasenose College, where a monument to his memory has been erected by the society over which he presided nearly twenty-five years. Bishop Cleaver was a learned, amiable, and excellent prelate, and published, besides a treatise, De Rhythmo Græcorum, many very useful sermons and charges.

MODERN HISTORY OF ST. ASAPH CATHEDRAL.

IN 1868-70 Sir Gilbert Scott restored the space under the tower, and the choir or chancel, the latter being made to resume its true Early English style, which had been destroyed in 1780; the Decorated window (with modern tracery) at the east end, however, remains. The Early English side windows were partly restored from jambs and other portions discovered in the walls. Those to the east were designed by Sir G. Scott. The ancient sedilia that were discovered were also replaced. The cradled timber roof was again uncovered, the plaster one being removed; many of the bosses, however, are new. The chancel was paved with encaustic tiles set in bands of grey mottled Anglesey marble; some of them reproduced old ones found during the restoration.

A new reredos, designed by Sir Gilbert Scott, was given by Mrs. Hesketh, of Gwrych Castle; it is of alabaster, representing the procession to Calvary, with arcading on either side.

The space beneath the tower was vaulted with oak, the plaster being removed. The Bishop's throne is here, at the eastern end on the south side. The stalls and portions of their canopies are ancient tabernacle work; but much of the work is modern, good, and not too rich. A new pulpit was erected opposite the Bishop's throne. The screen has been removed, so that the church is open from end to end; and open seats have been placed in the chancel.

In 1875 the nave was restored, and the roof raised and restored to its original style of oak vaulting. The clerestory was again opened, and windows re-inserted on the north side corresponding with those on the south. Thus the general appearance of the church has been very greatly improved.

The only modern monuments worth notice are those of Dean Shipley (died 1828), in the south transept, a seated figure; of Bishop Luxmoore (died 1830), in the north transept; of Sir John Williams, Bart. (died 1830), by Westmacott, in the south nave

ST. ASAPH CATHEDRAL: FROM THE SOUTH-WEST.

aisle; of Bishop Carey (died 1846), in the west end of the same aisle. There are numerous tablets to members of the Browne family, relatives of Mrs. Hemans, the poetess, and one to Mrs. Hemans herself, in the south nave aisle.

In the south transept is the effigy of a bishop, probably Bishop Anian (early 14th century), the hands broken off. In the north transept is a slab carved with a hare pursued by a greyhound; but without any inscription.

Modern stained glass was inserted in the east window in memory of Bishop Carey, in 1865.

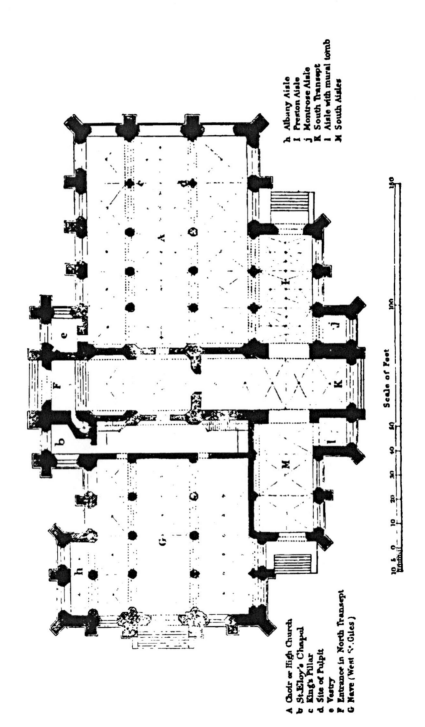

ST. GILES' TOWER AND STEEPLE, EDINBURGH.

THE SCOTCH CATHEDRALS.

In giving an account of the Scotch cathedrals it is impossible to pass over St. Giles's, Edinburgh. Although it is no longer used for the services of the Episcopal Church, nor contains the seat of a bishop, it is essentially a cathedral of the Scottish national Church, using the term as describing a principal church, and is connected imperishably with the religious history of Scotland.

Standing on a conspicuous elevation, on the south side of the High Street, forming one side of Parliament Square, it has witnessed some of the most stirring events in Scotch history, and after having undergone many spoliations and no little destructive "restoration," it has survived to receive a better renovation in 1879-83, under the auspices of the late Dr. William Chambers, the famous Scottish publisher.

St. Giles' was the ancient parish church of Edinburgh, and a church appears to have existed on the same site in the ninth century, when it was included in the Northumbrian diocese of Lindisfarne; at least, Edwinsburgh is mentioned in a list of churches belonging to that English See. St. Giles (Lat., St. Egidius) was by no means a native saint, but appears to have been born at Athens in the seventh century and to have lived in southern France, and to have died on September 1st, 721. His fame was spread widely by the Benedictine monks, and he figures as the patron saint of very many English churches. The reason for his adoption as such in Edinburgh is quite unknown.

The commencement of authentic history about St. Giles' dates from the Norman period of architecture, about 1120. It became a favourite church of the Scotch kings, who conferred substantial benefits upon the "vicar of St. Giles'." In the fourteenth century, however, it suffered grievous damage, not only from the devastations and fires occasioned during the English invasions of Scotland, especially in 1385, but also from the zeal of those who perpetuated their names or ideas by additional buildings, chapels, etc.; but the church had a continuous existence through all, although the Norman portions of the building became small by degrees, leaving at the end of the last century no more beautiful remnant than a doorway beneath the third window from the west end on the north side. This, unfortunately, was completely destroyed at the end of the last century, but from drawings which remain it is seen to have been a rich specimen of late Norman work, having four receding arches with carved capitals, and the outer arch having numerous grotesque carvings of beasts and birds, and grotesque heads. There is a record of the rebuilding of the church after the destruction wrought in 1385, for the municipality contracted on November 29th, 1387, for the building of five chapels in St. Giles', with pillars and vaulted roof, on the south-west of the nave. Early in the fifteenth century, among other additions was the Albany aisle, at the north-west corner of the nave, supposed to have been erected by Robert, Duke of Albany, second son of

ST. GILES'S, EDINBURGH, WEST END RESTORED.

Robert II., and Archibald, Earl of Douglas, who had starved to death the nephew of the former, David, Duke of Rothesay, in 1402. A pillar in the centre of this aisle sustaining the groined roof bears the shields of these evil specimens of church-builders.

In 1454 St. Giles' acquired a notable relic of its patron saint, in the shape of one of his arm-bones, bequeathed by William

VOL. III.   Q

Preston, of Gourton. The corporation of Edinburgh forthwith undertook the building of a new aisle extending from the Lady aisle, where the donor was buried, to receive his monument, and an altar for his chaplain to sing at; and they also granted the right of bearing the precious relic, whenever carried in procession, to his nearest kin. His monument has disappeared, but the Preston aisle remains, and will be described later. The right of bearing the arm-bone in procession was duly exercised until, in 1558, the last procession was held on 1st September, when it was attended by the Queen Regent; but when she had left the procession the mob broke it up, and destroyed a small image of St. Giles', which was carried in place of a full-sized one which had been stolen and burnt by zealous reformers. Four years later the accumulated treasures of the church and the jewelled case of the arm-bone vestments were sold by order of the municipality; It is not to be wondered at, therefore, that the clerical staff of the church, which had been made a collegiate establishment less than a hundred years before by James III., with a provost, curate, sixteen prebendaries, and other chaplains and large endowments, should have disappeared, their means of support being confiscated, and their services prohibited. The old paraphernalia had vanished in the storm, leaving nothing but pulpit and benches and bare walls.

This was the appropriate location for John Knox, the leader of the Scottish Reformation, who preached here for the first time at the end of June, 1559, and on the 7th July was elected minister of the Protestant inhabitants of Edinburgh. He preached for some years at St. Giles' twice every Sunday and three times in the course of the week. The marriage of Queen Mary to Lord Darnley in 1565 was the subject of one of his most impassioned harangues, followed by a personal attack upon the Queen, when he was brought before her at Holyrood. In 1571 the church was forcibly taken possession of by the Queen's party, and loopholes were made in the roof for the soldiers to shoot through; in June cannon were mounted in the steeple, and it was kept in a state of armed defence against the Regent Lennox. This state of things lasted more than a year, till a truce was proclaimed. Knox, who had been two years absent from Edinburgh, returned, but only to die on the 24th November, 1572. He was buried in the churchyard of St. Giles, the Regent pronouncing over his grave the memorable epitaph, "There lies he who never feared the face of man." The spot is now paved, and forms part of Parliament Square, but it cannot be exactly identified.

Already the Municipality of Edinburgh had begun to subdivide the great church, the western portion being turned into a Tolbooth, or place of meeting, for the Civil Courts. A stall in this place was assigned to Knox, who began to preach there on the 21st September before his death. The Reformation did not put a stop to the use of St. Giles's for business transactions, which were now chiefly carried on in the south transept. When the Regent Murray's tomb was erected, it was utilised, as had been the old Romish altar, for settling and signing bargains and paying money. It was so well known a place of resort for loungers, that the Scotch poet Sempill makes one of his characters say:—

"I dined with saints and gentlemen,
Ev'n sweet Giles and the Earl of Murray."

just as Londoners said that strollers in St. Paul's in want of a dinner dined with Duke Humphrey. It is not surprising, therefore, to find that "in the other parts of the building there were accommodated under varying conditions, a grammar school, courts of justice, a town-clerk's office, a prison, and a weaver's workshop. In an odd corner was kept the apparatus for public executions. It was a queer jumble, designed to meet public wants, with little regard to congruity."

In May, 1590, as part of the grand ceremonial of the reception of James VI. and his bride, Anne of Denmark, they attended St. Giles', and were preached to, the choir being specially fitted up, with a royal pew and seats for officials. It was frequently attended by the King and Queen for public worship, and the King addressed his subjects there several times, and even challenged the preachers' statements and opinions. On April 3rd, 1603, before his departure to assume the English crown, James was once more admonished from the pulpit and gave a farewell address to the people.

The reign of James's son, Charles I., introduced a still more stormy period in the history of St. Giles'. Under Laud's guidance, he decreed the re-introduction of Episcopacy into Scotland, and created Edinburgh a bishopric by charter (29th September, 1633), with St. Giles' for its cathedral, which the magistrates and town council were ordered to prepare for that purpose. The service-book prepared by Laud for the Church of Scotland, was used for the first time in St. Giles' on Sunday, July 23rd, 1637, and everyone has heard of the famous scene where Jenny Geddes threw her stool at the head of the Dean of Edinburgh, during the service in the south transept, the choir not having yet been fitted for Cathedral use. The tumult which this service occasioned, in the presence of many ecclesiastics and dignitaries, was followed by the drawing up of the Covenant in 1638, and by many a trouble which makes part of our national history.

JOHN KNOX'S PULPIT.
(*In the Museum of the Scottish Antiquarian Society.*)

Dr. Lindsay, the Bishop of Edinburgh, was assaulted, and barely escaped with his life. The service-book was used no more, and Presbyterianism regained its sway in the church. The short-lived cathedral status of St. Giles' was resumed in 1662, under Charles II., and continued until the Revolution of 1688, when it finally ceased to be, strictly speaking, a cathedral, though often popularly so designated.

Concurrently with the increase of Edinburgh, St. Giles' was

still more subdivided, till, in the middle of the eighteenth century, in addition to the Tolbooth Kirk in the south-west, there were the choir or High Kirk in the east, Haddo's Hole Kirk in the north-west, and the Old Kirk in the middle and part of the south side. The meetings of the General Assembly of the Church were held in the Preston aisle, and the central space under the tower, as well as the north transept, was occupied by the police-office. Outside it, towards the Tolbooth and the Luckenbooths, a number of sheds and shops were erected against the very walls of the church, and known as the Krames, in which glovers, mercers, and toy-dealers carried on their trade, and the smoke from which increased the blackness of the walls above them. These were not finally cleared away until after the removal of the Old Tolbooth in 1817.

"Before it was despoiled," says Dr. Chambers, "the vast interior of this grand old building, with its many pillars and groined roof, must have presented an appearance resembling that of a spacious English cathedral of the older class. The policy of cutting up and apportioning this handsome structure, on which so much architectural taste had been lavished, is inexcusable. The transformation was effected in a manner altogether tasteless. No care was taken to preserve the finer parts of the architecture. Rows of fluted pillars sustaining lofty arches were merged in the rough walls, which were erected lengthwise and crosswise to form the several compartments. The foliated base and capitals of pillars were hacked without mercy to bring them within the required line. Characteristic heads carved among the foliage were knocked off with hammers, and are found buried in rubbish beneath the floor. The erection of galleries in all the churches caused further dilapidation, as cavities for beams to sustain these galleries were dug in the sides of several pillars." Many of the buttresses had been greatly injured in building the outside booths, and most of the mullions and tracery of the windows had disappeared, and been replaced by clumsy wooden sashes. At last feeling was awakened to the necessity for improving St. Giles', but before taste had improved sufficiently to know what it was best to do. After several years' consideration the Town Council adopted Mr. Burn's plans for remodelling the church, and between

1829 and 1833 a very extensive "restoration" was carried out. Two aisles on the north side were taken down, and other two on the south-west, and many picturesque roofs and pinnacles were demolished. Worse still, the whole of the walls were recased with stone in a very debased style. Fortunately, the spire was left untouched. Internally the arrangements were considerably modified, but the choir remained as it was. The southern portion of the building was fitted up for the meetings of the General Assembly, and after a few years transferred to the use of the Old Kirk. The police-office was removed, and the space it occupied was made into a lobby common to all the congregations, who now all entered by a door in the north transept. The names of the Tolbooth Kirk and Haddo's Hole were discontinued, and the nave was occupied by West St. Giles' congregation. The fine old monument of the Earl of Murray was demolished, but the brass tablet, having engraved upon it figures of Justice and Faith, with an inscription by Buchanan, was preserved, and is now placed on the modern monument to the Earl.

Thus the structure remained till the recent restoration. The Town Council had seats in a gallery on the north side of the choir, while the Lords of Session occupied a corresponding gallery on the south side. The royal pew was in a gallery at the west end of the choir, having a canopy painted light blue and supported on four wooden posts. The whole church was fitted with plain deal pews of old-fashioned style. The atmosphere was musty in the extreme, owing to the soil beneath being crowded with human remains.

In 1872, after the subscription list started by Dr. Chambers had reached respectable dimensions, the work of restoration commenced with the choir, Mr. W. Hay being the architect. The galleries were removed throughout the building, and the fine old pillars were once more made visible, and repaired with stone where necessary. All the old pews and the huge dark pulpit and sounding board were removed. The royal pew and canopy were taken away as Crown property. The soil was cleared out to a depth of several feet, and all the human remains taken away and buried in a churchyard. A number of large gravestones that had formed part of the pavement were with questionable judgment handed over to a body representing the craftsmen of

Edinburgh. The walls of the choir and the groined roof were cleaned. New seats of oak were supplied throughout, with appropriate carving on the official ones. The Royal pew, at first placed at the west end (since removed to the back of the Preston aisle, with a special entrance in the south-eastern angle of the choir), is especially ornamental, and the whole are in keeping with the Early English architecture. A new pulpit of Caen stone, beautifully carved by Mr. John Rhind, of Edinburgh, was placed against the southern pillar nearest the east window. Instead of the Eastern arrangement found in English cathedrals, there is behind the Communion table a series of seven oak stalls for the members of the Chapel Royal of Scotland, beneath a corresponding set of stone canopies, supported on marble shafts. The aisles and passages have been laid with Moreton tiles bearing antique Scottish devices. The choir as thus renovated was reopened on 9th March, 1873.

The "Old Church" parish having been abolished in 1870, the southern portion of St. Giles', including the Preston aisle, was at length disused, and Dr. Chambers, who had already defrayed a large part of the expense of the previous alterations, undertook the further expense of its restoration. In February, 1879, the galleries and pews were removed, and various partitions and staircases taken down, thus throwing open the aisles. Under the floor there was found an indiscriminate collection of skulls and bones, mostly removed thither during Mr. Burn's restorations. These bones were now collected and examined by anatomists prior to burial in a cemetery. The Montrose aisle (properly Chepman's, south of the Preston aisle), in which the famous Marquis of Montrose was supposed to have been buried, had been walled off, and arranged in three stories, the lower a coal cellar, the middle containing a large stove, and the upper a plain room. These were cleared away, and the soil examined for relics of the Marquis, but none were found. When the partition wall was taken down, the arch was found to have been much damaged, a chimney having been run through the keystone of the arch, and about a dozen feet of the stone on each side had been cut away. The whole was repaired with new stone, and the original character of the walls restored. A handsome monument to the great Marquis has been placed in the chapel by the members of the clan Grahame. In the groined roof was discovered a finely carved boss bearing the arms of Walter Chepman impaled with those of his wife, on a shield held up by an angle. Chepman was the first Scottish printer (in 1507), and showed an energy in developing the art which makes him worthy to rank with Caxton. He died in 1532, after building this aisle, the altar in which was dedicated to St. John the Evangelist, whose emblem, the eagle, was found on a carved corbel on the west side of the roof. A tablet has been put up to his memory, bearing this inscription: "In the memory of Walter Chepman, designated the Scottish Caxton, who under the auspices of James IV. and his Queen Margaret, introduced the art of printing into Scotland, 1507; founded this aisle in honour of the King and Queen and their family, 1513; and died in 1532; this tablet is gratefully inscribed by William Chambers, LL.D., 1879."

The Preston aisle was fully restored, many pillars and arches requiring repair owing to the insertion of beams, and other injuries. Some of the bases and ornamental capitals required renewal. A new font has been placed in the west end of the church near the principal doorway. It is of Caen stone, on the model of Thorwaldsen's famous one at Copenhagen, a kneeling angel wreathed with flowers, holding a large shell.

Before restoring the south transept, the floor was examined for vaults, but only one was found, containing three leaden coffins besides a quantity of human remains. One of the coffins contained the remains of Alexander, fourth earl of Galloway, who died in 1690; but no other identifiable remains were found. This transept is notable as having contained the modern monument of the Regent Murray, a mural design in Caen stone, erected by John, eleventh earl of Moray, in 1864. This monument now stands a little to the west of its former site. Near the top is the old brass tablet with the emblematic figure of Faith or Piety on one side, with the motto "Pietas sine vindice luget;" on the other side a figure of Justice, with the words "Jus exarmatum est." This is followed by Buchanan's Latin inscription "Jacobo Stovarto Moraviæ comiti Scotiæ proregi vivo Ætatis suæ longæ optimo ab inimicis omnis memoriæ deterrimis ex insidiis extincto ceu Patri communi Patria mœrens posuit."

ST. GILES', EDINBURGH—THE CHOIR (*before the removal of the pulpit westward*).

The aisle immediately west of the south transept has also been cleared of the staircase with which Mr. Burn had filled it, although, unfortunately, its original two bays could not be restored. Mr. Burn had spared a fine arched mural structure, which he removed to a position under the remaining window. It consists of a Decorated Gothic arch over a flat slab, and is crowded with minute carved emblems and symbols of the Passion of Christ. It probably formed part of the altar of "The Holy Blood." The wall which Mr. Burn had substituted for the original arch has been removed, and a pointed arch on the church side again affords a view of the mural monument. The rest of the southern section has been restored with similar care.

Between 1880 and 1883 the restoration of the remaining portion of the building was completed, but, unfortunately, the munificent restorer died, almost on the eve of the reopening, which took place on May 23, 1883. The whole building is now thrown open as one church, the pulpit which had been at the south-east of the choir being removed to the first pillar west of the north transept, thus placing it nearly in the middle of the great area. The view of the interior is now impressive, especially from the west end, or from the Albany pillar in the south-west aisle, or the Murray aisle in the south, the labyrinth of stone pillars showing to great advantage in the latter positions. The main building, with aisles extending 196 feet in length by 70 feet in breadth, is flanked by three smaller buildings or aisles on the north, the Albany, the St. Eloy or Hammermen's, and by the Murray and Preston aisles on the south, forming a continuous range 122 feet by 22 feet, with small southern appendages we have described. The nave and choir are of five bays each, and the latter is terminated by the fine eastern window, which represents the Crucifixion and Ascension. The stone work is not highly finished or decorated, but it is a vast improvement on the old wash and plaster, which has been cleared away with the exception of the artificial ceiling of the nave and transepts. The main entrance to the church was till recently through the north transept, where a broad flight of steps leads to a vestibule cut off from the interior by a handsome screen of ornamental stonework. The fine doorway in the centre of this screen is flanked on either side by niches in which statues of John Knox and other Scottish worthies are erected. The organ, a powerful one, occupies the end of the south transept. Nearly the whole site of the old St. Eloy's chapel, on the west side of the north doorway, is now occupied by the new belfry turret; but the aisle of St. Eloy, in the Hammermen's Chapel, has been well restored, the carved boss which formerly was the keystone of the roof, having been replaced, and the window which has been built up having been reopened. The open screen of wrought iron work has been ornamented with medallions bearing emblems symbolical of the hammermen's art.

The exterior of St. Giles' has been repaired, and a new west doorway inserted since Dr. Chambers's death. Above it are niches with statues of notable persons connected with the church in the past, including Gavin Douglas, the translator of Virgil, John Knox, Bishop Forbes, Henderson the Covenanter, and others. The windows have been to a large extent filled with stained glass, in accordance with a settled plan. All are of late Decorated or Early Perpendicular style. The general plan of the windows illustrates Bible history throughout, and those in the choir depict exclusively events in the history of Christ. They have been executed by James Ballantine and Son, under the supervision of Mr. R. Herdman, F.S.A., and are very satisfactory. The clerestory windows in the choir are appropriated to the arms of the Incorporated Craftsmen of Edinburgh.

The Episcopal Church of Scotland having lost its old possession St. Giles's, has not until modern times been equipped with a substitute, which it has now acquired in St. Mary's Cathedral, situated in Manor Place, with its axis coinciding with that of Melville Street, from which its east end is well seen. It originated in a munificent bequest for the purpose by the Misses Mary and Margaret Walker, the latter of whom died in 1871. Sir G. G. Scott was chosen to be the architect, and the foundation-stone was laid by the Duke of Buccleuch on the 21st of May, 1874. The total cost when complete was over £130,000. The church is a cruciform one, mainly in the Early English style, with a lofty central tower and spire, 275 feet in height, and two smaller towers at the west end. It is one of the finest modern Gothic buildings in the kingdom, built of freestone from Dunmore and Polmaise. Both choir and nave have north and south aisles, and the total external length is 278 feet, the breadth at the transepts being 98 feet 6 inches. The latter are broad in proportion to their length, being 57 feet wide, including the aisles.

The west end, in Palmerston Place, presents an imposing façade, preserving the severe outlines of the Early English style, with a considerable amount of elaboration. The great west window, of four fine lancets, with a rose window above, rises high into the gable, and is flanked by the short western towers and their massive buttresses. The towers have double lancets in each of their three open faces, and an arcade of small arches above. They are intended to have spires upon them at a future date, rising to 210 feet. The western portal is a fine Early English one, gabled, as are the side arches, which harmonise with it, the shafts being of red Shap granite. The pediment over the portal has in its centre a seated figure of the Saviour, with a lamb supported on His left hand, and holding a key with the right, the whole surrounded by the verse, "Ego sum ostium; per me si quis introierit salvabitur." The spandrils contain figures of St. Peter and John the Baptist. Above the door lintel is a row of angels bearing a scroll with the inscription, "Tu es Christus filius Dei."

The exterior of the nave and its aisle shows five buttressed bays, each with double lancet windows, the clerestory being bold, and each bay having two double lancets. The roof is high-pitched. The south side has a portal in the second bay. The south transept has a portal with beautifully carved mouldings, and three large lancets, separated by massive clustered shafts, surmounted by a rose window, 24 feet in diameter, with geometrical tracery. Above this, five niches are occupied by statues of St. Paul, St. Luke, Titus, Silas, and Timothy. The north transept is similar, but without a portal, and the tracery of the large wheel window is of later style than the southern one, and is surmounted by a statue of David. The great tower rises square from the high roof of the church, having one stage with small lancets and massive buttress shafts at the corners, with flying buttresses to a turreted buttress at the intersection of the nave and choir aisles respectively with the transept aisles. In the second stage the tower becomes octagonal, at the height of 120 feet, the buttress-shafts at the angles becoming turrets against the four new sides,

ST. MARY'S CATHEDRAL, EDINBURGH, FROM THE SOUTH-WEST.

while two-light windows occupy the alternate faces. The spire (133 feet high) is likewise octagonal, with a lower stage lighted with four gabled windows, the sides corresponding to the turrets below having niches with statues of archangels. The weight of

INTERIOR OF ST. MARY'S CATHEDRAL, LOOKING EAST.

the tower is over 6,000 tons, the capstone and cross weighing a ton. It contains a peal of ten bells, presented by Dean Montgomery.

The exterior like the interior of the choir, is more ornamental than the nave. It has four bays, and the aisle windows are single, while those of the clerestory are triplets. The east end has the middle portion almost occupied by three tall lancets, surmounted by an arcade containing statues of the Virgin and the four Evangelists. The gable is flanked by massive turreted buttresses on either side, the aisles terminated with smaller turreted buttresses and two-light windows.

The interior of the Cathedral is very attractive, with its long row of arches, its high-pitched groined roof, and east and west lancets. The west lancets are filled with stained glass, the gift of Mrs. Gordon, of Cluny. Many of the other windows bear the arms of ancient Scottish families. The nave pillars are octagonal and circular, those of the choir of clustered shafts. There is the usual triforium below the clerestory (open in the nave and closed in the choir), and the design of the roof gives an appearance of great height to the interior. The nave and transepts are vaulted in oak, with richly moulded ribs and carved bosses. The lower arches, with their manifold clustered shafts, have a fine effect. The aisles throughout the central crossing and choir are vaulted in stone and concrete. The choir has two larger and four smaller pointed bays, and the height to the key-stones of the vault is 58 feet. The east end vaulting springs in an apse form from between the three east lancets; there is a low ornamental screen of marble and mosaic under the western tower arch, and the pulpit is against this, on the north-western side. The choir seats are beneath the tower, the gift of the ladies of Scotland. The reredos is an ornamental piece of alabaster arcading, with a middle arch containing a marble group representing the Crucifixion, by Miss Grant; it rises too high, blocking the lower part of the middle lancet. The organ, by Willis, is in the north transept. The massive alabaster font, supported by four red marble columns, and having carved on its sides the ark, dove, and fishes, is in the baptistery, under the south-western tower. North of the north-choir aisle is the library and chapter-house, with high-pitched roof. The Cathedral was opened in October, 1879.

Glasgow possesses a Cathedral, now used by the national Church of Scotland, which ranks with the best English Cathedrals in purity of style and excellence of design, the pre-

ST. MUNGO'S CATHEDRAL, GLASGOW, IN THE LAST CENTURY: FROM THE EAST END.

servation of which to our own days is due to the energy of the Glasgow incorporated trades in defending it from the Scottish Reformers. It is dedicated to St. Kentigern or Mungo, a saint of the sixth century, and friend of St. Columba, who is said to have founded in the year 560 a religious house or cell on the spot where the Cathedral now stands. From his time onward there was a religious establishment here, endowed by one of the Strathclyde princes with lands which were devastated by successive inroads of Picts, Scots, Saxons, and Danes. In the year 1115 David I., then Prince of Cumberland, made it a bishopric or restored it to that dignity, and appointed John Achaius, his chaplain, bishop. In 1123 a Cathedral was begun by him, and part of it was consecrated in 1136. Achaius died in 1147; his Cathedral was destroyed by fire about 1176, and Joceline, who became bishop in 1175, is the next great builder of the Cathedral, though what he built it is now impossible to tell, as only a small fragment of Transitional work, a few square yards of masonry at the south-west corner of the crypt now remains *in situ*, all the rest of the present building being of later date. Bishop William de Bondington (consecrated 1233) was no doubt the builder of the crypt and choir as they now stand. The nave was built later; its date is not ascertained, but part, at least, was built early in the thirteenth century. Bishop Lauder (consecrated 1408) built the chapter-house, which is entered from the crypt at the north-east corner, and also the upper part of the tower, the spire of which was probably completed by his successor, Bishop Cameron, who also built the vestry over the chapter-house. In 1491, during the time of Bishop Blackadder, the see of Glasgow was erected into an archbishopric by Pope Innocent VII. The Bishop did much to beautify the Cathedral, and constructed the crypt to the south of the transept, and the beautiful rood loft. During the Reformation troubles Cardinal Beaton took all the records and relics of the Cathedral to Paris, where they were afterwards lost during the French Revolution. The Cathedral itself barely escaped the Reformers' zeal, by reason of the protection afforded by the incorporated trades of Glasgow in 1578, who, however, agreed to the destruction of the statues of the saints. As with St. Giles', Edinburgh, worship in the Cathedral was by turns

Episcopalian and Presbyterian till at the Revolution of 1688 the latter gained permanent predominance. In 1650 Cromwell sat here and heard himself denounced as a "sectary and blasphemer," by Dr. Zachary Boyd. The crypt was at one time used as the Barony Parish Kirk, and the choir is still used as the High Church. About 1843 the Cathedral was "repaired and restored" by Mr. Blore, architect, under Government direction, but unfortunately the north-west bell tower, 120 feet high, and the consistory-house were removed.

GLASGOW CATHEDRAL: FROM THE SOUTH.

This fine church, standing on an elevated site 154 feet above the Clyde, measures 319 feet in length by 63 feet wide. The choir is 90 feet high, the nave 85 feet. The church has a special aspect, owing to the shortness of the transepts, which enhances the general effect of its length, and the central tower and spire are very handsome. There was this apology for the demolition of the north-western tower and consistory court, that they blocked up and injured the effect of the west end. It now presents a pure Early English type of front, with sparing ornamentations. The tracery of the west window was repaired, fresh mullions being inserted by Mr. D. Hamilton, in 1812. The west door is of great richness and beauty, being a double-pointed archway, with a square head to each opening, and the space above filled with niches. We cannot give detailed descriptions of the exterior of the nave and choir, but there being no extraordinary features, this is the less necessary. The general type is Early English, with numerous Early Decorated features, especially the nave. The transepts do not project beyond the line of the choir and nave aisles, but have corner turrets and buttresses, and large windows. From the crossing rises the beautiful square tower, with four-light lancet windows in each face, and turreted at the corners, with an open battlement; the spire is octagonal, with Decorated windows and two ornamental bands. It is 225 feet high. The east end presents a fine elevation, the four lancets rising high above the double lancets of the Lady chapel and its crypt.

The interior of the church is simple and grand, the effect being now enhanced by the stained-glass windows. A stone wall formerly cut the nave in two; but now the organ screen, between the eastern pillars of the tower, is the only division from end to end. The fine fluted pillars, the harmonious triforium and clerestory, and the lofty tower arches are the most notable features. The roof is a plain wooden vaulted one.

The organ screen was once a very fine work, and though greatly defaced by the Reformers, still has much beauty. The low and deep Perpendicular doorway, of several orders, is flanked by arcading which once contained statues. Above is a balustrade with pillars of tabernacle work, resting on grotesque figures.

The interior of the choir or High Church presents one of the finest Early English views. The main pillars have beautifully carved foliage in the capitals. The triforium gallery is continued through the exquisite piers of the eastern lancets. Beneath them are two large arches, behind the former high altar and opening into the Lady chapel. The roof is high-pitched and groined.

The Lady chapel, as it is erroneously called, at the east end of the choir, is of two bays in length, but is four bays wide, including the continuations of the choir aisles. Thus it forms practically an eastern transept. The east and west bays were used as chapels. The pillars are beautifully shafted, moulded, and the roof groined. At the south-east end is the monument to Archbishop Law. The tomb of the ancient family

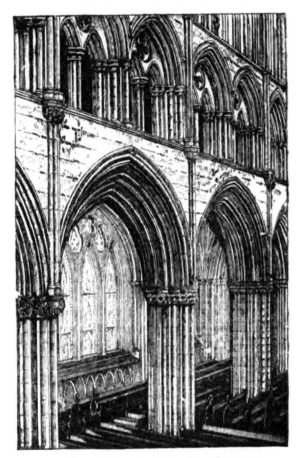

GLASGOW CATHEDRAL: ARCHES IN THE CHOIR.

of the Stewarts of Minto also remains on the south side of the choir, west of the entrance. The sacristy, at the north end of the choir, is 28 feet every way, the groined ceiling being supported by a pillar 20 feet in height.

Passing now back to the descent to the crypts, we enter by a flight of steps, perhaps the most extraordinary part of this remarkable building. From the fall of the ground eastward, it is entirely above ground, and is well lighted by a large number of lancet windows. The piers and groining are of the most intricate character, the most beautiful design, and excellent execution. The groins have rich bosses, and the doors are much enriched with foliage and other ornaments. "Here are to be found," says Mr. Collie, in his architectural account of Glasgow Cathedral, "piers of every possible form—square, round, and multangular, which are embraced by attached columns, having capitals of all varieties, from the simple moulding to the richest foliage." It was this crypt which was used by the congregation of the Barony parish, and which Sir Walter Scott has described in "Rob Roy." The crypt extends not only under the sacristy, but also southward, forming Blackadder's aisle, which it is supposed was intended to support an enlarged south transept. It became much injured by rain dripping through the roof, whence it was known as "the dripping aisle." This portion has been largely used as a burying-place in Glasgow, but contains no ancient monuments; that of Bishop Wishart is under the Lady chapel. The total length of the crypt is 125 feet, and it is 72 feet wide.

GLASGOW CATHEDRAL: THE LADY CHAPEL.

In 1856 it was resolved, under the auspices of Sir Andrew Orr, the Lord Provost, to embellish the Cathedral with stained-glass windows, and in a very short time subscriptions were promised for all the windows. The subscribers adopted a scheme by which the windows in the nave, transepts, and Lady Chapel were all executed at the Royal Establishment of Glass Painting at Munich, according to a scheme of subjects prepared beforehand by Mr. C. Heath Wilson. In the nave they are selected from the Old Testament, with certain exceptions illustrating the connection between the Old and New Testaments; the order of Biblical chronology being followed from the north-west window of the nave (relating to Adam) to the south-west window, which completes the Old Testament series. The great west window illustrates four great events in the history of the Jews: the giving of the

GLASGOW CATHEDRAL: THE CRYPT.

law, the entrance into the promised land, the dedication of the Temple, and the captivity at Babylon. The north transept window contains figures of prophets; while the south transept window illustrates the types and antitypes of the Saviour. The choir windows illustrate the parables and precepts of the Gospels, except one which illustrates the resurrection; while the great east window (given by the Queen) represents the four Evangelists. The windows of the Lady Chapel contain figures of the Apostles, with Saint Stephen and Timothy. The windows of the chapter-house illustrate acts of charity and mercy, and were designed by Mr. Henry Hughes, of London. The whole of the series, 81 in number, were completed in 1864. The result is perhaps the most beautiful and harmonious grouping of modern stained glass to be found anywhere; but on the whole the architectural features of the Cathedral are somewhat obscured by the great darkening it has undergone. The crypt especially has suffered.

Unfortunately the fittings and arrangements of the Cathedral are quite unworthy of its architecture, and have been termed disgraceful to the city of Glasgow. Part of the clerestory walls are two feet out of the perpendicular, and there are serious cracks in the tower arches.[1]

Passing still farther west, we find at Millport, in the Island of Cumbrae, near the entrance of the Firth of Clyde, the Cathedral of the Isles, a modern church which now represents the historic and ruined cathedral of Iona. It was originally founded as a collegiate church by the Hon. G. F. Boyle (now Earl of Glasgow), in 1849, in connection with Cumbrae College for clergymen and theological students, built by the same founder. The Collegiate Church having been made over to trustees for the Scottish Episcopal Church, was consecrated by the Bishop of Argyll and the Isles on May 3, 1876, and declared to be henceforward the Cathedral of the Isles. The Cathedral and college, which are in the Decorated style, are closely contiguous to the Earl of Glasgow's seat, "The Garrison," and are finely situated at the top of a succession of terraces. The south-western tower and spire are the conspicuous features of the building, together with the large west window, a fine Decorated window with geometrical tracery, filled with stained glass by Wailes. The tower and spire are beautifully proportioned, the tower having bold buttresses at three angles, and having triple lights in each face of the upper or belfry stage (which contains three bells and clock chimes). The spire is four-sided, surmounted by a large iron cross and a weather-cock. The entire range of buildings is constructed

---

[1] See Mr. Honeyman's paper before the British Archæological Association (*Glasgow Herald*, August 28th, 1888), and a paper by the same gentleman in the *Scottish Art Review* October, 1888.

of the delicately coloured freestone of the island, and does credit to the skill of Mr. Butterfield, the architect.

The building, which has no aisles, consists of nave, choir, and

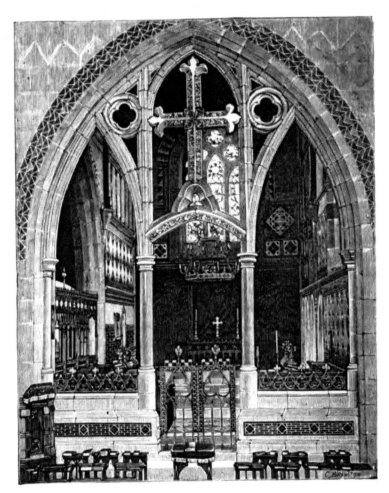

CUMBRAE CATHEDRAL: THE SCREEN AND CHOIR.

sanctuary, separated from the nave by a carved stone screen carrying tracery with a cross, with brass gates, the pillars on either side of them being of Aberdeen granite. The low wall of the screen between these pillars is surmounted by tracery in brass, containing a series of quatrefoils. The nave is entered by a south-western door, and consists of four bays, lighted on the south side by four stained-glass windows, by Hardman, the western representing Saint Ignatius and Saint Polycarp (memorial to G. W. Dasent, drowned at Oxford in 1872), the next representing St. Catherine of Egypt and St. Cecilia, the two nearest the choir depicting the four Latin doctors, given in memory of the Rev. John Keble. The whole of the walls of the choir, and the front of the screen and corbel of the chancel arch are adorned with encaustic tiles, with spaces in Parian cement for the introduction of pictures. The roof of the sanctuary contains representations of the ferns and flowers of the island. The windows are of stained glass by Hardman; the south-western representing the crucifixion, the next the resurrection. The east end of the chancel up to the base of the east window is covered with velvet hangings. The organ is in a vestry to the north, and beyond this is the chapter-house. On the east side of the college are two sides of a cloister (intended to be completed) adjacent to the chapter-house.

A new cathedral for the diocese of St. Andrews, Dunkeld, and Dunblane, dedicated to St. Ninian, was begun at Perth in 1849, and was consecrated in 1850, the choir, transepts, and one bay of the nave having then been built from Mr. Butterfield's designs. It was originally intended that the west end should have two towers; but in the design adopted in 1887 for the completion of the nave, there was substituted a single north-western tower. This work, making the nave four bays long, and the total length of the church 190 feet, is now (1888) being completed, including the building of the tower up to the base of the belfry story. Mr. Butterfield's complete design provides for a good belfry and spire, rising to nearly 200 feet. The style is a comparatively simple form of Decorated, most of the windows having triple lights. The west end abuts so closely on the wall of the barracks as to make a western entrance impossible; consequently a north doorway is inserted in the base of the tower.

The diocese of Moray, Ross, and Caithness has for its Cathedral a modern building at Inverness, erected in 1866-9, from the designs of Mr. Alexander Ross, of Inverness. It is a comparatively small church, in Decorated Gothic style, and its architectural

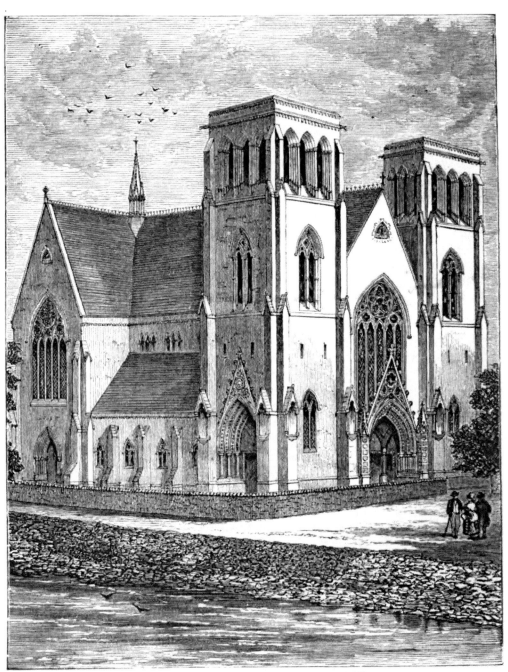

INVERNESS CATHEDRAL: FROM THE NORTH-WEST.

style may be sufficiently appreciated from our illustration; the east end is apsidal. The stone used is a light red sandstone, with dressings of cream-coloured freestone. The towers, carried up to 100 feet high, are intended to support spires also 100 feet high. The north tower contains a peal of bells. Under the south tower is the baptistery, with a white marble font copied from Thorwaldsen's, at Copenhagen. The nave has five bays, the arches having granite piers; its length is 90 feet, width 60 feet. The choir is 60 feet long. The total external length is 166 feet; width across west front, 72 feet.

We will now devote as much space as can be spared to a description of the remains of the numerous old Scotch cathedrals now no longer used by the Episcopal Church.

Dunblane Cathedral (in Perthshire) was made the seat of a bishop by David I., who built a Cathedral here about 1140, only the tower of which remains. Its peculiar position is explained by its having been at first a detached campanile. The nave is now roofless, while the choir is used as the parish kirk, having been repaired in 1873 by Sir W. Stirling Maxwell. The situation of the Cathedral, near the eastern bank of the river Allan, shows the west front greatly to advantage, with its deeply recessed doorway, and three tall lancets of two lights each, under a rose window, all in the best Scotch Gothic style. The nave is of eight bays, with aisles and excellent Decorated windows and arches, and measures 130 feet by 58 feet; the choir, also Early Decorated, and of six bays, is 80 feet by 50 feet wide, and retains its original roof. It has no south aisle, and the north aisle is extended to form a groined chapter-house. The tower, opposite the fifth bay of the nave, is 128 feet high. Its four lower storeys are Norman; the two upper are Decorated, having corbelled turrets and a parapet. This tower is surmounted by a small polygonal spire.

In the north wall of the choir is a fifteenth-century monument with effigy of Bishop Finlay Dermoch (died 1419), and in the chapter-house are the monuments of Malise, fifth Earl of Strathern (died 1271), and his countess, with gritstone effigies. Dunblane is also notable for its connection with Leighton (bishop from 1662 to 1669), afterwards Archbishop of Glasgow, who bequeathed his library of 3,000 volumes to Dunblane. It is still kept in a building near the church.

St. Andrew's formerly had a fine Cathedral, of which a remnant only now remains. The nave was formerly 200 feet long, and 62 feet wide, including the aisles; the choir, with aisles, was 98 feet long; and at the east end was a Lady Chapel 33 feet long, making a total length of 358 feet. Now there only remain

DUNBLANE CATHEDRAL: THE NAVE, LOOKING WEST.

the east gable, part of the west front, and a portion of the nave and south transept. In 1826 a quantity of earth and rubbish which had accumulated was cleared away and protected from further damage. The ruins show the usual Scottish combination of round-arched and pointed windows. The history of this see and

Cathedral and the other monastic and ecclesiastical ruins about it we have not space to detail.

The Cathedral of St. Columba, at Dunkeld, is another example of a fine building wantonly destroyed. The choir only has been

DUNKELD CATHEDRAL: THE NAVE, LOOKING WEST.

repaired, and is used as a parish kirk, the nave being left ruinous and unroofed. It stands on the site of one of the oldest Scotch churches, founded by Culdees driven from Iona, who brought with them the relics of St. Columba. The west front has a massive north-west tower of late fifteenth-century date, 96 feet high, and a large west window with a canopy twisted to one side to afford space for a circular ornament enclosing tracery. One peculiarity of the nave (of seven bays, and 120 feet long by 60 feet wide) is that the pointed main arches, with circular piers, are surmounted by a triforium with round-headed arches divided by mullions enclosing trefoils. The building of the nave extended from 1406 to 1465. The choir, which has no aisles, is 104 feet long by 27 feet wide. There are two monuments of bishops in the nave, that of Bishop Cardeny, who began the nave, being a beautiful canopied and sculptured one, in the south nave aisle. In the choir is the effigy of the wicked natural son of Robert II., known as the Wolf of Badenoch, who destroyed Elgin Cathedral, and who was buried here in 1394. In the chapter-house (on the north side of the choir) is a monument to John, the fourth Duke of Athole (died 1833), who contributed most of the funds for the conversion of the choir into a parish kirk. One of the most notable bishops of the see was Gavin Douglas, the translator of Virgil (1516-1522). In 1560 the Cathedral was despoiled by orders of the Duke of Argyll. In 1689, after Killiecrankie, the Cameronians and the followers of Claverhouse had a desperate fight here, the former occupying the Cathedral, which barely escaped destruction by fire.

The Cathedral of the Holy Trinity, Brechin, was founded by David I., in 1150, but has undergone much modification and rebuilding, including a ruthless adaptation of the nave, in the following fashion: "In 1806 the north and south transepts were removed, new aisles were built at each side of the nave, and one roof made to cover the whole, thus totally eclipsing the beautiful windows in the nave, and covering up the handsome carved cornice of the nail-headed quatrefoil description which ran under the eaves of the nave." The small choir, without a roof, is in a ruined state. The nave is now an incongruous kirk. The west end has still features of interest in the flowing Decorated tracery of the west window, the Decorated portal, and the massive square tower (dating from the latter part of the fourteenth century), in four stages, with considerable windows in the upper stage, surmounted by an octagonal spire, the whole reaching a height of 128 feet. But by far the most remarkable feature of the building is the round tower at the south-west angle, closely resembling the Irish round towers, and probably of eleventh or twelfth century date. It is 85 feet high to the parapet, of eight irregular stages, and covered by a short spire added later, 23 feet in

BRECHIN CATHEDRAL: WEST FRONT AND ROUND TOWER.

height, lighted by dormer windows. The diameter of the tower is more than 15 feet, and the masonry, while somewhat irregular, is old and massive. It formerly contained two bells. Six feet above the base is a round-headed doorway in the west aspect, with carved beaded mouldings, flanked by figures of saints, and having a crucifix carved above; it is now built up, and the tower is entered from the church.

In the "Auld Town" of Aberdeen the Cathedral of St. Machar, another of the successes of Scotch-Gothic art, has its nave, newly caparisoned, given up to the services of the Scottish national Church, while the transepts, choir, and Lady Chapel were destroyed by the Reformers in 1560, and by the fall of the central tower through its being undermined by Cromwell's troopers. Its west front, in massive stern granite, still remains fresh and powerful. The flat panelled oak ceiling is decorated with the shields and arms of kings, popes, bishops, and princes, who contributed to the expense of the building. St. Machar was one of the early Scoto-Irish missionaries, and he is said to have been a contemporary of St. Columba. The bishopric of Aberdeen was founded by David I., and the see received considerable endowments. By the middle of the fourteenth century the early Cathedral had been demolished, and in 1357 the present building was begun. The nave was completed towards the end of the century. The west front and the three towers were begun by Bishop Leighton (translated from the see in 1424). Bishop Elphinstone completed the great central tower and supplied it with fourteen bells in 1489. The west front was not finished till the time of Gavin Dunbar (1519-31), who built the north transept where his tomb was, and ceiled the nave with oak. Bishop Stewart built the chapter-house in 1532.

The west front is flanked by two massive buttressed towers with only very small openings, and these are capped by short octagonal spires with dormer windows, rising to 113 ft. 6 in. high. Over the round-headed portal (subdivided by two pointed arches) is a range of seven tall, narrow, round-headed windows close together, and all of the same height. The gable above has two round-headed windows. The nave, 126 ft. long by 67 ft. wide, including the aisles, has six bays with pointed arches, supported on circular piers. There is no triforium proper, but a triforium passage fronts the round-headed clerestory windows. The southern porch projects considerably beyond the aisle. The richly carved pulpit is the chief remainder of the former abundant carved work. Among several modern painted windows is one which has been inserted to the memory of the Aberdeen painters Jameson, Dyce, and Phillip.

The great central tower fell in 1689, the English soldiers having weakened it in 1652 by attempting to build a fort out of the choir stones, and by later endeavours to underpin it. Probably

ABERDEEN CATHEDRAL: FROM THE SOUTH-WEST.

the eastern portions of the church owe their destruction to their having been built of freestone instead of granite, like the western portion. In the ruins of the south transept there still remain the rich canopied tombs of Bishops Leighton (1424) and Dunbar (1518), a semicircular arch, richly decorated, covering the effigy in each case. It is singular to notice how in so many Scotch churches the Norman and the Early English arches remained, and were continually used at a time when the debased Perpendicular style was in full possession of the field in England.

The ruined Cathedral of the Holy Trinity, at Elgin, is generally acknowledged to have once been the most beautiful building in Scotland. The seat of the bishopric of Moray was transferred by Bishop Andrew Moray (1221-47) from Spynie to Elgin, where he dedicated his new cathedral in 1224, only a small part of which still remains, owing to a fire in 1270, and another in 1390, due to the Wolf of Badenoch, Alexander Stewart. The remaining portion of early work is a part of the south transept, where round-arched windows appear in the upper stage, above pointed lancets in the lower. The choir and other parts were built after the fire of 1270, and escaped that of 1390. In 1392 we find Bishop Bar imploring the king to compel the incendiaries to restore the church, which he calls the special ornament of the land, the glory of the realm, the delight of strangers and foreigners, and a subject of praise in foreign countries for the number of its ministers, its sumptuous decoration, its pious worship of God, its lofty bell-towers, its splendid furniture and countless jewels. Again, in 1402 it was burnt by Alexander of the Isles, after which every parish in the diocese had to pay a subsidy towards the rebuilding. A central tower was built by Bishop Innes (died 1414); but it ultimately fell, and was rebuilt by Bishop Forman (beginning about 1507), and had reached a height of 198 feet in 1538; but again in 1710 it fell, and was not rebuilt. Internally the building suffered in 1568, when the Privy Council ordered the roof to be stripped of lead to obtain funds to pay the troops. In 1640 the General Assembly ordered the interior to be despoiled, and the spoil included the beautiful and highly enriched rood-loft and the paintings thereon.

The main features of the splendid west front of Elgin Cathedral still exist, including the two towers, rising to about 84 feet, the round-headed west window under a pointed arch, now bare of tracery, and the magnificent portal with double entrance, somewhat as at Glasgow, surmounted inside by an arcade of pointed arches. The nave had six bays with double aisles, but only the bases of some of the piers remain, together with a portion of aisle walls and their flowing Decorated tracery. The transepts, 114 feet across, projected but slightly outside the nave aisles. The choir of four bays and two aisles had an ambulatory behind the high altar, leading into a Lady chapel. The beautiful clerestory of double lancets is more than matched by the exquisite double tier of lancets, five in each tier, separated by deeply recessed and beautifully carved piers, the whole surmounted by a large rose window and flanked by two beautiful turrets 60 feet high. There are many details of high interest which will repay the student. The whole church is 282 feet in length.

ELGIN CATHEDRAL: FROM THE SOUTH-WEST.

On the north side is the exquisite octagonal Decorated chapter-house, dating from early in the fifteenth century, 37 feet across and 34 feet high, the finely groined roof being supported on a beautiful central pier. There are seven flamboyant windows, each of four lights. There are still some of the old monuments existing, one an effigy of Hay of Lochbay, 1421. The south choir aisle is used as the burial-place of the Gordon family. Close by the Cathedral are several interesting ruins, including the remains of the bishop's palace.

Dornoch had a Cathedral, the seat of the Bishop of Caithness, built about 1230, but much injured in 1570 during an incursion of Highlanders. Much of it remained, though damaged and neglected, till 1836, when it was "restored" and practically

ELGIN CATHEDRAL EAST END.

destroyed. It was mainly Early English, with single lancet windows, except the west window, which has five lights. The church has a nave, choir, and transepts, and a low spiked spire. The choir piers are circular. In the choir is a monument by Chantrey to the first Duke of Sutherland; sixteen earls of Sutherland are buried here.

The see of Ross had once a beautiful Cathedral of red sandstone, at Fortrose, dating from the beginning of the fourteenth century, and of pure Decorated architecture. The greater part of it was destroyed by Cromwell. The chief remains now existing are the roofless south aisle and part of the chapter-house.

The Cathedral of St. Magnus, Kirkwall, formerly the seat of the Bishop of Orkney, remains more complete than any of the cathedrals last described, and is of remarkable interest, its foundation dating so far back as 1138, when the islands were a Scandinavian possession. It exhibits some of the best features of Norman architecture, although much of it was built after the Decorated period had passed away in England. Externally it is a very homogeneous building, having a nave of eight bays, a choir of four, with a presbytery of two bays, all with aisles, transept with eastern chapels, and central tower. The latter is 133 feet high, and the entire church is 218 feet long (internal); the height to the vault is 71 feet, and thus an appearance of great elevation is given to the interior.

The history of this cathedral is of considerable interest. It was founded by Rognvald, Earl of Orkney, in memory of his uncle the good Earl Magnus, who was murdered in the island of Egilsay, in 1110, by his cousin Hakon. Rognvald built the three western bays of the choir and the transept, with the base of the tower. The five eastern bays of the nave were built by Bishop William I., about 1160. In 1468 the Cathedral, with the islands, became part of the Scottish dominion, being given as security for the dowry of the queen of James III., daughter of Christian of Denmark. The three eastern bays of the choir, including the east window with its fine rose above four vertical lights, were built by Bishop Stewart, about 1511-25; he also gave the bells. The upper portion of the tower is Decorated, built by Bishop Maxwell, 1525. The west front and three western bays of the nave were the work of Bishop Reid about 1540. At one time the steeple was used for a prison, at another was defended as a fortress. In 1614 the Earl of Caithness was about to demolish the Cathedral, and actually destroyed the western portion of the ceiling. The Cromwellian soldiers used the nave as a barrack and stable. In 1671 the steeple was burnt by lightning, and the small square spire that now exists is comparatively modern. The Cathedral was, however, saved from destruction by the Reformers, and had Protestant Bishops down to the Revolution. In 1845 it was repaired and restored at the expense of Government, and in 1883 five windows on the south side of the nave were rebuilt. The nave is used for the worship of the Scottish Established Church. It is of the most massive style of Norman architecture, completed with triforium and clerestory. The circular piers with plain capitals, the semicircular arches with the plainest mouldings, and the simply groined roof are in perfect keeping with the rugged cliffs and boisterous weather of the Orkneys. The choir is of the same character, with a somewhat greater richness of moulding and clustered pillars. The Decorated east window is, of course, of a much later style, while the west front exhibits rich Decorated features in its arched and deeply recessed doorways, the central one being much ornamented with foliage, mixed with zigzag mouldings. The Decorated windows of the tower, too, tend to relieve the sobriety of the Norman design. The huge round tower of the ruined Bishop's palace near by (built by Bishop Reid) adds to the charm of the view.

In 1204 Earl Hakon was buried here after his defeat at Largs, but his body was subsequently removed to Trondhem. In 1290 the child-queen Margaret, the Maid of Norway, was buried in this church.

There is a large slab of white marble over the remains of Earl Robert, and fragments of the crocketed tomb of Bishop Tulloch (fifteenth century) have been found in the south choir aisle. A modern monument has been erected in the north transept to the memory of W. B. Baikie (died 1864), the explorer of the Niger, who was a native of Kirkwall.

For a series of beautiful views of St. Magnus, as of the other Scottish cathedrals as they were before the middle of the present century, every one interested in Scottish antiquities should consult Mr. R. W. Billings's masterly work the "Baronial and Ecclesiastical Antiquities of Scotland."

Whitherne, or Whithorn, in Galloway, was the seat of bishops of Galloway for more than a thousand years. It was noted as the site of the first white stone church (*candida casa*) in Scotland.

KIRKWALL CATHEDRAL: FROM THE NORTH

St. Ninian, who founded it in 397, was buried here, and his shrine became a famous place of pilgrimage. The present ruins date from the end of the twelfth and thirteenth centuries, excepting where they were modified for use as a parish church. They are now roofless, consisting of the choir and a round-arched west end, with a good south-west doorway.

The Cathedral of Iona is so well known, and has been so often described, that it is needless to repeat all that has been written about it. The present ruins, 160 feet long, date from the thirteenth century, being built of red granite. The nave and choir have no aisles, but there are a transept and a central tower 75 feet high, two windows of which have flowing circular tracery within a square heading.

The modernised kirk on the island of Lismore was once a cathedral for the diocese of Argyll; the Decorated choir only remains, and is absorbed into the parish church.

THE RUINS OF IONA CATHEDRAL.

ST. PATRICK'S CATHEDRAL, DUBLIN: EXTERIOR.

THE IRISH CATHEDRALS.

"WHATEVER opinion may be formed as to the dates of Irish buildings," says Mr. J. H. Parker,[1] "there can be no doubt of their very distinct national character, and that they are highly interesting, and deserve to be better known throughout Europe than has hitherto been the case." The Irish had no Roman buildings from which to learn architecture, and their early attempts were more related to the cromlechs and cairns of their ancestors, or at any rate predecessors, than to any other style. From an early period

---

[1] "Notes on the Architecture of Ireland," *Gentleman's Magazine*; collected in one volume in the British Museum.

conquests and domestic broils enfeebled Ireland's powers, and it was not till the English settled in Ireland that buildings of permanent architectural value were erected in Ireland, sometimes enclosing the rude masonry of early Christian cells or places of worship. In general these buildings are later in date than those of corresponding architecture in England. Yet there are not wanting distinctive Irish traits even in these.

The first place among the Irish cathedrals is justly due to the Cathedral of St. Patrick, extending between Patrick and Kevin Streets, Dublin; it has been a cathedral of the diocese of Dublin since the beginning of the thirteenth century, and in 1872 was adopted by the Synod of the (Disestablished) Episcopal Church of Ireland as a national cathedral, having a common relation to all the dioceses of the Church of Ireland, with stalls for the Archbishops of Armagh and Dublin, as well as the Irish bishops. It occupies the site of an early parish church, said to have been founded by St. Patrick. In 1190 the first English Archbishop of Dublin, John de Comyn, took down the old church, and built a collegiate church; it was dedicated in 1191. His successor, Henry of London, made the church a cathedral, and probably built the eastern part of the nave. It is supposed that Archbishop Fulk de Sandford built the Lady chapel. In 1362 part of the Cathedral was burnt, and it was rebuilt by Archbishop Thomas Minot, in 1372. He also built the north-west tower; the octagonal granite spire, which is quite uninteresting, was added in 1705. Previously to this the Cathedral had gone through many remarkable periods. In 1492 the Yorkists and Lancastrians came to blows in it, and the Earl of Ormond, after a conference with the Earl of Kildare, the Lord Deputy, fled into the chapter-house to escape the arrows of the archers. Dean Bassenet, in 1540, surrendered the revenues and estates of the cathedral to Henry VIII., and it was suppressed in 1547, reconstituted by Philip and Mary in 1554, and desecrated by the Cromwellians in 1651. In 1661 the French Protestant refugees were allowed to worship in the Lady chapel. Many other interesting events are recorded in the history of this Cathedral,[1] among which we can only mention

---

[1] See Canon Leeper's "Historical Handbook to the Cathedral Church of St. Patrick, Dublin."

the energetic deanship of Jonathan Swift (1713-45), and the munificent restoration by Sir Benjamin Lee Guinness, Bart., which was completed in 1865, having cost £140,000.

St. Patrick's is a complete cross church, both nave, and choir, and transepts having two aisles each. The choir aisles project east of the choir to a considerable length, flanking the low Lady chapel. The whole building may be described as Early English, though externally many of its features have suffered damage or

ST. PATRICK'S CATHEDRAL: INTERIOR, LOOKING WEST.

been modernised. The lancet windows and the plain buttresses are surmounted by late and inferior pinnacles. The turrets at the corners of the tower and elsewhere exhibit a notable Irish peculiarity, being formed of series of steps facing one another. The choir has flying buttresses over the aisles, and one of the buttresses at each angle is carried diagonally. The north and south aisles, says Canon Leeper, were completely rebuilt by Sir Benjamin Guinness, who added a north and a south porch, repaired the clerestory, entirely restored the triforium, removed the great west Perpendicular window, and set up a good Early English window of three lights in its place, rebuilt the flying buttresses, and placed stained glass in the windows. He also renewed the throne, the stalls, and other fittings of the choir, provided a new organ, completed the peal of bells, and placed an ornamental cross upon the summit of the spire. Much objection has been justly taken to various parts of the restoration, which have to a considerable extent made a new Cathedral, which looks even newer than it is.

It is generally agreed that the interior of the Cathedral has been more satisfactorily restored than the exterior. The nave, of eight bays, has its pointed arches supported on octagonal piers without regular capitals, there being merely a string-course running round the top of the pier, and the principal mouldings rising from corbels. The mouldings of the eastern arches are of much better Early English style than the western.

The choir contains the richly carved stalls for the Knights of the Order of St. Patrick and the prebendaries. The archbishop's throne and dean's stall are designed after those of Chester Cathedral. Within the communion-rails are two Gothic chairs, carved out of beams of old Irish oak, which formerly supported the roof. The pulpit, at the east corner of the north transept, leading into the choir, given in memory of Dean Pakenham (died 1863), is an octagonal one of Caen stone and Irish coloured marbles. Six finely carved figures, representing the Evangelists and the Apostles Peter and Paul, occupy the angles. An elaborate Decorated sounding-board has been placed over the pulpit. The organ, in the second bay of the north side of the choir, has been built by Bevington and Sons, utilising about three hundred pipes of the old organ.

In the baptistery, just west of the south porch, perhaps the most ancient part of the Cathedral, is the medieval square font, with a circular basin. Close to it is an effigy supposed to be that of Archbishop Fulk de Sandford (died 1256), who was buried in the Lady chapel. On the opposite side is Archbishop Tregury's granite tombstone (1449). The archbishop is represented in low relief in his pontifical robes. Dean Swift preserved this monument, found among rubbish in St. Stephen's Chapel (part of the Lady chapel). The floor of the baptistery consists of old encaustic tiles from the south transept. The small three-light window

ST. PATRICK'S CATHEDRAL DUBLIN: THE NAVE AND CHOIR, LOOKING EAST.

represents St. Patrick in the centre, St. Peter on the right, and St. Paul on the left. Beneath this is an old chest beautifully carved, formerly used to preserve many valuables. The massive stone figure of an ecclesiastic, long supposed to be Archbishop Comyn, is built into the wall on the right of the window, but there are reasons for believing that it represents St. Patrick. Here may also be seen the old door of the Lady chapel, and the old pulpit, used, among others, by Dean Swift. Above the baptistery there was formerly held the school of the Cathedral, dating from 1547.

The many important monuments in this Cathedral can only be briefly referred to. Beginning at the west end, on the right of the arch of the south-west porch is a head of Dean Pakenham, in limestone, and on the left that of Archbishop Usher. On the right side of the exterior, in the churchyard, is a statue of Sir B. Guinness, in a sitting posture, erected in 1875. Inside the porch, on the right side of the door leading into the robing-room, is a fine bust of Dean Swift, executed by Cunningham for Alderman Faulkner, his publisher, and given by the latter's nephew to the Cathedral. Beside the bust is Swift's monument, with his own famous inscription. He was buried here on October 22nd, 1745, "at the foot of the second column from St. Patrick's Gate (south-western)." Above, and on the right of the door before mentioned, is the inscription to Swift's "Stella," who was buried by torchlight on January 30th, 1727-8, close to Swift.

Near the west end, on the south side, is the lofty monument, of black stone and alabaster, of the Cork family, erected by Richard Boyle, Earl of Cork, early in Charles I.'s reign, and now containing sixteen figures of various members of the family, including Robert Boyle, the famous philosopher. This monument formerly occupied the position of the high altar, and was removed to the south side of the altar by Laud's influence and Stafford's co-operation. A fine statue, by Farrell, of Capt. Boyd, R.N., drowned in attempting to save a ship's crew at Kingstown, in 1861, is between the first two pillars of the north side of the nave.

In the north nave aisle, proceeding from the west, we find monuments to John Philpot Curran (bust by Moore, 1841), who died 1817; the Earl of Cavan; Archbishop Jones (died 1619); Carolan, one of the last Irish bards (died 1738); Dean Dawson (died 1842), the statue of the Marquis of Buckingham, near an old stone coffin; and a marble slab commemorating Samuel Lover, novelist and composer (died 1866). In the north transept, among others, may be noticed the monument of Bishop Meredyth (died 1597) and several regimental and military memorials. The Duke of Schomberg's monument is against the north front of the transept, and records Swift's epitaph, censuring the Duke's heirs who would pay nothing towards its cost. Archbishop Whately's (died 1863) memorial shows his recumbent figure, robed, by Farrell; it is in the north-east corner.

In the south transept, among numerous others, are the monuments of Archbishop Marsh (died 1713), Sir Mazière Brady (died 1871), Archbishop Smyth (died 1771), and Dean Swift's faithful servant Alexander McGee. Among those in the south choir aisle will be noticed that of the Rev. Charles Wolfe (died 1823), author of the famous poem on the burial of Sir John Moore. The brasses of Deans Sutton (died 1528) and Fyche (died 1537) and of Sir Edward Ffiton (died 1569) are well worthy of careful inspection.

Beginning with the Lady chapel, we will now note some of the stained-glass windows, most of which are modern. The east window of the Lady chapel (a triplet of lancets), a memorial to Dean Pakenham (died 1863), is a brilliant yet delicate work, by Wailes, of Newcastle. A three-light window at the east end of the south choir aisle is by Clayton and Bell, in memory of John Smith, Mus. Doc. (died 1861); the design illustrates Divine worship and praise, David being represented in the centre with his harp. In the east wall of the north transept is a window to the men of the 18th Royal Irish Regiment who fell at Sebastopol. Other windows, by Dublin artists, are in this transept. At the west end of the north nave aisle is a window in memory of Earl Mayo, assassinated in the Andaman Islands in 1872. The middle west window, by Wailes, illustrates the life and labours of St. Patrick. Opposite the north porch, in the south aisle, is a window in memory of Sir John Stevenson, Mus. Doc. (died 1833), erected in 1864 by Sir R. P. Stewart. He was the joint author, with Thomas Moore, of the "Irish Melodies."

Finally we may note the turret clock, which plays four hymn-tunes at intervals, and the ten bells, some not recast sin e 1670.

Christchurch Cathedral, a little west of Dublin Castle, has a longer history even than St. Patrick's; it is said to have been founded early in the eleventh century by Sihtric, king of the Ostmen (Danes) of Dublin, there being already "arches and vaults" situate there. Donat was the bishop who built this early Cathedral, apparently the nave, aisles, and a north chapel of St. Nicholas; he died in 1074, and was buried on the south side of the altar. The only remnant of this Cathedral is perhaps the portion of the crypt under the transept, ruder in masonry than the rest, and having rounded arches.

Laurence O'Toole became Archbishop of Dublin in 1162, and in 1163 changed the foundation of Holy Trinity into a priory. After Strongbow's invasion he combined with him and others to enlarge the Cathedral, adding a choir, central tower, and two chapels, probably the transepts. Of this church the transepts and two arches of the choir remain. During this time Archbishops Comyn, Henry of London, and Luke followed one another. In 1283 a fire destroyed the tower, chapter-house, and parts of the adjacent monastery. A long period of reconstruction followed, and it was not till 1329 that the stone tower was begun. Between 1349 and 1362 John de Paul, Archbishop of Dublin, built the chancel, the great east window, and three other south windows. In 1562 the stone vault of the nave fell, destroying the greater part of the south arcade and of the west front and south aisle. The southern arcade was replaced by a blank wall in the same year, and the stone roof by mean and naked rafters. The rest was a long time rebuilding. In 1588 the steeple cracked, and had to be taken down.

St. Mary's Chapel, on the north side of the choir, was built at a later date, and continued in use till this century, when it was converted into dwelling-houses. In 1831 there was a restoration which almost destroyed, at any rate concealed effectually, all the original work in the choir, injuring it greatly.

There was early a rivalry between this church, dedicated to the Holy Trinity, and the newer foundation of St. Patrick's; but in 1300 it was agreed that each church should be styled Cathedral and Metropolitan, but that the archbishops should be consecrated in Holy Trinity, and should be buried alternately in each church.

In 1541 Henry VIII. changed the "prior and convent of the Cathedral of the Holy Trinity" into a dean and chapter, and from this time it became known as Christ Church.

Before recounting the recent transformation of the Cathedral by Mr. Street, we shall give a summary of his account of its former structure.* The crypt furnished the most valuable indications, showing, as he believed, the outline of the choir before Archbishop John de St. Paul enlarged it. The crypt proper extends only twenty-

CHRISTCHURCH CATHEDRAL, DUBLIN: FROM THE SOUTH EAST.

five feet east of the central tower; it has a semicircular apse, and the aisle is continued round the apse; east of this are three small square portions or chapels. The crypt under the rest of the church follows its general plan, stopping short of the western bay of the nave, and apparently formerly extended under the south aisle.

* See Mr. Street's Report on the restoration, 1868, but especially the magnificent volume on "Christ Church Cathedral," 1882, by Mr. Street, with an historical sketch by the Rev. E. Seymour, and many exquisite steel and wood engravings and chromo-lithographs.

Mr. Street believed that this crypt was of uniform age throughout, dating from Strongbow's time, and that the whole of the choir was then built on the same plan, and so remained till the middle of the fourteenth century. All the eastern part was slightly earlier than the western, being Transitional Norman, though contemporary with Early English work in England. The nave appears to have been completed before 1225. It was only in agreement with what had taken place after the end of the twelfth century all over Europe that the short early choir should have been destroyed. At first a large Lady Chapel was built outside the Cathedral, at the north-east angle, and entered from a western porch; its axis was not parallel to that of the church. The choir was then extended to 102 feet (instead of about 30 feet) the south wall of the Lady Chapel being used, and the axis of the church being consequently deflected to the north. It was very inferior to the nave and transepts. When Mr. Street investigated the structure the old columns and arches of the south side of the nave were not discoverable, except a part of the eastern arch. The stone groining of the nave had fallen, and on the site of the old south aisle there were a series of vestries and a chapter-room.

On the south side of the choir was a modern entrance with a vestry, and on its north side were decayed buildings occupying the site of an old Lady Chapel. The central tower was supported on arches rudely wrought in limestone and covered with whitewash; the tower itself was solidly built, but mean and bad in all its details. The transepts had but one ancient feature externally, the south doorway (Norman), formerly in the north transept, and inside they had been much disfigured with whitewash, and had mean lath and plaster vaults. The north nave wall was in a dangerous state; the piers, built of small pieces of freestone with an interior of limestone rubble, were cracked and bulging in all directions. The triforium and clerestory were much out of the perpendicular. The groining of the north aisle had fallen, and the north aisle wall, being out of the perpendicular, had been propped up by an enormous mass of masonry outside, like a vast continuous buttress, thus closing (and preserving) all the windows. The south wall of the nave had been rebuilt with old pointed arches, and using up old stonework; but for its known history and the inscription, it might almost have been mistaken for the original wall. The west end was entirely modernised, having large buttresses and a mean round-headed window.

The choir was shut off from the rest of the church by a solid screen. Three old chevroned (Norman) arches, and a fifteenth-century piscina, and other fragments were the only old features left. The walls were covered with wretched plaster panelling, cornices, and pinnacles. The floor was badly paved, and the choir aisles had galleries. The organ was on the screen between the choir and the tower. Throughout the church not one ancient window remained open. Outside the church there was scarcely a single old wrought stone left; the tower was completely modern (*i.e.*, seventeenth or eighteenth century).

In 1870 Christchurch was fast falling into ruin, and the disestablishment of the Irish Church appeared to take away all hopes of its restoration. On March 31st, 1871, Mr. Henry Roe, of Mount Annville Park, offered to restore the building at his own charge, under Mr. Street's direction, Messrs. Gilbert Cockburn and Son being selected as builders. His liberality grew with Mr. Street's development of his designs, till at last he added all, or nearly all, the fittings of the church, and built the new Synod Hall for the Disestablished Church, the total cost being increased to £250,000. The restoration and rebuilding of the Cathedral was begun in 1871, and completed in 1878, the Cathedral being reopened on May 1st of the latter year. The *Saturday Review* of May 18th, 1878, says of the work, "Not a stone has been removed which was worth keeping, and every fragment of this ancient building has been preserved. We know of no modern restoration which is more legitimate or more interesting. It is the recovery of a great historical monument."

Beginning with the exterior of the west end, it is now once more of an excellent design. The new rich double-arched doorway, under a single larger arch, utilises a jamb of the original doorway; the tympanum has a carving of the Agnus Dei. The west window, of five lancets, the middle taller, and the others diminishing to the sides, has been rebuilt from the original jamb and details. Above is a rose window in the gable. The west front has adequate buttresses to nave and aisles, and short turrets at the corners of the gable, and the flying buttresses to the nave wall are visible, as well as the baptistery on the north side. The flying buttresses referred to are new constructions, due to the adoption of stone groining for the roof. The navé clerestory windows, with their peculiar triplets and arcades above, have been restored as they were undoubtedly built. The somewhat elaborate buttresses of the aisles, as well as their lancet windows, are also good restorations of the original design. The baptistery replaces an old chamber of unknown use; it has three bays externally, with two lancets in each, and elaborate buttresses.

STRONGBOW'S EFFIGY.

Both south and north transepts have been restored to their proper Norman Transitional style, with round-headed windows in two stages, above an old round-arched doorway on the south side, having fine shafts and chevron work. In the gable is a rose window, and it is flanked by two turrets, replacing bad ones, it is true, but scarcely the most successful part of Mr. Street's work. The central tower, while still retaining its main lines and masonry, has had much-improved belfry windows inserted, with triplet lights, and a new parapet and angle turrets, and a timber spire, slate-covered, have been added. It should be said that all the battlements have been renewed after the Irish step pattern. To the eight bells formerly in the tower four more have been added, including a tenor, nearly two tons in weight; also a clock with chimes, and a carillon machine, playing twenty-eight tunes.

The exterior view of the east end is very interesting and almost unique, the apsidal choir, the three square chapels, and the staircase turrets leading to the roofs combining very effectively with the tower, though the unequal sides of the apse are not quite harmonious. Most of the new external work has been done in costly hard limestone instead of the Caen stone originally used. Altogether, the exterior of Christ Church, if not nearly so effective as the interior, is superior to that of several English cathedrals.

Beginning a review of the interior from the choir, which has witnessed the most remarkable transformation, it is interesting that Mr. Street's surmises from the shape of the crypt should have received strong confirmation from the discovery of three old arches and other wrought stonework, giving the slope of the side of the apse. Thus the apse has been reconstructed, with two

CHRISTCHURCH CATHEDRAL, DUBLIN: THE CRYPT.

wider and two narrower arches and an eastern wider one, and the upper part of the wider portions has been furnished with two-light windows and arches. As so arranged, they come precisely over the old foundations in the crypt. The same essential style, late Transitional Norman, has been carried out in the triforium and clerestory, which in each bay are included within the same enclosing columns, and in all the rich and varied treatment of chevron, nail-head, and dog-tooth ornament is admirable. The wall spaces have been richly diapered with carvings and mouldings. The roofs of apse, aisles, etc., are vaulted in stone, and the principal niches are all richly chevroned, the new interior work being in Caen stone.

The eastern chapels and the aisles round the apse are elaborate and interesting and very effective. The walls are all arcaded below the lancet windows with richly carved capitals, and there is a continuous seat beneath. The coupled shafts round the apse have their capitals excellently carved by Mr. Taylerson from Mr. Street's designs, representing the Annunciation and subjects from the early history of Christ.

The transepts have been left in their comparatively simple guise, evidently the earliest part of the church. The old round-arched doorway (p. 279), though not in its original site (in the north transept), has not been removed from the south wall, and the fine chevron work and richly carved capitals are consequently undisturbed. A new chapel of St. Lawrence O'Toole has been built eastward from the south transept, on the discovered foundations of the old one. The effigy of St. Lawrence has been placed under one trefoiled recess, and that of a lady of the thirteenth century, found just outside this chapel, under a corresponding recess. The round arch opening into this chapel is of old stonework. Notable features in the transept are the pointed arches with chevron ornament opening into choir and nave aisles, the string-course above the lower stage, the round arches in the triforium, each enclosing two pointed arches, all enriched with chevron mouldings. The south wall is mostly new in its details, but has been left rough and unplastered. A stone vault has been added instead of the modern plastered one. The north transept, in place of the eastern chapel, has an eastern doorway leading into a little close. The north-west staircase has been restored, and now gives access to the organ-gallery. The old blocked up and dilapidated arches have been repaired and opened up, and some carved capitals which had been covered up have been once more exposed. A new organ gallery, stone groined, has been built across the northern half of this transept, so as to conceal its features as little as possible. The appearance of the entire transept, as well as the view through the Cathedral from east to west, has been remarkably improved by the raising of the tower arches ten feet by Mr. Street's most ingenious method, making the old arches support the tower till the new ones, very strong arches of brickwork in cement, abutting on Portland stone springers, had been inserted piecemeal above them. Then the new carved and moulded stone arches were inserted immediately under the brick arches. The piers were re-dressed, and clusters of marble shafts placed in front of them. The tower, like the rest of the church, has a stone groined roof, with an opening in the centre for the passage of bells.

CHRISTCHURCH CATHEDRAL, DUBLIN:
NORMAN DOORWAY OF SOUTH TRANSEPT.

The nave, the most beautiful part of the old design, has now fully recovered its beauty. The columns (now renewed or rebuilt) are even more elaborately clustered than those of Wells; eight filleted shafts are attached to a column, octofoil in section; and the shafts have a triple band in their centre. The capitals are all carved with exquisite conventional foliage of the thirteenth century; and they now show fresh, having been freed from the whitewash that had defaced them. The capitals on the south side are all new, and are no disgrace to the old ones. In one will be found, introduced by Mr. Thomas Earp, the emblems of the Evangelists, the angel, the winged eagle, the lion, and the ox. In another are the heads of the Primate, the Archbishop of Dublin, Mr. Roe, and Mr. Street. The upper part of the nave walls is equally beautiful and more original: clerestory and triforium are grouped in one design, and it may be said that the triplet in which it is designed is pierced at the upper part as a window, and below as a triforium. The groining shafts are continued from portions of the nave columns; but the work of strengthening the columns and the nave walls so as to be able to receive the stone vaults was one of the most arduous which Mr. Street ever undertook. The south nave aisle is entirely new, except fragments which were carefully made use of. The north aisle windows were reopened, and the new baptistery added. It has six bays of stone groining, carved on delicate clustered marble shafts, and with the wall arcading pierced for windows. A costly inlaid marble font, a rich pavement of encaustic tiles, a wrought-iron open-work door, and stained-glass windows make this a most effective addition to the church.

The two effigies supposed to be those of Strongbow and his son have again been placed side by side under one of the new arches on the south side of the nave. The former has details which prove it to belong to the end of the thirteenth century.

The pavement of the nave has been reconstructed from remains of the original pavement. There were sixty-three different patterns, and these have been copied and repeated, and having scarcely any plain tiles among them, make, as Mr. Street says, "probably the most gorgeous pavement of the sort ever laid."

The choir, including the space under the tower, has been divided from the nave by an open screen of stone, alabaster and marble, of five cinquefoiled arches, the centre largest, with a carved and perforated cornice. Over the doorway is carved an Agnus Dei, and above is a copy of the well-known cross of Cong. The gates are elaborate ones of brass. The carved oak altar, archbishop's throne and stall, the wrought-iron screen in the arches of

CHRISTCHURCH CATHEDRAL DUBLIN THE APSE AND EASTERN CHAPEL.

the apse are all worthy of their place in Christchurch. The pulpit, at the north-east corner of the nave, is of stone and marble, with statues of the four Evangelists in the niches.

The stained glass has been inserted, in accordance with a uniform scheme, by Messrs. Clayton and Bell, choir and transepts and chapels; Hardman and Powell, the nave, excepting the clerestory; and James Bell, nave clerestory. The nave aisle illustrates the types or figures of Christ in the Old Testament history; the west window of the nave has a fine tree of Jesse; the transepts have single figures of the twelve Apostles; the choir aisles illustrate the life of Christ; the Crucifixion is shown in the east window of the central eastern chapel, seen behind the altar, and also in the south transept; St. Lawrence O'Toole's chapel contains representations of the four patron saints of the United Kingdom; the clerestory of the choir contains the four Evangelists, the four Doctors of the Church, and the Ascension and Descent of the Holy Ghost in the central window. The baptistery windows, given by Mr. Street in memory of his wife, who died in 1876, have beautiful representations of saints. The clerestory of the nave has grisaille glass, with the arms of all the Irish sees which can be ascertained. Several windows are special memorials; the rest were the gift of Mr. Roe.

The Cathedral was reopened on May 1st, 1878.

Armagh Cathedral is celebrated as having been founded by St. Patrick himself in the fifth century A.D., but none of his building remains. A succession of fires and devastations have caused it to be again and again rebuilt; but some of the existing building is the work of Archbishop Sweteman, who in 1365 rebuilt the nave and its aisles, the piers, arches, and clerestory of which remain. The nave has four pointed arches on either side, and the aisles are lighted by Perpendicular windows. A massive but low tower rises at the intersection of nave, choir, and transepts. The west end has a triplet of lancet windows. During the last century the Cathedral was greatly injured both by neglect and by bad "restoration." Archbishop Stuart, in 1802, did still worse, erecting galleries and placing the altar at the west end. Another restoration took place in 1834, at the cost of Archbishop Lord John Beresford, under Mr. Cottingham as architect. He took down the wooden spire, rebuilt the piers and arches of the tower, opened out the clerestory, and straightened the arcade walls, which were seriously out of the perpendicular; but a great deal of lath and plaster was inserted, and much cutting away of the face of the old stonework took place. This year (1888) the reopening of the Cathedral after yet another restoration has taken place. The modern screen between choir and nave has been removed to the south transept, the whole of the nave, choir, and south transept have been reseated, and a new pulpit has been erected under the tower. The Cathedral contains numerous good monuments by Roubiliac, Chantrey, etc. The Cathedral is only 183 feet long, and 119 feet across the transepts.

The Cathedral of St. Fin Barre, Cork, is one of the most noteworthy examples of modern architecture. It occupies the site of the church built by St. Fin Barre about the beginning of the seventh century, which was succeeded by a later church, which was in a very decayed state, in the seventeenth century. In 1735 a new Cathedral was begun. It was naturally an inferior work, being built when it was, and in 1861 it was resolved to form a fund for building a new Cathedral. In 1862 the plan of Mr. William Burges, of London, was accepted, providing for the completion and roofing of the church without towers for a sum of £15,000. This building was completed in 1870, and consecrated on November 30th of that year. In 1875 Mr. F. Wise offered the sum of £20,000 to complete the central tower and spire, and Mr. W. H. Crawford £10,000 to complete the two western towers and spires. In 1877 Mr. Crawford further offered to complete the carving on the west front, including the statuary in the three portals, at a cost of £8,300. On April 6th, 1878, Bishop John Gregg laid the top stones of the western spires, and died on May 26th following. On October 23rd, 1879, his successor, Bishop R. S. Gregg, laid the topmost stone of the central tower.

This Cathedral is the most successful monument of Mr. Burges' great skill as an architect. It is French thirteenth century Gothic in style, with two western towers and plain octagonal spires, 180 feet high, with angle turrets, central tower and plain octagonal spire 240 feet high, also with angle turrets, large rose windows at west end and in north and south transepts, and semicircular apse and ambulatory. The total internal length is 162 feet 6 inches, and width with aisles 56 feet 6 inches; the transept is 81 feet 6 inches across, and 24 feet 8 inches wide, but only projects 12 feet 6 inches from the nave aisles. The apse is 28 feet 6 inches long, and the ambulatory is 11 feet 6 inches wide. The nave roof rises to 68 feet. The lantern of the central tower rises 101 feet above the pavement of the choir. A large number of the windows have already been filled with stained glass, many as special memorials. The oaken bishop's throne, given by the clergy and laity of the diocese, as a memorial of Bishop John Gregg, at a cost of nearly £1,500, is 46 feet high, and is very elaborate. On the three wooden panels enclosing the seat are carved twenty heads of eminent prelates who have filled the see of Cork, beginning with St. Fin Barre. The upper part is turreted and crocketed, and has appropriate carved emblems. The mosaic pavement of the apse is of remarkable design, by Mr. Burges, illustrating Matt. xiii. 47, and the parables of the sower, the lost sheep, and the grain of mustard-seed. This costly work, executed in Paris by Italian artists, was one of the last gifts of Bishop John Gregg. The lectern, given by the ladies of the diocese, is a most elaborate and beautiful one. All the internal details were most carefully designed and superintended by Mr. Burges. Some parts of his designs are not yet carried out for lack of funds. For full details Dr. Caulfield's Handbook should be consulted. The doorway which we represent is the only ancient feature in the building, having been removed from the old building.

ANCIENT DOORWAY: CORK CATHEDRAL.

The churches or ruins of churches in Ireland that were formerly, or are now, cathedrals are exceedingly numerous, and their full

CORK CATHEDRAL.

description would fill a separate volume. Among those which contain noteworthy features we may particularise those of Cashel, Clonmacnois, Cloyne, Kildare, Kilkenny, Limerick, Lismore, Londonderry, and Tuam. Only at the first two of these are there still existing round towers, or belfries, of the type frequently found dating from considerably before the English conquest of Ireland. There is a very early Norman arch in Killaloe Cathedral, with diamonds, spirals, and chevrons. Cormac's Chapel, adjacent to and earlier than the present Cathedral of Cashel, is a most interesting Norman Church, having a transept formed by two square towers at the junction of nave and choir. The barrel vaults, the square apse, and the latter being not median but at the S.E. angle of the nave, and many other features make the church quite unique. It dates from about 1127. Scarcely later is the chancel of the old church of Tuam with its fine arch and triplet east window.

DOWNPATRICK CATHEDRAL.

INDEX TO ST. PAUL'S CATHEDRAL.

Anne, Queen, Statue of, 13
Bacon, Sculptor, 19
Bells, 13, 24
Bell Tower, Old, 2
Bird, F., Sculptor, 3, 12
Bishop of London's Palace, 2
Bishop's Throne, 18
Charles II., 9
Choir, 14, 15, 18
Choir Screen, 18
Clock, 13
Cloisters, Old, 2
Cost, 20
Crypt, 15, 26
Decoration, 19, 22
Design of St. Paul's, 10
Dimensions of Old St. Paul's, 4
Dome, 14, 15, 16, 17, 18, 22
Elevation, 11
Exterior, 10-15
Fire, the Great, 7
First St. Paul's, 1
Gatehouses, Old, 2
Interior, 15-30
James I. at St. Paul's, 6
James II., 9
Lantern, 14
Library, 16, 27
Milman, Dean, 21
Modern History of, 21-30
Monuments in Old St. Paul's, 6, 7
" Modern, 19, 24
" National, 19, 24, 25

Mosaics, 22
Nave, 14, 15
Nelson, Lord, 15, 24, 27
New St. Paul's, Building of, 9
Organ, 18, 22
Paul's Cross, 2, 22
" Walk, 4
Portico, 10, 11, 12
" of Transepts, 13
Portland Stone, 10
Pulpit, 18
Railings, 22
Reredos, New, 27-30
Restoration, 21-26
Second St. Paul's, 1-7
Spire, Old, 4
Stalls, 18
Steeples, 13
St. Faith's Church, 2, 3
St. Paul's School, 3
Thornhill, Sir J., Painter, 18
Tower, Old Central, 4
Towers, 12, 13, 24
Transepts, 13
Vaulting, 15
Wellington, Duke of, Monument of, 24, 25
Wellington, Sarcophagus of, 27
West Front, 10-12
Whispering Gallery, 16
Windows, 22, 23
Wren, Sir C., 9, 11, 12, 16, 17

INDEX TO PETERBOROUGH CATHEDRAL.

Abbey, History of, 31-34
Abbots, Privileges of, 36, 37
Apse of Choir, 44, 46
Bishops, 45
Cathedral, Building of, 35
" History of, 35, 36
Choir, 40, 43, 44
Clerestory, 42
Cloisters, 45
Decoration, 46
De Vecti, Martin, Abbot, 35
Dimensions, 45
Diocese, 31
Establishment, 37
Exterior, 38-41
Interior, 41-45
Lady Chapel, 40

Lantern, 41
Lawrence, St., 31
Medeshamsted, Monastery of, 31-34
Modern History, 46-49
Monk, Bp., 37
Monuments, 48, 49
Nave, 39, 41, 42
New Building, 49
Organ Screen, 44
Pulpit, 46
Tower, Central, 41, 43, 47
Towers, Western, 39, 40, 41
Transepts, 40, 41, 43, 46
Triforium, 42
West Front, 38, 39
Windows, 46

INDEX TO CHESTER CATHEDRAL.

Abbey, History of, 52-54
Altar, 73
Bells, 65
Bishops, 63
Bishop's Throne, 61, 75
Brassey Memorial Chapel, 75
Canon's Vestry, 74
Cathedral, the Norman, 54, 55
Chapter-house, 58, 61, 66
Chester, Early Christianity in, 50
Choir, 58, 60, 65, 71
   „ Screen, 71
Clerestory, 57, 59, 60, 66
Cloisters, 61, 79
Dimensions, 62
Diocese, 62
Establishment, 62
Exterior, 56-59
Interior, 59-61, 68-80
Lady Chapel, 58, 65, 77

Modern History, 64-82
Monuments, 68, 78, 79
Mosaics, 75, 81
Nave, 57, 58, 59, 60
Norman Remains, 54, 55, 74
Organ, 60, 65, 70
Pavement, 72
Porch, West, 56
Pulpits, 65, 68, 71
Refectory, 59, 61, 81
Stalls, 71
St. Werburgh's Shrine, 61, 65, 75
Tower, Central, 59, 66, 77
Transept, North, 60, 64, 66, 68
   „ South, 57, 60, 70, 71
Vaulting, 68, 71, 72, 74, 75
West Entrance, 56
West Front, 56
West Window, 56
Windows, 56, 58, 59, 70, 77, 78

INDEX TO CARLISLE CATHEDRAL.

Bishops, 88, 89
Chapter-house, 88
Choir, 85, 87
Clerestory, 85, 86, 87, 88
Dimensions, 90
Diocese, 90
Early History, 83, 84
East Window, 85
Establishment, 90
Exterior, 84-86
Interior, 87
Law, Bp., 92
Modern History, 93

Monuments, 90
Nave, 85, 87
Organ, 96
Roof, 87, 93
St. Catherine's Chapel, 86, 88
Stern, Bp., 91
Tower, 86
Transepts, 85, 86, 87, 93
Usher, Abp., 91
West Front, 84
Window, East, 85, 89, 93
Windows, 93, 96

INDEX TO RIPON CATHEDRAL.

Abbots, 101
Building, 101
Chapter-house, 109, 114
Choir, 104, 105, 107, 113, 114
Clerestory, 103, 104, 106, 107
Collegiate Church, 97
Crypt, 108
Dimensions, 108
Early History, 97-100
East End, 104
Establishment, 109
Exterior, 102-106
Interior, 106-108
Library, 109
Longley, Bp., 110
Modern History, 111-116
Monuments, 108
Nave, 103, 105, 106, 111, 113
Organ, 107, 115
Painting, Fresco, 115
Screen, 107
Stalls, 107, 108
Tower, Central, 105, 106, 107, 115
Towers, West, 102, 111, 113
Transepts, 103, 105, 107, 115
Vaulting, 107, 113
West Front, 102, 113
Wilfrid, St., 97-99
Window, East, 104, 107, 111
Windows, 115, 116

INDEX TO MANCHESTER CATHEDRAL.

Both, John, 121
Chantries or Chapels, 123-125, 127-129
Chapter House, 130, 133
Choir, 128
Clerestory, 126
Collegiate Church, Building of, 123
            „   Foundation, History of, 118-123
De la Warre, Thomas, 118-120
Diocese, 117
Exterior, 125, 126
Font, 133
Fraser, Bp., 117
Huntington, John, 120
Interior, 126-130
Jesus Chantry, 129, 133
Lady Chapel, 124
Lee, Prince, Bp., 117
Modern History, 131-135
Monuments, 135
Nave, 126, 133
Organ, 135
Porch, South, 126
Reredos, 135
Roofs, 135
Screens, 124
Stanley, Bp., 125
Stanley Chapel, 124, 133
St. George's Chantry, 127
St. James's Chantry, 128
St. John the Baptist's Chantry, 129
St. Mary's Chantry, 130
St. Nicholas' Chantry, 127, 133
Tower, 125, 133
Wardens, 120-123
Windows, 135

INDEX TO SOUTHWELL CATHEDRAL.

Chapter-house, 145, 153, 154
Choir, 145, 147, 152, 153
Christian, Mr. Ewan, 139
Clerestory, 142, 149, 152
Cloister Passage, 154
Collegiate Body, 140
" Church, 137-139
Dimensions, 155
Diocese, 137
East End, 147
Exterior, 140-147
Gateways, 155
History of, 139
Interior, 147-155
Lectern, 153
Library, Former, 145, 153
" Present, 153
Monuments, 153
Mosaic Pavement, 150
Nave, 142, 143, 147, 149
Norman Church, 138

North Transept Chapel, 145, 150, 153
Organ, 152
Organ Screen, 152
Palace of Archbishops, 155
Paulinus, Abp., 138
Porch, North, 143
Restoration, 139, 140
Roofs, 143, 145, 147, 149, 150
Sandys, Abp., 153
Spires, 142
Stalls, 153
Tower, Central, 142, 143, 145, 149
Towers, West, 142
Transeptal Chapels, 145, 147
Transepts, 143, 149, 150
Triforium, 149, 152
Vestibule of Chapter-house, 154
West Front, 142
Windows, East, 155
" West, 142
" of Chapter-house, 154

INDEX TO NEWCASTLE CATHEDRAL.

Bells, 160
Building, 158
Chapel of the Incarnation, 163
Chapels, 163
Choir, 162
Dimensions, 164
Diocese, Ancient, 157
" Modern, 158
Exterior, 159-162
Font, 163, 164
History, 158, 159

Interior, 162-164
Monuments, 164
Nave, 162
Norman Church, 158, 159
Paintings, 163
Reredos, 163
Restorations, 158, 159
Steeple, 160
Tower, 159, 160
Windows, 162, 193

INDEX TO WAKEFIELD CATHEDRAL.

Bells, 168
Choir, 168
Clerestory, 168
Dimensions, 170
Diocese, 165
Exterior, 168
Galleries, 166, 169
History, 166
Nave, 168
Norman Church, 166
Organ, 166, 169

Pilkington Chantry, 170
Porch, South, 168
Reredos, 166, 170
Restorations, 166
Roofs, 168
Screen, 170
Spire, 166, 168
Stalls, 170
Tower, 166, 168
Windows, 166, 168, 170

INDEX TO WELSH CATHEDRALS.

Anian, Bp., 198, 211, 212
Bangor, 197
BANGOR CATHEDRAL, 197-210
  Chapter, 203
  Chapter-room, 207
  Choir, 201, 202, 207
  Dimensions, 202
  Exterior, 199-201
  Font, 210
  History of, 198, 199
  Interior, 202
  Modern History, 205-210
  Monuments, 209
  Nave, 200, 201, 202, 209
  Norman Cathedral, 206
  Organ, 207
  Reredos, 209
  Tower, Central, 207
     " Western, 200
  Transept, 200, 201, 208
  Windows, 200, 201, 206
Bangor, See of, 197, 203
Bulkely, Bp., 199
Caerleon, See of, 171, 172
Cleaver, Bp., 205
Daniel, Bp., 197
Dubritius, Abp., 171, 185, 194, 197
Dyfryg, Abp., 171, 185, 194, 197
Godwin, Bp., 196
Hervens, Bp., 197, 198
Hoadley, Bp., 203
Kentigern, Bishop of Glasgow and St. Asaph, 211
Llanbadarn, See of, 185
Llandaff, Bishops of, 185, 186, 195, 196
LLANDAFF CATHEDRAL, 185-196
  Chapter, 195
  Chapter-house, 187, 190
  Choir, 191
  Dimensions, 195
  Exterior, 187
  History of, 185-187
  Interior, 190
  Lady Chapel, 185, 186, 187, 193
  Modern History, 187
  Monuments, 194
  Nave, 188, 190, 191
  Norman Arch, 193
  Presbytery, 192, 193
  Pulpit, 191
  Reredos, 193
  Throne, Bishop's, 191
  Towers, 186, 187, 188, 190
  West Front, 188
  Windows, 188, 190, 191, 192, 194

Llandaff, See of, 185, 195
Lloyd, Bp., 199
Malgo Conan, Prince, 197
Menevia, 172
Pearce, Bp. Zachary, 204
Prichard, Mr., 187, 193
Restoration of Bangor Cathedral, 205, 210
Roberts, Bp., 199
Rossetti, Mr. D. G., Pictures by, 193
Rowlands, Bp., 199
St. Asaph, 210
St. Asaph, Bishops of, 212, 213, 215, 218

ST. ASAPH CATHEDRAL—
  Choir, 214
  Dimensions, 215
  Early History, 211, 212
  Modern History, 219-221
  Monuments, 219, 221
  Nave, 214, 215, 219
  Tower, 214, 215
  Transept, 214, 215
  West Front, 213
St. Asaph, See of, 216
St. Caradoc, Shrine of, 182
St. David, 171
St. David's, Bishops of, 177

ST. DAVID'S CATHEDRAL—
  Chapels, 174, 176
  Choir, 174, 176, 180
  Dimensions, 176
  Early History, 173
  Modern History, 179-183
  Monuments, 176, 182
  Nave, 173, 174
  Rood Screen, 176, 179
  Screen, 176
  Tower, 174, 175, 180
  Transept, 174
  West Front, 173, 183
  Windows, 180, 181, 183
St. David's, See of, 171
St. David's Shrine, 182
St. Teilo, Bp., 185, 194
Sampson, Abp., 172
Scott, Sir G. G., 205, 206
Sherlock, Bp., 203
Skeffington, Bp, 199, 200
Urban, Bp., 185
Ward, Mr., of Bath, 186
Watson, Bp., 196
Welsh Church, The, 185

INDEX TO SCOTCH CATHEDRALS.

Aberdeen Cathedral, 256, 257
Badenoch, the Wolf of, 254, 258
Beaton, Cardinal, 241
Blackader, Bishop, 241
Bondington, Bishop de, 241
Brechin Cathedral, 254-256
Cathedral of the Isles, 247
Chambers, Dr. William, and St. Giles's, Edinburgh, 224, 229, 235
Chepman, Walter, the Scottish Caxton, 231, 232
Covenanters, 228
Cumbrae Cathedral, 247-249
    Windows of, 249
Dornoch Cathedral, 260, 261
Dunblane Cathedral, 251
Dunkeld Cathedral, 253, 254
Elgin Cathedral, 258-260
Fortrose Cathedral, 261
Geddes, Jenny, 228
GLASGOW CATHEDRAL, 239-247
    Crypt of, 244, 245
    History of, 239-242
    Windows of, 243, 245-24.
Glasgow, Earl of, 247
Inverness Cathedral, 249-251
Iona Cathedral, 264

Joceline, Bishop of Glasgow, 241
Kentigern, St., 241
Kirkwall Cathedral, 261, 262
Knox, John, 226, 227, 234
Lismore Cathedral, 264
Magnus, Earl of Orkney, 261
Millport, Isle of Cumbrae, Cathedral of, 247-249
Montrose Aisle, St. Giles', 231
Mungo, St., 241
Murray, the Regent, 227, 230, 233
Perth, St. Ninian's Cathedral, 249
Preston Aisle, 231, 232
Reformation in Scotland, 226, 227
Rognvald, Earl of Orkney, 261
Round Tower of Brechin, 255
St. Andrew's Cathedral, 252
ST. GILES', EDINBURGH, 223-235
    History of, 224-229
    Restoration of, 230-235
    Subdivision of, 229
St. Mary's Cathedral, Edinburgh, 235-239
St. Ninian's Cathedral, Perth, 249
Tolbooth, Edinburgh, 227, 229
Whitherne Cathedral, Galloway, 262.

INDEX TO IRISH CATHEDRALS.

Armagh Cathedral
Christchurch Cathedral, Dublin, 272-282
Cork Cathedral, 283-285
Downpatrick Cathedral, 286
Early Irish Architecture, 265, 266
Guinness, Sir B., and St. Patrick's Cathedral, 267
St. Fin Barre, 283

Laurence O'Toole, St., 272
ST. PATRICK'S CATHEDRAL, DUBLIN, 265-271
    History of, 266
    Monuments, 270, 271
    Windows, 271
Street, Mr., 273-282
Swift, Dean, St. Patrick's, 270